SAGE was founded in 1965 by Sara Miller McCune to support the dissemination of usable knowledge by publishing innovative and high-quality research and teaching content. Today, we publish more than 850 journals, including those of more than 300 learned societies, more than 800 new books per year, and a growing range of library products including archives, data, case studies, reports, conference highlights, and video. SAGE remains majority-owned by our founder, and after Sara's lifetime will become owned by a charitable trust that secures our continued independence.

Los Angeles | London | New Delhi | Singapore | Washington DC

Filming Reality

Filming Reality

The Independent Documentary Movement in India

Shoma A. Chatterji

 www.sagepublications.com
Los Angeles • London • New Delhi • Singapore • Washington DC

Copyright © Shoma A. Chatterji, 2015

All rights reserved. No part of this book may be reproduced or utilized in any form or by any means, electronic or mechanical, including photocopying, recording or by any information storage or retrieval system, without permission in writing from the publisher.

First published in 2015 by

SAGE Publications India Pvt Ltd
B1/I-1 Mohan Cooperative Industrial Area
Mathura Road, New Delhi 110 044, India
www.sagepub.in

SAGE Publications Inc
2455 Teller Road
Thousand Oaks, California 91320, USA

SAGE Publications Ltd
1 Oliver's Yard, 55 City Road
London EC1Y 1SP, United Kingdom

SAGE Publications Asia-Pacific Pte Ltd
3 Church Street
#10-04 Samsung Hub
Singapore 049483

Published by Vivek Mehra for SAGE Publications India Pvt Ltd, typeset in 10.5/12.5 Minion Pro by RECTO Graphics, Delhi and printed at Saurabh Printers Pvt Ltd, New Delhi.

Library of Congress Cataloging-in-Publication Data

Chatterji, Shoma A.
 Filming reality : the independent documentary movement in India / Shoma A. Chatterji.
  pages cm
 Includes bibliographical references and index.
 1. Documentary films—India—History and criticism. I. Title.
 PN1995.9.D6C437   2015   070.1'8—dc23   2015022116

ISBN: 978-93-515-0287-6 (HB)

The SAGE Team: Shambhu Sahu, Saima Ghaffar, Anju Saxena and Ritu Chopra

'I most humbly dedicate this work to every single Indian film-maker, academic writer and technician who created, shaped, honed that razor-sharp knife called 'independence' of the documentary movement in India over the past four decades through their sustained research, painstakingly created films, solely through their determination to keep the movement go ing despite roadblocks—official, social and political—to prove how powerfully the real can be aesthetically and authentically portrayed through the language of cinema through celluloid and all its modern variants.

Shoma A. Chatterji

Thank you for choosing a SAGE product!
If you have any comment, observation or feedback,
I would like to personally hear from you.
Please write to me at **contactceo@sagepub.in**

Vivek Mehra, Managing Director and CEO,
SAGE Publications India Pvt Ltd, New Delhi

Bulk Sales

SAGE India offers special discounts
for purchase of books in bulk.
We also make available special imprints
and excerpts from our books on demand.

For orders and enquiries, write to us at

Marketing Department
SAGE Publications India Pvt Ltd
B1/I-1, Mohan Cooperative Industrial Area
Mathura Road, Post Bag 7
New Delhi 110044, India

E-mail us at **marketing@sagepub.in**

Get to know more about SAGE

Be invited to SAGE events, get on our mailing list.
Write today to **marketing@sagepub.in**

This book is also available as an e-book.

CONTENTS

LIST OF IMAGES ix

ON A PERSONAL NOTE xi

CHAPTERS

Chapter 1: Introduction: Why Independent Films? **1**

Chapter 2: Of Lives and Histories: Known and Lesser Known **24**
Introduction 24
Lives: Known 24
Lives: Lesser Known 65
Conclusion 73

Chapter 3: The Ethnographical Film: A Cinema for the People, by the People **75**
Background 75
Introduction 76
Gathering Momentum 77
Case Studies 80
When Does an Ethnographical Film Become an Investigative Film or a Political Statement? 103
Conclusion 134

Chapter 4: The Ray Factor **136**
Ray's Documentary Films 136
Films on Ray 144
Conclusion 149

Chapter 5: The Milestone Makers **152**
Introduction 152
Anand Patwardhan 153
Amar Kanwar 156

Rakesh Sharma 158
Sanjay Kak 162
Ajay Raina 167
Ranjan Palit 171
Supriyo Sen 174
Joshy Joseph 177
Krishnendu Bose 180
Other Pillars 183
Conclusion 184

Chapter 6: Dialogues in Diversity: Women Film-makers **186**
Introduction 186
Criteria of Choice 188
Conclusion 210

Chapter 7: Positive Documentaries on Sustainable Development **213**
Introduction 213
Some Examples 214
Conclusion 237

Chapter 8: Out of the Box **239**
Introduction 239
Out of the Box 240
Conclusion 273

Summing Up **274**

BIBLIOGRAPHY 284

INDEX OF FILMS 287

INDEX 294

ABOUT THE AUTHOR 299

LIST OF IMAGES

2.1.	*Celluloid Man*: P.K. Nair	47
2.2.	A Poster of *An American in Madras*	50
2.3.	Tagore behind the Window	55
2.4.	The Saroj Khan Story	61
2.5.	Tom Sharma in Film: *Making the Face*	71
3.1.	*If It Rains*	80
3.2.	Gour Khepa Lost in His World	83
3.3.	A Production Still of *Bottle Masala in Moile*	87
3.4.	*Divine Drums*	95
3.5.	Little Magazines Stall at the Kolkata Book Fair	101
3.6.	*Apna Aloo Bazar Becha*	112
3.7.	*Bilal*	113
3.8.	*Loha Garam Hai*	115
3.9.	On Location of *Crosswinds Over Ichamati*	119
3.10.	*Whose Land Is It Anyway*: The Director and His Crew on Location	121
3.11.	*Known Strangers*: Janardhan Rani and Chapal Rani	125
3.12.	A Poster of *Sons and Daughters*	128
5.1.	*In Camera*	172
5.2.	*Way Back Home*	175
5.3.	Damayanti Tambay in a Still from *Hope Dies Last in War*	176
5.4.	Mahasweta Devi Singing at Nandigram	178
5.5.	*Tiger—the Death Chronicles*	180
5.6.	A Production Still from *The Forgotten Tigers*	182
6.1.	*Gulabi Gang*	207

7.1.	A Poster of *Ek Ropa Dhan*	217
7.2.	*Johar—Welcome to Our World*	223
7.3.	*Earth Witness*: The Director on Location with Locals	228
7.4.	*Have You Seen the Arana*	233
8.1.	*King of India*	243
8.2.	*Nakusha—The Unwanted*	251
8.3.	*Ocean of Tears*: Bilal A. Jan on Location	256
8.4.	*110002*	258
8.5.	Superman of Malegaon	259
8.6.	*Char—The No Man's Island*	261
8.7.	A Poster of *Flickering Angels*	263
8.8.	*Our Family*	266
8.9.	Gautam Sen in *A Poet, A City and A Footballer*	270

ON A PERSONAL NOTE

The first documentary film that made a deep impact on me was Anand Patwardhan's *Bombay: Our City* (1985). I watched it at a hall in a building on the other side where the Siri Fort Complex stands when I had gone to cover the International Film Festival of India (IFFI) in Delhi many years ago. The film shook me up from my 'happy' world of feature films and brought me face-to-face with a cinema and a world I knew little about. What shocked me more was watching Anand passing a handkerchief around among the audience after the screening to put in what they could. Was this the way a film-maker had to garner funds because his film could not get a theatrical release through proper channels? Why? What was the reason behind such brazen casteism within cinema where mainstream cinema was celebrated and promoted and awarded across the world and documentary cinema was discarded by the wayside? These were the 'voices in the margins' I was touched by and remain touched till today.

Later, I watched an abbreviated version of S. Sukhdev's *Nine Months to Freedom—The Story of Bangladesh* (1972) and was amazed at the risks these film-makers took just to do what they truly believed in and wanted to share it with the people they made it for—the Indian on the street—like me. The word 'documentary' for me meant nothing more than the newsreel shown before each screening of the main film or an occasional 'story' film by the Films Division. I did not know that there was a 'movement' going alongside the newsreels both within and without the Films Division. After 30 years of watching hundreds of independent documentaries by makers ranging from Mani Kaul through Uma Segal to Meera Dewan, and through Gulzar to Jill Misquitta to Madhusree Datta, I felt that I should collect my ideas, conceptions and information on the films I had seen again and again, the film-makers I had interviewed in great detail, the books and essays I had read and put all this together in the form of a book. It took another five years for the idea to gain flesh and blood and acquire a life of its own.

The first in-depth piece I wrote on a documentary film was on *Voices from Baliapal* (1988), which was screened in the office of a press club near Flora Fountain in Mumbai many years ago. The piece was published without any editing or rewriting in the Sunday supplement of *The Financial Express*. I cut my teeth in 1979–80 when I did my internship as a journalism student.

The independent documentary is the most dynamic and ongoing form of cinema known to the world and especially in India. Once you hear about a film such as Sunanda Bhat's *Have You Seen the Arana* (2013), then you are suddenly confronted with a stunning film such as Bilal Jan's *Ocean of Tears* (2012) or Nishtha Jain's *Gulabi Gang* (2012). By the time you have watched them closely and repeatedly and written about them at length, another 50 films have come out of the editing room, ready for screening. So, just putting everything together took two long years of gathering all that I had written after the computer came in. The features I had written before the computer, such as a long review of Uma Segal's *Sheher* (2009), Madhusree Datta's *I Live in Behrampada* (1993) and Ranjan Palit and Vasudha Joshi's *Voices from Baliapal*, are lost.

I am grateful to all the film-makers who have made it possible for me to even think of writing a book on their movement and their work. I refrain from mentioning names because some names are prominent, some names are known to some and some names are anonymous, not because they did not fare well but because they made few films that faded from history for lack of screening facilities, funding and an audience. It would be unfair to take a few names and leave out the rest. But the gratefulness extends to even those who have passed yonder and those I could not nail down for an interview because they remained out of reach. Many film-makers, younger than me, young and very young, have become personal friends, though we might not meet or be in communication as our lines of work are different and so are our ages, mobility and physical disposition.

I extend my thanks to all the film-makers who have willingly and freely given me dozens of scanned images from their films for use in this book and even agreed to give me letters of authorization if the publishers needed these. I extend my personal thanks to film-makers who willingly couriered me DVDs of their films so that I could watch them again and again, pause to take notes and all this for free. Among them, the names I can recall right away are of Joshy Joseph, Deb Ranjan Sarangi, Sourav Sarangi, Nishtha Jain, Sunanda Bhat, Shivendra Singh Dungarpur, Karan Bali, Bilal Jan, Akanksha Joshi, Jyotsna Khatry, Vaidehi Chitre, Arindam Saha Sardar, K.P. Jayasankar and Anjali Monteiro of the Tata Institute of Social Sciences (TISS), Mumbai; Nilanjan Bhattacharya, Ajay Raina, Ritesh Sharma, Pankaj H. Gupta, Subha Das Mullick and Dhananjay Mandal.

This book might not have been possible had I not watched dozens of documentaries at the Mumbai Academy of the Moving Image (MAMI) festival in Mumbai, at IFFI and Film Utsav festivals across the country from 1986 to 1999 when I was a regular participant as a press delegate. In some cases, I got the opportunity of interacting with some of them, such as the late Uma Segal in Hyderabad in 1986 through Deb Ranjan Sarangi in 2000 or thereabouts. Other sources of viewing are traced back to my regular attendance at the Mannheim-Heidelberg Film Festival from 1988 through 1999 and the Oberhausen Festival of Short Films twice where Indian documentaries were selectively screened and bagged awards. I saw Amar Kanwar's *A Season Outside* at Oberhausen and interviewed him too. Once, Mani Kaul was part of the international jury at Mannheim and a wonderful interview came out of our first meeting. Several years later, I caught up with Mani Kaul again during a three-day conference on sound in cinema organized by the School of Sound, London, where both of us made presentations. An exciting interaction followed, which for me, was a wonderful learning experience.

My deep gratitude goes to Shambhu Sahu, my commissioning editor at SAGE, who kindly went through the first draft and asked me to send over the final; to Elina Majumdar, who gave me the courage to send in my editorial queries to Mr Sahu and Saima Ghaffar at SAGE who have been involved in giving the book its final look.

I am also deeply grateful to journalist Frederick Noronha and the e-group he created and moderates, namely docuwallahs2.com, and allowed me to become a member though I am not a film-maker. I often reached out to everyone in the group with questions they might have thought to be naïve, foolish and funny, but they cooperated every time I posted a query. I take my hat off to all my journalist friends who became wonderful documentary film-makers. I have not been able to write about their films because I have not yet had the opportunity of watching their work. Among them are Altaf Majid and Utpal Borpujari, each a National Award winner. I also take my hat off to Joshy Joseph, a documentary film-maker who writes prolifically and brilliantly on cinema in general and documentary films in particular.

My thanks reaches out to every editor of newspapers and online journals I contribute to for generously having given me the space and the opportunity to write about documentary films and film-makers. Among the print media, the papers that published my documentary cinema pieces are *SCREEN* of the Indian Express Group; *Times of India*, Kolkata; *The Financial Express*, Mumbai; *The Free Press Journal*, Mumbai; *The Statesman*, Kolkata; *One India One People*, Mumbai; *Teragreen* (The Energy and Resources Institute), Delhi; *Vidura*, the quarterly journal of Press Institute of India (PII) published from Chennai; and *Grassroots*, also published by the PII from Chennai. Among online publications, I am honoured by editors of www.IndiaTogether.org, www.TWFIndia.in and www.upperstall.com for having permitted me to write about many documentaries I had watched over the years.

I am more than grateful to my husband Ajoy, who, for most of the 50 years we have shared, gave away his right, sometimes with irritation, sometimes without turning a hair, but mostly with resignation to my space and set me free to think, ideate, write and rewrite without making culinary and other similar demands husbands are generally prone to make. We have had our storms and our floods and our rainbows but finally have settled down to watch the sunset together.

It took me five long years to put this work together in fits and starts because within these five years, I wrote three more books on cinema, by which time I had gathered the courage to go ahead with this one. This is by no means an exhaustive study of independent documentary films because that would span thick volumes and many years to compile. If there are omissions, they are all mine. I have tried to sustain my objectivity as much as I could, but the very fact that I chose this subject to write on, means that I am extremely biased towards the independent documentary movement.

ON A PERSONAL NOTE

My prayers go to my late parents, Asoka Gangopadhyay and Sumita Gangopadhyay, who forever egged me on to leave something concrete behind, other than children, for future generations to fall back on. My deep love is for our 14-year-old grandson, Ishaan, who kept erasing away sentences while I worked on this book. It made the trouble worth it.

This is just a small stone cast in the huge ocean of writing that waits to be created in the years to follow. I remain grateful to my potential readers who, I hope, will be informed and somewhat educated from the content that follows in the pages of the book, though I cannot promise entertainment unless we redefine the meaning of 'entertainment'.

The quotes of the film-makers in the entire book, unless otherwise mentioned, wherever not accompanied by a footnote or reference, are based on the author's interviews with the film-makers—personal, telephonic and/or through e-mail.

1
INTRODUCTION
Why Independent Films?

The word 'documentary' poses many challenges in providing definitions. "The use of the term 'document' in the word documentary is a contentious matter, though the other nomenclature—non-fiction—is even more problematic. The moral insinuation of both of these has been plaguing the genre since its very inception. The former implies proof of authenticity, while the latter asserts the privilege of being factual. These implications, in turn, lead us to a kind of linearity, a fixed text, a representation of 'the' truth, which comes from the tendency of treating 'fact' or 'authenticity' as truth," writes activist-documentary film-maker Madhusree Datta.[1]

The word 'documentary' was used for the first time in 1914, with reference to *In the Land of the Head Hunters* (1914), a film about American Indians. But beyond the realistic was the magical. That same year, a 22-year-old film student from the US named Jessica Brothwick, spent a year in the Balkans. "During the cholera rage in Adrianpole, everything connected with that terrible disease was painted black," she wrote later. She continued, "While the scourge was at its height, I went down into the gypsy quarter to take a film. The people in this part of the city had never seen a camera before, and when they saw me pointing my black box at various objects, they thought I was operating some wonderful new instrument for combating the disease which was destroying them. Quickly surrounding me, they came and knelt upon the ground, kissing my feet and clothing, and begging with dreadful pathos that I should cure them."[2]

Documentary's founding father, John Grierson—to whom we shall return—defined it as the "creative treatment of actuality". Over time, this definition has emerged with its limitations because all 'actuality' is not necessarily a 'documentary' film. A promotional film, for instance, may shoot actual people and sequences in order to prove a point or fulfil an agenda. But it is certainly not a documentary film. The air hostess who guides you on safety rules on the video in a flight is real but is not a documentary. Besides, when a documentary is aimed at projecting future happenings in the light of what has happened in the past, the past may be available from archival clippings. But the future will need to be dramatized perhaps with actors. It will still qualify as a documentary, though.over time, this is often called docu-fiction.

Michael Rabiger, who has written some of the most outstanding books targeted at documentary film-makers, gives a concrete example. In *The War Game* (1965), Peter Watkins took the disastrous incidents that happened in the World War II bombings of Dresden, Hiroshima and Nagasaki to use them to hypothesize a major nuclear attack on London. "Until someone invests a time machine, documentaries about the past or the future have to use actors. This means that fictional characters and scripts are not automatically excluded from the documentary," writes Rabiger.[3] If fictional features were to be kept away from actual fact, Mani Kaul's *Siddheshwari* (1989) would never have seen the light of day. Or, an 'abstractly' conceived *Khayal Gatha* (1989) by Kumar Shahani would never have been made.

The word 'movement' suggests a sense of fluidity, of moving forward, of an ongoing journey that never ends, that is ambivalent unto itself, that, amoeba-like, can stretch itself to any shape it wishes to. The environment that is counterproductive in different ways does not deter the activists from leaving the field in search of greener pastures in the mainstream or television. Sometimes, the movement falls sick for lack of breathing space. At times, it stops to take stock of its bearings but finally catches on, surfacing from the depths of imminent death not only to survive but also to go on and sustain through new challenges.

INTRODUCTION

WHY 'INDEPENDENT' FILMS?

Independence from What?

The word 'independence' is a loaded word filled with political, social and financial implications. It also extends to independence to freedom of expression and from censorship before, after and during the making of a given film. This 'censorship' paradigm is complex that involves the active and passive participation of individuals and groups, administrative bodies and political-vested interests who do not wish a given film to be made for their own reasons. Right to freedom of expression is a constitutional right that is countered by the Board of Film Censorship in India. One the one hand, while the Constitution grants this fundamental right, there are offices like the Central Board of Film Certification (CBFC) ready with their sharpened scissors to order cuts that might break the intention of the film to send out a given message, or expose things some parties would hate to have exposed, or ban the film entirely from screening. Documentary film-makers desperately fight for this independence from such vested interests.

In an ambience of political control veiled as democracy, Someswar Bhowmik's *Cinema and Censorship: The Politics of Control in India* is a landmark work on the politics of control. The word 'control' links itself to a dictatorial form of order, where the citizen's right to freedom of expression is not denied, it just does not exist. So, why and how does the concept of control operate in a democracy? Bhowmik raises a very relevant and topical question—why should censorship that functioned mainly as an instrument of political and informative control during the British rule sustain for more than six decades after independence in the world's largest democracy producing the largest number of films? In 1999, the veteran Polish journalist, Ryszard Kapuscinski commented, "In a dictatorship, censorship is used; in a democracy, manipulation". Though this was with reference to Western experience and sensibilities, it would apply equally well to film censorship in India.[4]

Independence to What?

The film-makers dedicated to their individual causes and agendas desire the freedom to voice their comment, dissent, discordant notes of observation, exploration and investigation through the language of their choice—cinema—in order that this reaches the mass audience not only in India but across the world. They crave the independence to work and exist and breathe in an open world where they can function free of fear and fetters. It is difficult but not impossible.

The authoritarian climate-committed documentary film-makers work and live in, has many manifestations. On the one hand, it involves the quiet takeover of our democratic institutions, and on the other, the open violence of organized mobs. Independent and alternative film-makers believe that this fight to create, sustain and promote independence is not about films and censor certificates but is a larger fight to hold on to their rights and their democratic norms. These film-makers maintain that in its present form, censorship violates the essential rights of citizens. They therefore seek to intervene by promoting the screening of documentaries, and generating discussion on the politics and aesthetics of film-making. As film-makers, public opinion is an important part of their struggle, and they believe it is essential to energize a strong screening culture. They are aware that the best way to guard their rights as citizens is to speak clearly, speak honestly and speak from all corners of the country.

Some independent documentaries portrayed moments and issues of political injustice. Some of these films were given a more nuanced treatment by a number of feminist film-makers. But, the limitations of the earlier language of expression were slowly becoming visible. Questions were raised about finding a new form to articulate political concerns. Film-maker Saba Dewan describes her earlier films, *Dharmayuddha* (1989) and *Nasoor* (1991), as protest films made in the midst of the late 1980s' and early 1990s' identity politics.[5] In accordance with the language and objectives of the documentary genre of that time, "they sought to expose hidden faces of reality". Dewan adds, "While I believed in the issues of the earlier protest films, their form was predictable and did not excite me as a film-maker. Along with making political documentaries came the need to work with images and form and to think of documentary as an aesthetic medium. If I do a film, then it has to satisfy the political person as well as the film-maker in me."

The movement gained momentum and speed, garnered itself for action and defined itself as a movement with a cultural–political identity of its own, its bloody head unbowed under bureaucratic pressures, official red tape and irrational and politically motivated censorship. More people committed themselves to the documentary—in form, content, style, choice of subject and approach—notwithstanding the paucity of funding and the almost total absence of exhibition outlets. Slowly, the source of funding expanded.

"Being independent in a business that demands complete adherence to established practice can never be easy. Yet the tribe of intrepid Indian film-makers who choose to exist outside the system and make documentaries about social and political issues of import has only swelled in both quantity and quality in the recent times. Needless to say, Indian cinema is much the richer for it. In fact, Indian cinema wins more global accolades these days for the work of its independent documentary film-makers than for the output of their better known, better publicized counterparts who operate within the mainstream fiction film-making space," writes journalist Saibal Chatterjee.[6] Gargi Sen says, "Both in terms of form and substance, today's documentary makers are able to experiment far more than ever before. These are exciting times indeed. What is really heartening is the sharp increase in the number of women film-makers in this space."

It is still an ongoing journey that is changing its destination and its route with the changing demands of time and circumstance. It stands independent of every other kind of cinema such as mainstream cinema, promotional and advertising films, propaganda films commissioned by political parties as part of their electoral campaigns, educational films aimed at screening in educational institutions and corporate films commissioned by corporate houses for in-house training programmes. It stands distanced from the intellectual arrogance of parallel cinema and is far removed from official media.

AIMS

1. To do away with a chronological history of the movement and to focus instead on the ongoing struggle among autonomous documentary film-makers towards sustaining and taking forward their independence of functioning, making, financing, exhibiting and distributing their films

across issues, geography, cultural, gender, communal and casteist differences as may obtain in the world.
2. To explore the independent documentary cinema movement in India post-1980s when the movement began to acquire an identity of its own and many films got recognition abroad.
3. To detail a descriptive and analytical detail, spanning roughly the period beginning from the mid-1980s to the present time through different genres, film-makers and subjects rather than through a sequential narration of history.

Further, this work aspires to provide detailed information, education and to some extent, an exploration into different areas of film-making where the film-makers are trying to reach far beyond the profit motive and are picking, choosing and writing about films that are not purely a commodity to be marketed and sold to a mass-centred ticketed audience in regular theatres. It is cinema that does not include the box office within its purview, not because theatre release is not possible, but because they need to make some statements about issues and subjects and address these to niche or selective or invited screenings. Cinema for these film-makers have a different meaning even if they are, at times, using a very form as entertainment, such as a particular dance form that is fading away, as the subject of the film.

The descriptions and comments on the films are necessarily of different length because the films themselves are of different lengths and depths, though there are exceptions where a less than average-length film might call for lengthier exploration than a long film that has said everything within a few minutes.

RATIONALE FOR THE STUDY

In an era of globalization where the world can be shrinked to fit into a television set or on a tablet or even a cell phone, it is significant to look at the independent documentary film movement in India as placed within a larger universe and from a different perspective. The independent documentary cinema is alive and flourishing every passing moment. It refuses to be killed, injured or damaged for stringency in funding, scarcity of exhibiting space, distribution support and so on.

At this juncture, the author felt that a study of a genre-centric and director-centric study in place of a historical, descriptive and chronologically-sequenced story on this movement would perhaps become a frame of reference for film studies' students and scholars, film-makers and film institute students for future research and analysis.

Around 2014, this independent movement is roughly more than three decades old. It is therefore, in the fitness of things, to look back on these 40 years of the movement that is going ahead despite the pitfalls, struggles and blocks—financial, political and administrative—besides the lack of proper and necessary distribution platforms.

The time frame of this work begins roughly in the 1950s for the historical backdrop and then moves on to the 1970s to the present day, including films screened in 2014. Language of the films is of no consequence, and films in all Indian languages and dialects, including English, have been included for the study.

Criteria for Choice of Films

The principal criteria for choice of films discussed in the book is the author's familiarity with these films through (i) intensive and extensive viewing of most of the films chosen, (ii) interviews conducted on a one-to-one basis with most of the film-makers discussed in the pages either through face-to-face interaction or through telephonic conversation or through e-mail discussion, (iii) proceedings documented at panel discussions at different film festivals by the author either as a participant or as an observer or as a reporter and (iv) films the author has written about at length through the past 35 years as a film journalist involved in writing about the movement.

Does this mean that films the author has not watched do not find place in this study? No, a handful of films find place by virtue of the debates they raised, the significance of the film-makers concerned whose some work the author might be familiar with but not exhaustively, and last but not the least, films that lent themselves smoothly to a definite genre of films to make the study more inclusive than exclusive. The author has weeded out films that do not find a place in the book by virtue of their lack of focus in uncovering 'truth', or pretending to be honest yet being more propagandist than honest and so on. The films have been chosen with great care because the author found them to be honest in exploring and uncovering what the makers felt was the 'truth'. For example, sometimes a critic is placed in the horns of a dilemma about deciding whether a given film is 'honest' or is 'pretending' to be honest. Here, a subjective decision needs to be taken on one or the other.

Docu-fiction has been included because these are based on real life and blend the real with fiction for want of actual documentation, or while projecting the future or depicting incidents and happenings, real people would not agree to feature in. For example, it would be difficult to create the psychology of fear in women unless there was some structuring of fiction woven into real-life interviews with real people. The National Film Awards bestows awards to docu-fiction under the 'documentary' segment because there is no separate category for docu-fiction.

A CLASSIFICATION INTO GENRES

Classifying and categorizing of independent documentary films was perhaps the most formidable task the writer had to encounter in breaking up the work into genre-based chapters. Because independent documentary films defy genres of any kind by their narrative content, the form, approach and most importantly, the ideology of the film-maker that often spans several genres. No documentary film-maker works with any specific genre in mind. We—viewers, critics and film scholars—impose genre labels on the films.

To quote from an interview of Anand Patwardhan by Francis Miquet at the Montreal Film Festival,[7] Patwardhan says, "I do not see myself as being excessively political and I have never identified myself with narrow ideological dictums. I was never clearly a Marxist when everyone called themselves Marxists and I have not become an anti-Communist now that everyone is anti-Communist. My background is a mixture of Left philosophy and Gandhi. Some consider class struggle and pacifism and humanism to be mutually exclusive but this tension actually appeals to me. When I make films, I do not have a hidden agenda outside of the film itself; but at the same time, I come to film-making with my own ideas and my own way of interpreting the world. I am never 'objective'. I have chosen sides, if you will. Sometimes my views change in the course of making a film but usually the intuition that led me to film is confirmed."

The independent documentary has widened itself to combine presentation with social concern, picturization and comment. The ideological stance offers a political comment, by suggestion or articulation or visualization. In this sense, an ethnographical documentary may also present a cultural matrix within which, given people live and work and flourish or do not flourish. A biographical documentary can be a sad humane comment on loneliness and a growing sense of alienation as three films on Badal Sircar subtly reveal. It can also demonstrate the history of a given musical instrument such as the harmonium one gets to learn in a film on a talented harmonium artiste in Kolkata who played the instrument solo, though it is generally understood to be an instrument that accompanies and supports a vocalist's performance and not performed solo.

For example, Anand Patwardhan's *Bombay: Our City* unwittingly unfolds the lives and pains of slum dwellers of Bombay, the rag-pickers of the city who, by themselves, define a major ethnic group in Indian metros of today's upmarket, branded-and-packaged India. By the same argument, Jill Misquitta's *The Clap Trap* (1993), a film on junior artistes in Mumbai cinema, is an ethnographic film in one sense because it deals with a specific group of marginalized people exploited by the system. In another sense, it is a political indictment on a corrupt, manipulative system that exploits this group financially, socially and even sexually, using their elusive hopes as the plank for exploitation and abuse. The zeroing in on the lives of two junior artistes, one male and one female, who came to become stars and reduced themselves to 'extras', forms another layer that makes it a human, individual document. Taking these three approaches in the same film together, one makes it a strong political comment on celluloid.

Genres overlap, cross each other, blur borders and also separate into different categories within the same film. But if artificially created, it makes for a new way of looking at the same film at different times by the same person and different film at the same time by different persons.

The National Film Awards bestowed by the Directorate of Film Festivals under the Ministry of Information and Broadcasting has itself broken up non-feature films into genres. It gives greater scope for awards for contribution to different ideological statements made through different subjects. Awards are bestowed for films entered under different sections such as the (i) Best Anthropological/ Ethnographic Film, (ii) Best Biographical/Historical Reconstruction Film, (iii) Best Arts or Cultural Film, (iv) Best Promotional Film, (v) Best Environmental Film (including agriculture), (vi) Best Film on Social Issues, (vii) Best Exploration/Adventure Film (including sports), (viii) Best Investigative Film and (ix) Best Film on Family Welfare.

Exclusions

This book has kept away from a few genres—if they can be called thus. These are (i) the adventure film documentary, (ii) documentaries on scientific subjects and (iii) historical documentaries, unless some of them overlap with the biographical documentary or are included in the 'Out-of-the-Box' chapter.

The elimination is based on the author's lack of adequate knowledge of familiarity with and understanding of these genres and her unfamiliarity with the works of film-makers who work exclusively in these fields such as Mike Pandey and his entire family. This writer has also kept away from 'educational films', though some film-makers such as Chhandita Mukherjee (*Another Way of Learning*) have contributed significantly to this field. There are hundreds of 'promotional' films thrown up in the guise of 'educational' documentaries. The category of Promotional Film is ambiguous and its agenda is not very clear to this writer, though it is included in the National Film Awards. The reason for keeping this genre out is that the films within this might be commercial or advertisement films, backed by solid funding and ambivalent agendas. The book also does not include 'political' documentaries as a genre because according to the author, every documentary has a 'political' stance, hidden or expressed, direct or indirect, stated or understated. So the author believes that the categorization of a separate genre on 'the political documentary' is an all-encompassing word that defies classification.

The author has excluded films made by non-resident Indian (NRI) film-makers and/or Indian film-makers who made films with international support in terms of funding, distribution and so on. This decision is based on the author's conviction that these are the 'outsider's films, such as documentaries made by Mira Nair or Deepa Mehta or a film such as *Born into Brothels* (2004), because besides offering an 'outsider's' view of the subject, they also might offer a distorted, unrealistic and/or sensational view of the subject or issue'. The other reason is that even a good documentary on Amartya Sen has been kept out because Suman Ghosh is an NRI. For any NRI, the funding and accessibility to his subject might place resident film-makers at a comparative disadvantage. Any NRI has access to greater funding and grant avenues than his home colleague. He can interact directly with the subject more easily than can the desi film-maker. With adequate funding at his disposal, he can extend the time of film-making if and when he has to. The author has also kept away the censorship conflicts around many films featured here that are already much discussed and debated elsewhere and need not be repeated here as this might detract from the aims of this study.

This book is entirely from the subjective point of view of a film critic, so this work has kept strictly away from the following:
1. Methods, technologies, thought processes and judgements that a director must use throughout the fascinating process of making a film.
2. The human, psychological and technical knowledge that dictates and backs the work of a documentary film-maker.
3. A view of the artistic process.
4. Detailed and applicable terms on how to engage with the conceptual and authorial sides of film-making.
5. Offering or suggesting practical tools and exercises that might help a film-maker discover his or her artistic identity, develop credible and compelling documentary films.

TOWARDS A COUNTER-MOVEMENT FROM WITHIN FILMS DIVISION AND WITHOUT

Films Division, established in 1948 by the Government of India, was the main film-making and film-producing body committed to maintaining "a record of the social, political and cultural imaginations and realities of the country". Before the advent of television, these films were shown in private cinema theatres and in government organizations, and later broadcast on the State-owned television network.

While most of the films produced in the first few decades after independence were 'educative' tools to push forward sociopolitical agendas of a pedagogic State, there emerged, by the mid-1960s, a generation of film-makers who brought in subtleties to the cinematic craft by pushing aesthetic boundaries, while producing a critique of the nation-state. The films in this curation are open to multiple readings, as cultural artefacts, as historical documents, as State propaganda and its subversion, as an account of the birth of a nation and of 'nation-building' and as documentary film texts that created formal and aesthetic innovations.[8]

While films such as *Freedom Marches On* (1949) and *Hamara Rashtragaan* (Our National Anthem) (1964) are pedagogic in their ambition, documentaries such as *Naya Daur* (New Era) (1975) and *Face to Face* (1967), while furthering the State project of nation-building, also seem to question the very idea of 'India'. A more formal experimentation with image and sound can be seen in films such as *This Bit of That India* (1975) and *Explorer* (1968), while *Flashback* (1974) is a reflection on the documentary film movement, and explores the relationship between cinema and the nation-state, and what it meant to make films 'back then'.

The dominant trend in documentary film-making by the Films Division, politically correct, socially neutral and myopically informative, was countered in the late 1970s. The notion of nation state was significantly challenged by the Naxalite movement and other organized political formations from the Left and Left of Centre ideologies. Independent political documentaries from local regions were born. Famine was shot, so was homelessness, state atrocities, migration, women as victims of domestic and sexual violence, and issues of landownership became important. In the period following the Emergency, a number of political documentaries were made. Gautam Ghose, Utpalendu Chakrabarty, Anand Patwardhan, Suhasini Mulay and Tapan Bose are some of the significant names from that period. They all came from a shared political background.[9]

They knew their subjects, their terrain. They wanted to make films in order to prove and disseminate what they already knew as truth. They began to challenge the benevolent perception of the State through a series of films, critical of the State. Yet even as there was an attempt to question the State, the aesthetics and the language were often similar to the earlier films.[10] They had the kind of confidence in their arguments that allowed them to hold a mid-shot of an interviewee for minutes. These films were mainly edited on the basis of dialogue tracks—polemics reigned supreme.

"In these films, instead of a benevolent State, there was the rogue State. Instead of trying to define the citizen, there were citizens as victims," points out Gargi Sen, documentary film-maker and co-founder of the Delhi-based documentary distributor, Magic Lantern Foundation. Yet many of today's film-makers had their first experience of seeing documentaries at this time, though they would go on to raise questions about them later. Sanjay Kak, one of the most outstanding documentary film-makers in the country, saw his (Sanjay Kak's) first documentary in the 1980s in a darkened classroom in his Delhi college—an Anand Patwardhan screening, *Prisoners of Conscience* (1978), on political prisoners in the time of the Emergency. "Anand was one of the first persons to go criss-crossing the country to show his film with such energy," says Kak. "After the screening, I realised that it was possible to do this. Yet, apart from a few films, the scope for seeing documentaries was limited, and we often made our films long before seeing many others..."

By the end of the 1980s and the turn of the 1990s, several parallel streams of documentary cinema came about. The Films Division commissioned film-makers to make documentary films of different genres, but the subjects could not be controversial or critical of the government and its policies. Significant film-makers invented their own imaginary and aesthetic lines of creativity to make documentaries of their choice in their own way. Examples are Mani Kaul's *Dhrupad* (1983) and *Siddheshwari* and Satyajit Ray's *The Inner Eye* (1972). Non-governmental organizations (NGOs) in increasing numbers began to commission the making of documentaries to perpetuate their cause without turning the films into propaganda and publicity machines. Earlier in their career, Delhi-based film-makers Saba Dewan and Rahul Roy, worked on several such films. Often these films would be driven by their own agendas, which circumscribed their scope and creativity. "These commissioned films co-opted the language of protest that was associated with earlier non-commissioned independent films, but their concerns were restricted and within the state's limits," Dewan recalls.

From the Eighties onwards, there were many 'methods' floating around. The 'all-knowing activist voice-over' was being used and discredited at the same time. Some said it was okay if the line was correct, the message clear and the heart firmly in the left place. Inspire or expose injustice! Others vehemently disagreed. The image was irrelevant; it was the politics that mattered. Both however, made beautiful films. These documented magnificient moments in the lives of struggling people and political movements and carried the stories of these struggles all over the world," wrote Amar Kanwar.[11]

Funding made to people outside the Films Division and other state departments remained, by and large, restricted to 'politically correct' films by their very definition, or to eminent feature film-makers who, by making documentaries for Films Division, would be adding respect and dignity to the organization itself, apart from enriching its archive library. Examples of such films are Girish Karnad's *Lamp in the Dark* (2009), Gulzar's *Pandit Bhimsen Joshi* (1992), Priya Dutt's *Nargis* (1991), documentaries by Adoor Gopalakrishnan, Gautam Ghose, Buddhadeb Dasgupta, Mrinal Sen, Satyajit Ray and so on. Film-makers, who are within Films Division, keep making 'politically correct' films for different governmental departments. Rarely does this official body permit slightly radical films such as Nilita Vachani's *Eyes of Stone* (1990).

There have been some significant exceptions. Mani Kaul's *Siddheshwari*, based on the life of renowned *thumri* singer Siddheshwari Devi, is one of the most unusual films to have been produced by the Films Division. Kaul rejects two holy tenets of documentary—linearity and exposition—and focuses on how the singer came to be immersed in classical music. He gets Mita Vashisht to play the singer and depict key events in Siddheshwari's life (such as her early years of training and her struggle to survive as a single mother). He juxtaposes these re-stagings with recreations of Siddheshwari's memories and epiphanies. Is it a documentary or is it fiction? Kaul, who was one of India's foremost experimental film-makers, had no easy answers.[12]

What Kind of Documentaries are Being Made Today?

"It has never been easy to characterize the precise difference between documentary and fiction films. That the documentary uses fact and fiction is too simplistic an explanation. There are fiction films that are based on what could be called solid facts. And there are documentaries that foray into fictional construction to state a fact. Ghastly Indian realities that are reported as news every single day and eagerly lapped up by an equally ghastly readership, present a world that will be difficult to fictionalize into a film, let alone made into a documentary. That is the state of our reality and fiction. Paradoxically, Indian life is at the same time choking on the 'feel good' stuff churned out by proponents of commerce, their advertising wizards and of course the state itself. They make one doubt, if at the end of it all, the reality might be nothing more than a piece of fiction," said Kaul.[13]

Today, many young film-makers with their courage and dedication to the cause of cinema are rising in numbers, audience reach and variety in subject matter, approach and presentation. Most of their films highlight our ignorance of life beyond our thickly insulated and fiercely protected urban life. Their films dig out the criminal inequality in the distribution of resources. They underscore the gross misuse, abuse and violation of human rights as well as the apathy of NGOs, the government and even foreign voluntary agencies to the plight of the marginalized. In India, the term 'marginalized' refers to people in the small and unorganized sector, disadvantaged groups such as children and destitutes, underprivileged working women and also groups and agencies who work with and for these people. We increasingly feel that the lives and achievements of these people, their aspirations and struggles, have been kept out of mainstream television on grounds that they do not offer entertainment value. The independent documentary movement sheds light on these lives and struggles.

"Perhaps the greatest problem which any historian has to tackle is neither the cataclysm of revolution nor the decay of empire, but the process by which ideas become social attitudes," wrote J.H. Plumb in the *New York Review of Books* many years ago. The film-maker today finds himself in the horns of a similar dilemma; whether to mirror the impact of dramatic social change on the people in general and the marginalized in particular; whether to reflect the change itself; or whether to use the language, the technique and the aesthetics of cinema as a medium of self-expression—an expression which encompasses that change within the film-maker himself. The following chapters will try to explore and resolve some of these questions.

Several factors are responsible for giving the independent documentary a place of its own, a place of respect in the marginal environment of economic bankruptcy and poverty of viewership. These are:

1. International documentary film festivals where Indian documentary films have won awards, bringing the films and their makers in the limelight.
2. The Mumbai International Film Festival for documentary, short and animation films (MIFF) started in 1990. It offers an international platform to Indian documentary film-makers who can command a good audience at least once.
3. Many documentary film festivals organized by film-makers themselves across the country every year defining genres, or to highlight a topical issue such as environmental film festivals, a festival of films on adventure films, a festival of films on wildlife, a film festival screening documentaries on fine arts, artists and performing arts such as the Jatin Das Centre of Art, Bhubaneswar.
4. Films for Freedom (earlier called the Campaign Against Censorship) is an action platform of over 300 independent documentary and short film-makers from across India who hold that freedom of expression and the right to information (RTI) are essential to the survival of a vibrant democracy. In an in-depth article in *Frontline*, film-maker Anand Patwardhan wrote[14]:

> As MIFF 2004 approached, the government knew that many films on the carnage in Gujarat exposing the ruling party's complicity were in the making and could embarrass it on an international stage. Perhaps to circumvent this, an amazing new rule was introduced stipulating that all Indian films should have a censor certificate. Foreign films were exempt from this rule. Documentary film-makers across the country were galvanized into action. Over 275 filmmakers exchanged ideas, drew up action plans, organized a Campaign Against Censorship (CAC) and threatened to boycott MIFF if the censor certificate requirement was not withdrawn. As a result, of a united and popular campaign, the rules for MIFF were amended again and the censorship clause was withdrawn. The film-makers were nevertheless apprehensive that there would be an attempt to introduce censorship through the back-door, that is, by eliminating 'uncomfortable' films from the festival through a manipulated selection. Their fears

came true. MIFF 2004 rejected some 30 of the most outstanding new Indian films made on a range of themes—primarily political. Included in the reject list were several films on state complicity in the Gujarat violence and many excellent films on communalism, caste and gender, sexuality and the environment. Quite a number of these have already been screened at major international festivals and won awards.

Finally, the protesting film-makers consensually decided to screen the 'rejected' films at some venue near the MIFF, and the films withdrawn from MIFF joined the screening list. This gave birth to what is now a new festival called Vikalp—Films for Freedom. The festival along with screenings continues till this day.

5. The Social Communications Film Conference organized by Roopkala Kendro, under the West Bengal Government is held annually. This however, has of late, lost its audience pull because it has been totally politicized by the ruling party and is run practically by government-appointed executors and administrators who have little interest in and knowledge of the documentary movement in India. Roopkala Kendro holds a Social Communication Cinema Conference annually in the month of February. "The focus in not on information but on the multi-layered reality of people's lives and the output should also have an input of entertainment for the thinking mind," said former CEO and Director, Anita Agnihotri, IAS. The ball was set rolling way back in November 1988. With a letter addressed to Gopi Arora, the then Secretary to the Government of India, Department of Information, Satyajit Ray had enclosed a project report prepared by the then young film-maker-cinematographer Gautam Ghosh in consultation with some Italian film personalities. The report contained the framework and plan for production of and training in making of educational and documentary films which, felt Ray, would create an environment of conscientious film-making in the Eastern Zone. The combined vision of these two talented film-makers propelled by the initiative of the Government of West Bengal crystallized into

an understanding between the Government of India and the Italian government. The outline of the project was laid down in 1995 and was named Roopkala Kendro. It is an Indo-Italian Cooperation project and 1995 marked Roopkala Kendro as a registered society. The objectives are (i) producing social communication cinema on video and (ii) training aspirants to this kind of cinema.
6. The banning of powerful political statements by the CBFC and other government bodies at the central and state levels that exerts a kind of 'negative' influence, a 'bouncing back' of the film, through widespread dissemination in the media, creating a demand for such films to be screened privately across the country.
7. Foreign funding and sponsoring agencies such as the Jan Vrijman Fund of the Netherlands, BBC's Channel Four and similar other organizations where Indian film-makers have made a mark.
8. The Public Service Broadcasting Trust (PSBT) based in Delhi offers funding and screens films they have produced and funded at an annual festival hosted by the Trust. PSBT also offers annual fellowships to film-makers and researchers in cinema and television. It collaborates with Doordarshan and its various channels to telecast these films. PSBT is a non-governmental, not-for-profit trust with the mission to create and sustain a credible space for public service broadcasting in India that is independent, participatory, pluralistic and democratic, distanced from commercial imperatives and state/political pressures. We work to mainstream the Indian documentary and empower independent film-makers by commissioning and mentoring films from across the country. On last count, the list on the PSBT website shows 417 documentaries and short films made over the years. Every year, PSBT commissions 100 films directly from independent documentary film-makers. Half of these films are made by women and 65 per cent of funded films are made by new film-makers. Since communication between PSBT and the film-makers is direct, the intrusion of agents, middlemen and production companies is ruled out completely.

Commissioned films reflect a wide variety of themes from gender and sexuality, through globalization, conflict, contemporary politics, education, health, development, environment, wildlife, profiles in courage, livelihood, agriculture, culture and tradition, children, diversity, history, ethnography, anthropology, art and craft, biography, to HIV-AIDS and so on. PSBT also organizes an annual film festival entitled Open Frame Film Festival and Forum organized in partnership with UNESCO, Prasar Bharati—the national public service broadcaster—INPUT (International Public Television) and the India Habitat Centre, New Delhi. The festival organizes workshops and forums for training documentary film-makers and aspirants, thereby widening the horizons of the programme. PSBT offers media fellowships from time to time to initiate and encourage in-depth research on contemporary media programming and its impact.

9. In 2006, some cultural activists got together and pooled contributions from the people of that town to arrange a film festival called The Cinema of Resistance, a kind the Hindutva-dominated Gorakhpur was not used to. The festival became an annual affair in Gorakhpur and entered its ninth year in 2014 in a row. It created perceptible ripples in the local cultural scenario and punched a few holes in the right places. But what was definitely not foreseen at the start of the journey was the proliferation of Cinema of Resistance festivals, which over years, grew roots in more than 10 cities spread across seven states. Inspired by the Uttar Pradesh (UP) experience, chapters were born in Bihar, Rajasthan, Chhattisgarh, Madhya Pradesh, Uttarakhand and West Bengal. The movement has taken its first steps in four more states, namely Haryana, Delhi, Odisha and Andhra Pradesh, as local teams crystallize. Cinema of Resistance campaign has dedicated itself to alternative film screenings, film distributing and film-making practices. It is aligned squarely with people's struggles. All these festivals have been organized solely on people's funding, with No governmental or corporate sponsorships.

Sanjay Joshi, one of the founders of this movement and National Convenor, Jan Sanskriti Manch (JSM), writes in his paper *Gorakhpur to Kolkata: Eight Years on the Road of Resistance* "The no-sponsorship model in turn helped fashioned a curation policy aligned with local politico-cultural needs. A curator funded by big foundations and CSR wings of companies or NGOs can well overlook local issues but a curator who runs by the direct support of five hundred people can't afford to be detached from the people's expectations from a cultural initiative like the *Cinema of Resistance*. This gets reflected in the documentaries, shorts and feature films we curated for our festivals. The integration of other art forms like theater and music also came organically, as had been JSM's founding traditions. To put it in short, we did not envisage *Cinema of Resistance* as a film-screening exercise for the sake of it. Rather, we wanted to build a platform with cinema as the primary medium, to amplify the voices of people's movements on the ground and to use cinema as a medium to initiate debates and dialogue to challenge the market-driven discourse on 'development', 'progress' and the 'ideal society' we strive for. Naturally, we tried to integrate all the other art forms at our disposal, to this end of making our festivals a platform for the oppressed and marginal voices. The documentary helped in raising the issues directly and to break the dominant to watch *Gangs of Wasseypur* (2012) or a *Love, Sex Aur Dhokha* (2010) would not go for Anand Patwardhan or Sanjay Kak documentaries with the same readiness. Our job is to try and change this culture."

In keeping with the spirit, this festival does not sell tickets across the counters. The festival is open to all and free. To quote Sudhir Suman from *Hard News* (Cinema of Resistance, 18 October 2011) "The festival showcases films which portrays the struggle of people for a better life and 'lifestyle'; it celebrates resistance to all forms of hidden and overt oppression. These are films which are a call to the conscience, and yet, they are not crass, propagandistic or didactic: they speak epic, nuanced, sensitive tales of stories which are not spoken in the mainline realm of cricket, entertainment, celebrity and television grandstanding. These are films on the plunder of natural resources by multinationals, the slow, relentless barbarism faced by the tribal people in India, hunger deaths of peasants, the unreported struggles by Manipuri and Kashmiri people for their democratic rights."

CHAPTERS BREAK-UP
Chapter 1. Introduction: Why Independent Films?
Chapter 2. Of Lives and Histories: Known and Lesser Known
Chapter 3. The Ethnographical Film: A Cinema for the People, by the People
Chapter 4. The Ray Factor
Chapter 5: The Milestone Makers
Chapter 6. Dialogues in Diversity: Women Film-makers
Chapter 7. Positive Documentaries on Sustainable Development
Chapter 8. Out of the Box
Summing Up

CONCLUSION
The documentary film, in all its vastnesses that embrace and envelop it today from educational films to the reconstruction of a fact or a historical event, is perhaps the main basis of revolutionary film-making. Every image that documents, bears witness to, refutes or deepens the truth of a situation is something more than a film image or purely artistic fact; it becomes something that the system finds indigestible.[15] Besides, in India, the question of cultural, linguistic, ethnic and lifestyle diversity dictates the norms and issues a documentary film-maker is concerned with. Which language should he choose to make his film in? If he uses English, unknown to a majority of Indians, his film will be incommunicable to a majority of his audience. If he does not make it in English, it will demand the additional responsibility and expense of subtitling for an international audience. If he fills it with talking heads, it will be boring to those who, within the domain of a factual non-feature film, are looking for some entertaining insights and relief, never mind if the term 'entertainment' here signifies a larger universe than it does in case of the fiction film. If he chooses a particular individual, say an eminent personality in West Bengal, where every issue and person is politicized, the personality's political leanings, articulated or understood or by implication, might block the film-maker's honest intentions of making a documentary on the given subject. He might withdraw from his design of making the film because he fears pre-censorship, censorship and post-censorship problems. Where will he go? Who can he turn to? When and how? The struggles of film-makers working in different genres and film-makers who use their film-making

and films as a language of rebellion, resistance and revolt will perhaps offer some information to the readers of this book. At least that is what it aspires to achieve.

Satish Bahadur, who taught film appreciation at the Film and Television Institute of India (FTII), Pune, from 1963 to 1973, in response to a question on financing documentary films in an ambience when governmental funding was almost drying up said, "Filmmakers will have to beg, borrow or even steal if needs be. The artist has to set his own limits and work out the framework within which he can function. To what extent he is willing to stick out his neck is what it boils down to. The committed film-maker has always faced problems; it is only the degree that varied. Every generation has had its Mahabharata. However oppressive the conditions, some cultural truths always filter down to the next. The persistence of human culture is based on the sheer dignity of man and his ability to survive with dignity. Humans have always supported the creation of works of art. That is what sustains the artist ultimately."[16]

Questions of voice, authority and authorship, have become a serious concern among documentary film-makers and anthropologists. Who can represent someone else, with what intention, in what 'language,' and in what environment, is a conundrum that characterizes the postmodern era. In this essay, I explore some of the responses to these problems by focusing on the relationship between documentary/ethnographic filmmakers and the people they film—in particular, the development of cooperative, collaborative and subject-generated films."[17]

NOTES

1. Madhusree Dutta, *In Defence of Political Documentary*, Infochange Film Forum, online magazine, http://infochangeindia.org/film-forum/news-a-views/in-defence-of-political-documentary.html (last accessed on 17 December 2011).
2. Ibid.
3. Michael Rabiger, *Directing the Documentary*, 4th ed. (USA: Focal Press, 2004), 4.
4. Shoma, A Chatterji, "Censorship—Fragmenting Cinema," in *100 Years of Jump-cuts and Fade-outs: Tracking Change in Indian Cinema* (Delhi: Rupa Publications, 2014), 279.
5. Sonam Joshi, "Turning Around the Camera," *Caravan*, 1 April 2010.
6. Saibal Chatterjee, "Gutsy Reels, Real Voices," *Tribune*, 5 July 2009, Chandigarh, Sunday Cover Story.
7. Francis Miquet, "From the Polemical Heart," taken in December 1995, *Spectrum India* (29 January to 5 February 1996), 5.
8. http://www.csds.in/sites/default/files/Banner/FD%20Zone%20Details.pdf

9. Ibid.
10. Joshi, *Turning Around the Camera*, 2010.
11. Amar Kanwar, "The Search," Festival Brochure—Films for Freedom, Bangalore, 2004, 25. Organized by Vikalp—an initiative of Campaign against Censoship.
12. Nandini Ramnath, "Reel Change, Revolution Flows from the Lens of a Camera," *Time Out*, Mumbai, online magazine. Also available online at https://mlfblog.wordpress.com/2010/01/. Last accessed on January 26, 2010.
13. Ibid.
14. Anand Patwardhan, "Parallel Festival of Documentaries", *Frontline* , volume 21, issue 4, 14–27 February 2004.
15. Bilquis Zafirul Hassan, *Mohasiron Ka Shahar* (City of Sieges), translated from the Urdu by Diba Zafir (Seagulls, 5 April–May–June 2002).
16. Thomas Abraham, "Who's Afraid of the Commercial Wolf?" Interview with Satish Bahadur, *Spectrum India* (29 January to 5 February 1996), 3.
17. Jay Ruby, "Speaking For, Speaking About, Speaking With, or Speaking Alongside: An Anthropological and Documentary Dilemma," *Visual Anthropology Review* 7, no. 2 (Fall 1991).

2
OF LIVES AND HISTORIES
Known and Lesser Known

INTRODUCTION

The biographical documentary takes several forms. The first belongs to the segment that celebrates some of the greatest Indians who have contributed to Indian history, culture, language, economy and so on. The second concerns lesser-known individuals whose names are lesser known or not known at all but their contributions need to be documented for the archives such as *Arzoo* (2009) by Shashi Gupta who documents the contribution of Sulekha Ali to child victims of the Gujarat communal riots. There is another area of the biographical that records individual struggles and triumphs over physical disabilities, mental issues, social obstacles, family hurdles and so on. There is a fourth category that subscribes to a recreation or revisiting of historical time such as Lalit Vachani's *The Salt Stories* (2008). Vachani's film falls somewhere along the continuum of a biographical and a historical film because it focusses on how Mahatma Gandhi and his initiation of the historical Dandi March impacted people living along the road of the Dandi March today.

LIVES: KNOWN

The Films Division

Perhaps one of the greatest contributions of the Films Division (FD) is its massive output of biographical documentaries. Besides films made by producers within the FD, the organization also has in its priceless archive biographical documentaries made by prominent film-makers beyond the borders of FD such as Buddhadeb Dasgupta,

Gulzar, Chidananda Dasgupta, Shaji Karun and so on. The best part of these excellent biographical documentations of great lives is that they defy genre classification as typically biographical films. Nor do they succumb to the temptation of turning into celebratory tributes that lack perspective and are simply idolatry.

Kumar Shahani's *Khayal Gatha* and *Bhavantarana* (1991) are two of the most outstanding documentaries exploring the history of the *Khayal* and documenting the life of the Odissi dancer and scholar, the late Kelucharan Mohapatra, respectively. He played around with the form in the former film, turning it into a blend of abstractions and conc rete expressions without being loud about the chronological history of the Khayal School of Music. *Khayal Gatha* stressed on the aesthetics of the film rather than on factual information, investing the concept of the documentary with a new dimension.

Shot entirely on actual locations in Orissa, *Bhavantarana* takes us on a journey into a lush, green mantle of enchantment enriched by the fluid movements of a girl in green, dancing away against the sea in the midst of the trees. There is no commentary. The asymmetrical narrative is often broken by text cards quoting from the Rig Veda, Mahabharata, Taitareya Upanishad, Guru Kelucharan himself and Anand Coomaraswamy. Instead of taking the audience away from the subject, this placed the film more in perspective raising it to spiritual and philosophical dimensions in addition to the one that dance, music and rhythm has for all of us. Shahani is very low key in his use of colour, light, music and sound not permitting them to sidetrack his main subject—Guru Kelucharan Mohapatra. Yet they become a part of his cast—they perform and they make the final product a work of art and a finely honed example of craftsmanship.

Gulzar's documentary, *Pandit Bhimsen Joshi* is as much a biographical documentary as it is a historical one because alongside tracing the life of the great vocalist, it also traces the history of one school of Hindustani classical music, namely, the Kirana Gharana. Gulzar added his aesthetic touches to the film, with feather-light, suggestive strokes when in one shot, the camera focusses on the pair of slippers Panditji wore, lying outside the door to his *riyaaz* (practise) room. Warm images of Panditji sitting with his family at the dinner table, introducing the members one by one to the maker, dot the film. The 45-minute film unfolds small bytes of information.

It spells out the determination of a man to find out in whatever way possible, the guru he was searching for. "I ran away from home at the age of 11 not because my mother refused me a spoonful of ghee when we were eating. It was just an excuse to run away from Gadag which did not have the guru I could learn from. There was just one music teacher who could only impart elementary music lessons I had already learnt. I had made up my mind earlier. I was looking for an excuse to run away in search of the right mentor."

Artificial classifications of the documentary format into genres are a misnomer because all genres are subject to considerable overlapping thus often lending themselves to varied interpretations, blurring the dividing line between one genre and another. Gulzar's documentary on Pandit Bhimsen Joshi is as much a biographical documentary as it is a historical one because alongside tracing the life of the great vocalist, it also traces the history of one school of Hindustani classical music, namely, the Kirana Gharana, without which no history of Hindustani classical music styles can be complete.

Arun Khopkar's *Colours of Absence* (1993), on cubist-abstract painter Jehangir Sabavala, unfolds the painter's evolution to become one of the most outstanding among contemporary painters in India. However, in terms of sheer form of expression, it can be termed an experimental documentary considering the way in which Khopkar interweaves his narrative with his subject's views on nature through variable chromatic light, through sound effects that sometimes relate directly to the visuals and sometimes create a contrapuntal tension, aiming to capture the spirit of the paintings. In this sense, it is also an art-centric, aesthetic documentary. It is also an archival film that forms part of India's art history.

Problems arise when biographical documentaries are made on celebrated film-makers themselves. It is difficult to document their lives, their aesthetic approach, their choice of subject, etc. because the documentary, filming such a person, is constantly dogged by questions of his own creativity, ingenuity, aesthetic expression and research. *A Dream Takes Wings* (2000), on D.G. Phalke, popularly known as Dadasaheb Phalke, was directed by Gajanan Jagirdar, with archival footage from Phalke's life, probably cinematographed by Phalke himself, clippings from some of the 95 films and 26 short films he made during his career.

B.N. Sircar (1995), directed by Nishith Banerjee, is a biographical film about the founder of the once-famous and now historic New Theatres Ltd., the production banner and its two studios that changed the history of Bengali and Hindi cinema in the country forever. The film traces what drew the interest of Sircar, a foreign-trained engineer, to film-making and how he produced 150 films under his production banner in Hindi, Bengali and even Tamil, making path-breaking films such as *Devdas* (1935) and introducing the audience to some of the greatest talents Indian cinema has seen. P.C. Barua, R.C. Boral, Pankaj Mullick, Bimal Roy, K.L. Saigal and Nitin Bose are just a few names that found their feet and bloomed in New Theatres.

B.D. Garga's ***Creative Artist: Satyajit Ray*** (1974), shot in black and white (B&W), is mainly a coverage of Ray's approach to film-making, his strategy of shooting, directing his actors, preparing before a shoot, discussing and debating with his cast and crew, all done when Ray was shooting *Mahanagar* (1963) with Madhabi Mukherjee and Anil Chatterjee. Garga's styling of the biographical documentary is original as it does not go through the routine paces of place and date of birth, early childhood, his father's passing away and so on. The film offers an unusual insight into the mindscape of one of the world's greatest film-makers at his prime.

U.B. Mathur's ***Hrishikesh Mukherjee*** (2008) is a simple, straightforward, very conventional documentary on this extremely successful film-maker who redefined the term 'wholesome family entertainment' for mass audiences in the country. With clips from *Abhimaan* (1973), *Aashirwad* (1968), *Anand* (1971) and *Namak Haraam* (1973), how without using voyeuristic strategies of sex and violence in his films, Mukherjee could get his message across to reach his target audience.

Cinematically and aesthetically speaking however, the best film in this bunch was Shaji Karun's tribute to his mentor in the film ***G. Aravindan*** (1999). Karun began his career as cinematographer for Aravindan and shot the film after the sudden and untimely demise of the great, but extremely low-profile film-maker. Karun later became an independent film-maker in his own right and this gives the film that extra touch of aesthetic sensibility and social concern not usually witnessed in biological documentaries. With archival clippings from Aravindan's early life, still photographs picked from the family album, Karun uses colour to shoot an actor shot from behind to personalize Aravindan and his enduring love for nature in all its beauty. The film mentions how in *Kanchana Sita* (1977), Aravindan used nature to symbolize Sita instead of using an actor to play the character in his original interpretation of Sita in captivity.

Brij Bhushan's celluloid essay, *Anil Biswas* (2004), whose songs featured in Indian films from 1935 to 1965, offered personal confessions by the talented Biswas who says at one point, that he copied generously from his 'father' Rabindranath Tagore, and found nothing wrong in it as it is alright for a 'son' to pick his 'father's' pocket. One comes to learn of Biswas' long stint with All India Radio (AIR), his successful career in Bombay (now Mumbai) cinema followed by another long and successful stint in Delhi where he settled down for the last 20 years of his life. Biswas is extremely candid and natural in front of the camera. The film remains silent about his desertion of his first wife and the children born out of his earlier marriage. This amounts to a violation of the truth, an essential element of a biographical documentary, because it projects Meena Kapoor as his only wife.

Clips from *Doctor* (1940) and some other films that featured Mullick as an actor-singer formed part of the celluloid essay *Pankaj Mullick* (1980). The film appears to have been shot during the last days of his life. It offers a very intimate picture Mullick, the family man, close to his wife, daughter, son-in-law and grandson. Some more focus on the singer as a music director and a little emphasis on some songs of Tagore he put to music would have made it a more complete film. One classic example is Mullick reportedly having set Tagore's "diner seshe ghumer deshe" to music when Barua wanted to use it for a New Theatres' film. Stills of Mullick winning awards for his contribution to music formed part of the film.

Jagadish Banerjee's *Salil Chowdhury* is a film portrait of the dedicated music composer. Salil Chowdhury was an outstanding composer, an accomplished and gifted arranger, poet, storyteller, playwright, writer, an intellectual and a humanist. A master multi-instrumentalist, he acquired mastery over both string and reed instruments and also the flute. The film focussed mainly on his Gana Sangeet and his compositions for Hindi films that remain archived often because of their songs and music. The film left his personal life out of the film except for his childhood in Assam, captured in fictionalized flashback and presented him as music director and lyricist. Sadly, there is little mention of his deep involvement with the people's theatre movement where Gana Sangeet played the most important role.

Naushad Ali—The Melody Continues (2008) was the best of all the biographical documentaries. It pays a musical tribute to Naushad Ali, one of the greatest music directors of Indian cinema, and gives a brief account of the achievements of the departed soul. The film opened with shots of the composer just before his demise, taken by his grandson. Naushad's personal inputs go back to his childhood in Lucknow, where his maternal grandmother brought him up, the chasing of his musical dreams in Mumbai intercut with beautiful anecdotes and clips from some of the best musical scores of his long career. The music director offers a glimpse of the essential quality of not letting fame and glamour go to one's head. One interesting anecdote is about his interaction with K. Asif when the latter asked him to score the music for *Mughal-e-Azam* (1960). The Salim–Anarkali romance had already been immortalized in Filmistan's biggest hit Anarkali with brilliant music by C. Ramchandra. "How would you achieve the same thing within the same situation?" I asked him, said Naushad. Asif was confident that he would do it differently and come out triumphant. "*Phir unhone sheesh mahal banwaya*," said Naushad.

Film-maker, music director and scriptwriter Satarupa Sanyal made a 35-minute documentary *Immortal Martyr Jatin Das* (2009), produced by the FD. She has sketched a portrait of Jatin Das, the young man first drawn to Gandhian ideals of non-violence to shift to armed revolution by acquiring expertise in making bombs under the guidance of another freedom fighter, Sachindra Nath Sanyal. Das was arrested as one of the 10 accused who robbed the railway treasury on 9 August, 1925 from a train in Kakori in Uttar Pradesh. He was later transferred to Mymensingh Jail where he and his colleague Pannalal Mukherjee underwent a 20-day hunger strike to protest the mistreatment of political prisoners. They were later transferred to the notorious Mianwali Jail in west Pakistan but were released in October 1928.

The biographical archive of FD will go a long way in educating aspiring film-makers, students and cine buffs in tracing the mindset of these artists for whom cinema was not just a commodity to be advertised, promoted and sold to the market but to be imbibed, ingested and understood forever.

Beyond FD

Lalit Vachani's ***Natak Jaari Hai*** (2005) is a nostalgic journey into the struggles, evolution and commitment of Jana Natya Manch, also known by its acronym Janam founded as an offshoot of the Indian People's Theatre Association (IPTA). The film moves back and forth through time, space and people, offering priceless vignettes into the character and persona of the late Safdar Hashmi, through archival footage where he belts out a line of song, joking about his actor's total lack of voice, tune or rhythm.

Natak Jaari Hai moves at its own pace, through time, space and people, as the camera closes in on a specially put up proscenium performance of Janam's first street-theatre production, *Machine*, a satire on industrialization that reduces the human being into the mechanical predictability of an assembly line or a machine. Shot in B&W, the silhouetted figures of the actors, standing in a row behind each other to resemble a single machine, their mechanized voices coming out as if through a toneless and pitchless recording instrument, captivates the audience with its sheer intensity. Vachani retains the black-and-white format for the flashbacks into Janam's past when Safdar was alive and captures him with his group, taking light potshots at some of his actors who cannot sing to save their lives but must if they must be a part of agitprop theatre.

Vachani travelled with the group to Kolkata in 2004 where they had gone to present and perform *Bolo Kya Banoge Tum*. Other clips from milestone plays of the group such as *Yeh Dil Mange More Guruji, Who Bol Uthi* and so on are also there while there are archival clips with Hashmi himself performing in *Halla Bol*. The film is dotted with snippets of information such as the fact that since 1973, when the group was formed, till 2005, Janam has done 15 proscenium plays and given 7,500 performances of 66 street plays; that one lakh workers had gathered to watch a street performance of *Machine* in October 1978; and that *Aurat* became a part of the women's movement when it was first performed in 1979. Vachani talks to almost all the members of the group who have remained with Janam till date beginning with Malashree, followed by Sudhanva who joined the group in 1987, "just a couple of years before the death of Safdar," the ever-smiling Uttam who came all the way from Murshidabad in West Bengal with stardust in his eyes but stayed on to become a part of the movement, without regrets, and of course, the young Sarika who was impressed during a workshop in her college and decided to pitch in.

Natak Jaari Hai winds its way through the slums, rough roads of the countryside as the group travels to perform somewhere else, to street corners, to come back to the same place—Sahidabad—where Hashmi was chased during a performance of *Halla Bol* and finally battered to death way back in 1989. The play was about the government's repression of the workers' organs for economic struggle. During the show, Mukesh Sharma, supported by the Congress Party as well as a crowd of Congress supporters, arrived at the scene, armed with guns and bamboo poles. They began a confrontation, which led to the murder of Safdar. Hashmi was killed because he dared to stage a street play on behalf of the Centre of Indian Trade Unions (CITU), which challenged the then ruling party's mafia politics in Delhi's slums.

Vachani keeps away from the politics of the movement and focusses on its existence at present, its evolution and its sustenance. The red flag does make its appearance during some of the plays and the Leftist stance is visible right through the film. Yet, there is no propaganda in or through the film, for or against the group. Though his choice of subject is openly subjective, Vachani tries his best to maintain an objective distance, and quite surprisingly, he succeeds.

Malashri opens an album of black-and-white photographs that offers the audience a brief glimpse into their lives together in a no-nonsense, matter-of-fact manner, completely devoid of dramatics. Though the film does tend to focus on the Leftist leanings of Janam, this in no way interferes with Vachani's ability to alienate himself from the political ideology of the group or from the messages it seeks to project through its plays. This is a very difficult task for a documentary film-maker who tends to get sucked into the vortex of a powerful subject such as Janam. *Sabse khatarnaak hota hai hamaare sapnon ka mar jana* was an adage Safdar lived by. It is a famous line from a poem created by the Punjabi poet Pasha. This line applies precisely to the film *Natak Jaari Hai* as well. It is a film of endless journeys through a dynamic movement that seeks to reach an undefined destination stretching to infinity.

Vision Unveiled (2010) is a documentary on painter Wasim Kapoor produced by Manibrata Das, which unfolds, layer by slow layer, the life of a healthy boy who grows up watching the puja drummers perform on the streets from the window of his house or watching movies on a home projector within a darkened room, through a twist of destiny that changes his life completely. The expression of wonder written on his face is a perhaps a pointer to his great fascination for the stars who people the tinsel world of cinema, his first love.

Vision Unveiled offers more than a glimpse of an artist and painter. It is the story of a man who rose above the obstacles destiny imposed on him when he lost the use of his legs but who, instead of wallowing in a life of self-pity, redefined his life all over again, choosing to express himself with his palette of colours and brush on canvas. Wasim Kapoor is a familiar sight at every imaginable event in Kolkata, be it someone else's art exhibition or an event organized by the Spastic Society of India's city branch or even a glitzy film premiere. The unassuming nature of his earthy character carries no aura of the talent he has. However, *Vision Unveiled* does not dwell on this side of the artist's personality. Rather, by fictionalizing his childhood and early youth with actors drawn mainly from Bengali television, Das chooses to focus on the artist's success despite his physical handicap.

Wasim Kapoor's track record as painter goes back by 35 years and his oeuvre is enriched by an amazing versatility in range and choice of subject matter. From portraits of film stars to Jesus Christ in different moods and from varied angles, Kapoor has done it all. Offering a multi-layered perspective, the film explores the different aspects of Kapoor's creative persona tracing the trauma he underwent as a child when he lost the use of his legs. The film moves more or less fluidly between and among his fictionalized childhood to Kapoor himself talking about his life, work, inspiration, experience to celebrities talking about Kapoor, the man and the artist. He talks about his first encounter with Debiprasad Roy Choudhury who, impressed with the works of a young Wasim, volunteered to write the introduction to the catalogue for Kapoor's first one-man show in Kolkata.

It is indeed rare to encounter a film critic making a bio-documentary on a film-maker. But then, one has to concede that both the critic, namely Chidananda Dasgupta, and the film-maker Mrinal Sen, are distinguished men in their own fields. The alternative universes they seem to carry around in their cerebral heads define their lives. Therefore, surprising though it might appear at first glance, as you warm up to the fact, you learn to cope with the reality. Interestingly, Dasgupta is a film-maker too, in his own right, just as Mrinal Sen claims to have had some interesting phases in his life as a journalist. Dasgupta made a documentary, *Mrinal Sen* (2001), produced by the PSBT.

"Over its footage of 30 minutes, the film focusses on Sen's technique and his ideas, ideology and conception that led him to choose his subjects for his films. I should have thought of this earlier, but strangely, it escaped me. While I was researching for a book on Mrinal Sen, the PSB System offered me a proposal to make a few biographical documentaries on some film-makers, I jumped at the chance. That is how this film came about," said Dasgupta about his documentary on Mrinal Sen.

Shot over seven days, the film has a detailed interview of the film-maker by Dasgupta's daughter Aparna Sen. "I wanted a film-maker to be the interviewer who is familiar and has deep regard for Sen's work as film-maker. Aparna has worked under Sen's directorial wand as an actress and has done an in-depth interview with him for the magazine she used to edit. Besides, she is a film-maker herself. She is articulate too. I wrote down the questions she had to ask. She made improvisations whenever she had to. This has invested the interview with an air of spontaneity. The interview was shot over a three-day spread of shoots," said Chidananda. "I decided to zero in on Mrinal's own voice, his manner of breaking away from conventional norms of film-making, his dynamism and his vibrancy, his casual indifference to the traditional grammar of cinema to evolve his own individual style and language in my film," he summed up.

The other strong element is capturing the ambience of Calcutta (now Kolkata), the city with an evolving history of its own. "Whenever one tries to recall the 'voice' of middle-class Calcutta as captured on film, the first name that comes to mind is that of Mrinal Sen. His films offer a microcosm of middle-class Bengali life in Calcutta, their problems, their hypocrisy, their pain and sorrow, their class struggle. So I, my Chief Assistant Aniruddha Dhar and my Cinematographer Shirsa Ray wandered around the streets of Calcutta, took interior shots of the Town Hall, and some shots from inside a tramcar, traversing through streets frequented in the past by Mrinal himself who led many and *adda* with his friends of yore," informed Dasgupta. The film carries archival clips from some of Sen's films. "But this has been one of my main stumbling blocks because many of Mrinal's films have just vanished without a trace. Such as *Punascha* (2014)—a telling comment on the man-woman relationship—which was a film much ahead of its time. So I had to make do with whatever was available. But I cannot say I am unhappy about the project," he surmised. Not very long ago, DD National, within its celebratory programme for 100 Years of Indian Cinema, featured a documentary on Mrinal Sen by Ramesh Sharma called *Mrinal Sen—Portrait of a Director* (1999).

It took FTII alumnus Anup Singh six long years to finally be able to put his documentary *Ekti Nadir Naam* (The Name of a River, 2002) on the screen. "Refugee?" Ghatak asks repeatedly in his films. "Who is not a refugee?" This forms the crux of this film, which can be interpreted as a fictionalized documentary on film-maker Ritwik Ghatak. The film sets out to find answers to the question Ghatak posed in and through his films, in a myriad different ways, mostly angry, often restless, reflecting the state of his schizophrenic mind, forever vacillating between his roots—Bangladesh and the city that was the base of his uprooted identity—Calcutta. "The film is about the life and cinema of Ritwik Ghatak," says its maker Singh. "Although a contemporary of Satyajit Ray and Mrinal Sen, Ghatak's films are posthumously receiving international attention as arguably the most relevant and moving cinema of our time," he adds.

Singh thus discovers that, "He has the rare fluidity of being able to slip though all boundaries made lucid with every film with the music in them. The music of *The Name of a River* seeks to invoke the cultural memory of a civilization. Its ancient calls and melodies hold the resonance of its future. It is a music that carries the textures and the movements of vast journeys. The songs of the nomadic Bauls (wandering minstrels), of the classical singers concretize the vast journeys of the Sufis of Persia and the Middle East through the Sind, Punjab and Bengal. The Sufis fused Muslim and

Hindu philosophy into a direct, joyous relationship with the divine. In their voice there is as much the desert and the mountain as there is the river," Singh sums up, emotionally moved by his own experiences of making such an ambitious and challenging film.

Singh begins the tribute by borrowing the title of his film from a Ghatak film, never mind the fact that he fragments it and takes only a part. Singh takes out the 'Titash' from Ghatak's *Titash Ekti Nadir Naam* (1973) to invest his film with a more universal canvas. This spans within itself, a world view of cinema, theatre as a Leftist movement, and life which constantly flows back and forth between the question of the refugee's identity, as perceived through the life of Ghatak himself. K.K. Mahajan's cinematography blended into Sanjay Choudhury's musical score, with bits and pieces of songs taken from the original soundtrack of Ghatak's films, makes *Titash Ekti Nadir Naam* a beautiful celluloid tribute to the master, who, like the river he identified so closely with, continued having the last laugh long after his death. An analysis of his comments forms the essence of Singh's film. Produced by National Film Development Corporation (NFDC) of India and the British Film Institute, London, the film had its world premiere at the London Film Festival last November.

The film reaches its peak when the camera and crew travel all the way to Bangladesh on the banks of the river Titash, where Ghatak shot *Titash Ekti Nadir Naam*. Two Bangladeshi actresses, Rosy Afsari and Kabori Sarwar, recall, while making *peethas* (a sweet prepared with rice powder and/or sweet potatoes) on an earthen oven, how Ghatak made them go through pain that would strip them of their starry auras to grill them for their roles in his film. The film closes, albeit a bit suddenly, against the Kolkata skyline with its jagged borders of housetops and terraces, browned and rusty with age and neglect. A church in the backdrop with the top of a masjid a bit further away suggests the end of the journey. However, did Ghatak want his 'journey' to ever end?

Eka Ebong Kayekjon (2000) that translates as *Alone and A Few Friends* is an 80-minute documentary based on the life and works of contemporary Bengali literature's greatest icon, Sunil Gangopadhyay. Gangopadhyay who passed away last year is a cult figure in Bengal and also in India, since many of his works are available in Indian translations.

Shot and presented in video format, the film is directed by Gautam Barman who also scored the music. The name *Eka Ebong Kayekjon* has been inspired from one of Sunil's own works. Conceived and produced jointly by Sahana Sen and Alakananda Banerjee, *Eka Ebong Kayekjon* stands testimony to the evolution of a dreamy-eyed boy from a middle-class Bengali family growing up to become one of the most famous literary giants in post-modern Bengal.

The film explores the dual identity of Sunil, the writer. Sunil as Sunil Gangopadhyay, poet, novelist, short-story writer and playwright; and Sunil writing under the pseudonym Neellohit, nickname Neelu, where he creates beautiful satiric prose, writing in the first person, as a 27-year-old youth, a pathological liar, a weaver of tales, who never grows old or up, whose adventures and explorations find fruit through his journeys into the unknown. Neelu could be described as a modern-day version of the wandering minstrel of Bengal, the Baul who wanders from village to village, and singing songs woven around his travels. His mind is as wandering as is his body, his soul, a moving spirit. This 'mustard seeds under the feet' characteristic can be identified with the real-life Sunil who is crazy about travelling to places known and unknown. Among his most memorable journeys, Sunil mentions his meeting with his ideal, T.S. Eliot, during one of his first visits to the UK.

The film has a captivating opening scene showing Sunil ambling along the sand-beaches of Puri. A poem of his is recited in the voice-over. The film closes on the same note, in circular fashion, on the Puri beaches, with Sunil distancing himself from the foreground to dissolve into a small dot of humanity in the infinite expanse of the horizon. With some disciplined and merciless editorial clipping of, say, 20 minutes of footage, *Eka Ebong Kayekjon* would make for an impressive biographical documentary, a significant contribution to the country's cultural archives.

Four different documentaries have been made over time over Third Theatre creator Badal Sircar. The films are—Sourav Sarangi's *Collage*, *Pakhira* (Asim Choudhury, Sibananda Mukherjee and Debashish Chakraborty), *Third Theatre in Bangla* in two parts, directed by Goutam Sharma and Swapna Dutta's *Ebam Badal Sircar* (2008). Swapna Dutta's *Ebam Badal Sircar*, a 47-minute documentary, looks at Sarkar from a different angle. We find the octogenarian engaged in freewheeling conversations with a group of children. It is a process of discovery on both sides. In course of this interaction, we are gradually introduced to Badal Sarkar as the eminent theatre personality, as a keen social commentator even at 80 plus, as the grandpa next door. Rare archival photographs provide the perspective while he reflects on his experience or explains his philosophy of theatre. The background scores used in the film are from Badal Sarkar's compositions, played by the child artistes. The other films mainly focussed on his 'third theatre' practice. Shot in B&W, they suffer from lack of preservation that has affected the quality of the prints.

As playwright and director, Badal Sircar evolved and defined his individual content, form, aesthetics and philosophy he called 'Third Theatre', which, in course of time, became synonymous with his name. Third Theatre is that kind of performance that recognizes, establishes and continuously reinforces maximum intimacy between actor and spectators. His strategy and methodology appeared simple and uncomplicated. However, peeping behind the apparent simplicity was a philosophy that made theatre a performance for the people, of the people and, in a manner of speaking, even by the people. He began by performing in small halls and with benches and stools to create varied shades of relationship between actors and spectators. He moved on to the open streets, gardens, parks, everywhere, turning the whole world into a stage without any reference to Shakespeare. He drew theatre out form the confines of the folk and the urban styles and into the Third Theatre to expose us to an unconventional theatrical dimension of free theatre, courtyard productions and village theatre.

The Last Lady (2002) is Alok Das' personal tribute to Lady Ranu Mukherjee who enhanced and enriched Calcutta's world of art and culture with her personal contribution to it. The camera opens on the lush green mantle that makes up the gardens of the famous Mukherjee house in Calcutta. The film closes with a shot of the horizon, a boat meandering across the Ganges in coloured silhouette, as lines from a Tagore song, "tobu more rekho…" in the rich voice of Suchitra Mitra mark the end of the film.

The film steers clear of the gossipy references surrounding the lady. Was this steering away from personal observations and intrusion into privacy a conscious attempt? "Yes, it was," says Das, who produced, directed and scripted the film. "I did not wish to focus on anything else except the Lady and her artistic creation—The Academy of Fine Arts," he added.

The film subtly points out the striking contrast between the infinity of art and the finiteness of life by placing Lady Ranu on a wheelchair with an attending nurse in the midst of her spacious living room chock-a-block with some of the best antiquities in art and sculptural creations in the archives of this Indian collector. Her priceless contribution to the history, geography and culture of Calcutta is the Academy of Fine Arts, residing in the heart of the city, in the midst of a beautiful garden replete with sculptures and artworks, leading to four art galleries at front and an auditorium for staging plays and performances in the rear. Though the Academy was originally founded in one corner of the Indian Museum, in 1933, Lady Ranu got actively involved with it from 1947 and later shifted it to its present premises, as living testimony to the beautiful heritage architecture of a bygone day.

Melody in Mass, a documentary produced by the Bosu Cultural Academy and directed by Jagannath Chatterjee on noted sculptor Debabrata Chakraborty offers an intriguing combination of a low-profile director exploring a low-profile subject, a rare event at a time when blowing one's own trumpet is the name of the game. Jagannath Chatterjee is a low-profile person who occasionally makes telefilms and documentaries that leave a distinct mark of his individuality as a film-maker. He is passionate about films, but also holds a job to fall back on, since manipulations and strategies are beyond him. *Melody in Mass* spans the works and life of sculptor Debabrata Chakraborty whose oeuvre is as masterful as it is versatile in terms of choice of subject, medium, theme, size and aesthetics. He earlier made a documentary on the famous dentist Dr R. Ahmed, named *Portrait of a Pioneer* produced by the Indian Dental Association in 1995.

Explaining his motivation, Chatterjee says, "In our humble, hum-drum existence, the term 'art for art's sake' sounds like a trite phrase until you meet Debabrata Chakraborty who lives in Bally, on the outskirts of Calcutta. He is docile, with eyes withdrawn, slightly fatigued, but his inner self is bedrock of strength and tough resolve. His home and studio are strewn with plaster, wood, aluminium, stone, fibreglass and other materials—each a piece of beauty and rhythm with its contours, charm, spell, delicacy and grace. The melody that emanates from each of them is mellifluous and seeps into our souls. But what triumphs above everything else, is the inner beauty of one of the finest human beings I have ever met. Some of the most notable of art critics such as Shobhan Shome has compared his works with those of Henri Moore and Rodin. I persuaded some of them to speak into the camera and they did."

Padatik (The Footsoldier) is a 60-minute documentary on Tapan Sinha directed by Bapi Banerjee and produced by the Eastern India Cinematographers' Association. The film opens with strains of the Tagore song "amaar mukti aloye aloye ei aakashey," a song Sinha used in his film *Atithi* (1966) many years ago. The lines of the song are a fitting tribute as they are a metaphor for Sinha's life. "My freedom lies in the light of the open sky," goes the rough translation of the lines. 'Light' here represents the light Sinha shed through his films among his audience for many decades. 'Freedom' symbolizes the infinity of his greatness that is liberated through death but reaches far beyond mortality. 'Open sky' is a metaphor for his infinite horizon in films and in film-making.

The film traces the historical backdrop of world cinema within which Tapan-da found inspiration for a new kind of cinema. In 1948, the film points out, the form and content of cinema found a new definition and meaning with Vittorio De Sica's *Bicycle Thieves* (1948). This film laid the foundations of what came to be known as neo-realism in cinema, which, in the course of time, influenced several Indian film-makers such as Satyajit Ray, K.A. Abbas and Bimal Roy. Partly because of the use of nonprofessional actors and partly for economic reasons, these films were shot without sound and the dialogue was synchronized back in the studio, a process that gave the director greater freedom in capturing what was happening spontaneously in front of the camera. Sinha also was influenced by this school of cinema. *Ankush*, Sinha's first film, was released in 1954. Ray's *Pather Panchali*, released the following year, made international history and, as a result, *Ankush* went unnoticed. The film points out that Sinha made 44 feature films on the widest range of genres not done by any Bengali and, probably, even Indian film-maker to this day.

Tapan Sinha, who often appears in the film answering queries from his sick bed, when asked what made him switch over to direct and compose the music for his films himself after having worked with some of the most celebrated and gifted music personalities, says, "I have worked with some of the best music composers in the country like Hemanta Mukhopadhyay, Ali Akbar Khan, Ravi Shankar, etc. Their music was very good and there are no two questions about it. But after a point of time, I began to feel that their musical score ran parallel to my film and did not blend into the story or the theme. Somehow, I was not satisfied. So, I began to bank on Tagore for my own musical scores. I really do not credit myself for music compositions in my later films. It was all Tagore from beginning to end." But Arati Mukherjee begs to differ and says that Tapan-da was a gifted music composer. "It is his basic modesty that makes him under-rate himself."

Padatik is generously dotted with archival clips from Tapan-da's films *Raja, Atithi, Safed Haathi* (1978), *Atanka* (1986), *Jhinder Bandi* (1961), *Wheel Chair* (1994), *Louhakapat* (1958), *Apon Jon, Jotugriha* (1964), *Khaniker Atithi, Sagina Mahato* (1971), *Adalat O Ekti Meye* (1982), *Bancharamer Bagan* (1980), *Nirjan Saikate* (1963), *Hatey Bazarey* (1967), *Kshudhita Pashan* (1960) and many others. His personal life is kept completely out of the scenario, perhaps at Sinha's request.

Remembering Bimal Roy

Remembering Bimal Roy is a 55-minute documentary film made by his only son, Joy Bimal Roy, collating his memories of a father he lost when he was only 10, talking to people in the industry who worked with this great film-maker, such as Dilip Kumar, Nabendu Ghosh, Kamini Kaushal and Gulzar, not forgetting to question eminent personalities who were children when Bimal Roy passed away. Among them are Javed Akhtar and Ashutosh Gowarikar who admitted that *Lagaan* (2001) was a tribute to Bimal Roy and his *Do Bigha Zamin* (1953). Bimal Roy's wife, the late Manobina Roy, talked about the film-maker as a husband and as a father. Joy has created an effective celluloid collage.

"I got to know him mainly through his films," says Joy. "For me, they are pure magic…haunting, evocative and timeless yet simple and easy to understand." The making of the film became a journey within and helping him understand why his father was so driven and how he achieved immortality in a short lifespan of 54 years.

Joy intercuts the film with archival clips from *Sujata* (1959), *Do Bigha Zamin* and New Theatres' *Mukti* (1937) which Bimal Roy cinematographed. There are many still photographs from the Roy's family album, catching Roy in his varied moods, smoking away—he was a chain smoker—Bimal Roy with Jawaharlal Nehru, Bimal Roy as leader of India's first film delegation to Russia, Bimal Roy holidaying with his family; they offer a glimpse into the life of a great man and his pursuit of excellence.

Remembering Bimal Roy effectively encapsulates the man and the film-maker. He spoke very little Hindi and yet created a portfolio of some of the finest films in Hindi, shot completely in black-and-white, with melodious music, strong storylines and brilliant acting. Many of them still stand on a solid edifice of a beautiful screenplay scripted by Nabendu Ghosh who passed away recently. "I discovered that the man was like his films. His life mirrored the purity of his films like a clear reflection of his beloved river Padma in Bangladesh," Joy sums up.

One wishes the film mentioned Bimal Roy's love for literature. His works were soaked in their rich literary source—from Sarat Chandra Chatterjee through Tagore to Munshi Premchand and Salil Choudhury. Joy also failed to mention that the Bimal Roy banner gifted Hindi cinema with some of the best film-makers in the generation following him. Three names that come up at once are Hrishikesh Mukherjee, Gulzar and Basu Bhattacharya. He gave directorial breaks to many strugglers who, however, failed to make the best of the opportunity. These are actor Asit Sen, Moni Bhattacharya (*Usne Kaha Tha*, 1960) and Arabinda Sen (*Amanat*).

Two Cameramen—Two Films—Subrata Mitra and Soumendu Roy

"The movie camera places on celluloid whatever it sees in real life. These images are not wholly real. Man operates the camera. The camera and the man together create a new world on the screen canvas. Three dimensional images become two-dimensional though traces of the third dimension remain. It works both ways—when the camera tracks back, indoors, it captures little details that went unnoticed before; on location, it brings to life the richness of nature. When it tracks forward, it captures the grains on the skin of a smiling face, and unseen realities enter the circle of one's vision. The spectator's eye and the camera's eye become one and the same."

These come across in the voice-over when *Soumendu Roy* begins. The cameraman keeps playing, exploring, capturing, innovating, freezing images with his magic machine that is his paint brush, making what the lens sees his canvas, the colours of nature his palette. These are thoughts that surface when one watches two documentaries on two of the greatest cinematographers India has ever produced—Subrata Mitra and Soumendu Roy.

Arindam Saha Sardar, a young, low-profile and film technique-crazy self-taught film-maker-archivist has made these one-hour-long documentaries. The bond these two cinematographers share is the film-maker they cut their tooth in cinematography with—Satyajit Ray. While Mitra began his career with Ray's *Pather Panchali,* Ray asked Soumendu Roy to take on the cinematography for Ray's documentary on Tagore and *Teen Kanya* (1961), his film based on three Tagore short stories.

Subrata Mitra opens with a voice-over of a brief sketch of Mitra who rose from humble beginnings to milestone achievements in a career filled with historic landmarks in lighting. It switches over to a nostalgic conversation between two cinematographers of two generations, Adinath Das, Dean and Academic Head at Satyajit Ray Film and Television Institute (SRFTI), Kolkata, and Soumendu Roy, his first disciple. They discuss Mitra's struggle to attain excellence in cinematography. The film is stranded together with interviews of renowned stalwarts such as cinematographers Purnendu Bose and Ramananda Sengupta and editor Dulal Dutta, who recount their interactions with Mitra at work, in experimentation and in real life, narrating anecdotes people would never have known had this film not been made.

Other than the famous innovation of bounce lighting 10 years before Sven Nyquist, *Subrata Mitra* zeroes in on an incident in Darjeeling during the shooting of Ray's *Kanchenjungha* (1962), his first film in colour. A team from Bombay was shooting Lekh Tandon's *Professor* (1962) at the same time. Dwarka Divecha, the noted cinematographer who was director of photography (DOP) for *Sholay* (1975), was the cameraman. The team was stuck for days on the hills. They could not shoot because of the moodiness of the mist. However, Mitra continued to shoot *Kanchenjungha* in the same environment. A surprised Divecha asked him how he could manage to work within the whimsical moods of nature. Mitra said that it was precisely the misty environment that he wanted and he got the visuals within this mistiness. *Kanchenjungha* is a milestone in colour photography for cinema done in Eastman Colour, looked down upon by big production houses in Bombay. *Subrata Mitra* is an impartial tribute, not a flattering celluloid celebration of a great artiste.

For *Charulata* (1964), shot in a relatively confined studio space with Bansi Chandragupta having designed the period sets, Mitra faced the possibility of multiple shadows created by the lighting needed to shoot the interiors of Charu's home. After many experiments, Mitra got wooden boxes approximately 3' × 2' in size. He got the box fitted with 27 household lamps of 100 watts each in three rows with separate switches for each row and a master switch for all the lights, a tissue paper covering the open side of the box. The whole box was then fit into a usual 2 kilowatt light stand. It was fascinating to see the quality of sophisticated, shadowless light that came out of these crude wooden boxes. This lighting replaced the earlier form of bounce lighting and turned into a trend among cinematographers in Bengali cinema. *Subrata Mitra* was declared the winner in the competition section of India Gate Festival 2011, Italy, organized by Performing India.

Soumendu Roy is shot in B&W. When the two films are juxtaposed, one discovers the difference between mapping the life of a living technician on celluloid and documenting the work of a genius who is no more among us. *Soumendu Roy* has been shot as one long interview almost totally on location in Khanyan near Burdwan in Kolkata, at C. Ghose Studio in Albert Hall itself and in the premises of Roopkala Kendro, other than some shots in Roy's home. Roy answers very thoughtfully to the structured questions posed by his interviewer, Kalyan Bandhu Mitra. The narration is more in the form of reminiscences from the first person perspective of Roy. The opening frame is mounted against the backdrop of a Mitchell camera, the camera with which Roy began his independent journey. One can hear the whirring sound of the reel turning as the credits come up and the subtitles begin. The film then pauses on an Arriflex to close on digital camera, marking the technological journey of this great cameraman. The film closes on the strains of *Alo Amar Alo* (1971) reflecting on this man who had painted with light all his life.

Roy comes across as the man he is in real life, modest to a fault, articulate about his conceptions, relaxing on the open fields of a natural garden, seated in his apartment or taking a cup of tea at the coffee house. He admits that he has had to make compromises for family needs, but adds that these were few and far between. One is surprised to learn that he never cinematographed a Hindi film though he had worked for a few Tamil films. He looks upon Subrata Mitra, whom he assisted for years together, as his mentor and guru. When asked about having had to work on limited budgets and little equipment, Roy explains that it is not only a big challenge to work within infrastructural and monetary limitations but also a great learning experience lavish budgets cannot teach you. The footage acquires colour when Roy begins to talk about *Ashani Sanket* (1973), his first work in colour. It goes back to B&W when the film returns to base. He talks about his memorable work in Tarun Majumdar's and Tapan Sinha's films among others.

The ghost-like figure of Satyajit Ray is seen hovering around the filmscapes, more in *Soumendu Roy* than in *Subrata Mitra*. *Subrata Mitra* is more of a biographical documentary than a technical lesson in cinematography. *Soumendu Roy* is more a technical lesson than a biographical documentary. We learn about the detailed tools that go into the complex world of cinematography—different grades of lenses in red, yellow, green, etc., the meaning of latitude in terms of camera movements and angles and the difference between colour and B&W. As Roy reminiscences about his work for *Postmaster* (1964), *Monihar* (1966) and *Samapti*, a hidden window to Ray's world opens. Roy explains how Ray insisted that a film be shot according to the mood of the story. "As the story of *Postmaster* is sad, he wished that I shoot the whole story within a cloudy atmosphere. *Monihar* was shot largely within the confines of a beautifully decorated home and the story had an eerie air about it so my lighting had to be in keeping with that mood. *Samapti* had to be bright and sunny because it was a happy story with a lot of the comic and the funny."

When a film makes history, its director attains immortality. The actors' faces become famous. However, the technical experts, such as the cinematographer, editor, art director and sound designer, whose contribution to the final product is no less than the rest of the team, go unrecognized and unnoticed because they work behind the camera, away from the limelight. Film-makers have shown little interest in documenting the lives of technicians in Indian cinema. Arindam Saha Sardar has made it his life's mission to start a series of documentaries of technicians whose work can mark a model, ideological lesson in cinema technique for film-makers and film students of tomorrow.

Bansi Chandragupta

Saha Sardar has also made a documentary on art director Bansi Chandragupta who worked with Satyajit Ray in his earlier films and was noted for making the maximum aesthetic use of minimum material resources. *Bansi Chandragupta* is a wonderful unfolding of this simple man who hardly spoke because his mind was busy creating designs and his hands were forever engaged in doing up sets or sketches himself. Shot entirely in B&W with the exception of clips of films originally shot in colour, the film takes us on a highly informative journey back to a time when art direction did not have modern technique that it has today. The journey is both nostalgic and emotional for those who have worked with Chandragupta and for those familiar with his work.

Chandragupta is one of the very few technicians who did extremely well even after he left the Ray camp and migrated to Bombay (now Mumbai) though he left a part of himself in Calcutta. "May be we did not have the kind of experimentation Bansi had. But that does not take away from him his absolute focus on the job at hand which brought excellence in the final product—the film," says art director Kartick Bose. Hiran Mitra, artist and art director who has done a beautiful sketch of Chandragupta for the film reminisces about the dedication of this man. "He is the first art director in India to introduce plaster-of-paris in art direction. He painstakingly undertook the 'weathering' of sets after they were constructed for his first Ray film *Pather Panchali*. He used the technique of 'filling' to design the floors of the court of the King of Halla for *Goopy Gyne Bagha Byne* (1969). His hallmark was that he could produce the best effect at minimum cost. It was a beautiful white floor with a big, circular *alpana* (particular type of art or painting done on horizontal surface to mark an auspicious occasion) design in the centre."

Chandragupta began his career in another film before he joined the technical team of *The River* (1951). He worked closely with production designer Eugene Lourie and learned the craft of designing for film. Ray asked him to join the Calcutta Film Society. Chandragupta won the Filmfare Award for Best Art Direction three times, once for *Seema* (1972), for *Do Jhoot* (1976) and for *Chakra* (1982.) He was awarded the Evening Standard British Film Award posthumously for the Best Technical/Artistic Achievement in 1983. In an interview, when Dharmaraj was asked whether he had shot *Chakra* on actual locations, he said "yes." Chandragupta was very angry. He confronted Dharmaraj and asked him why he had lied because the entire film was shot on a set designed and executed by Chandragupta.

His last film was Aparna Sen's *36 Chowringhee Lane* (1981). Sen dedicated the film to his memory. "I was surprised when he brought a whole lot of pictures of cats for my film *36 Chowringhee Lane*. When I asked him why, he said that he needed just the right cat for Violet Stoneham's pet I had described in my script. The thought had not even occurred to me before that. He had seen me growing up as a kid so when I decided to direct my first film, I knew who would do the art direction for my film," says Aparna Sen.

"Sometimes, directors like Ray and Mrinal Sen would get irritated because he would make them wait till he finished with the sets before the camera could roll. He would ask us to keep the director waiting with some excuse," informs Soumendu Roy. He adds that Chandragupta would often hold the reflectors to help Soumendu without blinking an eye though it was not his job at all. "He was a very good photographer, so he knew where the reflector had to be held, how and at what time, as I was adjusting the lighting for a given shot," says Roy.

"When I called him for *Balika Badhu* (1967), I warned him that I would not be able to pay him much. He agreed. But as shooting began, I was a bit surprised looking at the sets he had designed because I knew I had a shoe-string budget. One of my production team told me that Bansi-da was spending money out of his own remuneration. Can you imagine the commitment?" asks film-maker Tarun Majumdar. His most accomplished work that marked him out were the sets he conceived, designed and executed for Ray's *Charulata* (1964), *Nayak* (1964) and *Shatranj Ke Khilari* (1977). His design of the then interior of a railway compartment for *Nayak* was so flawless that most viewers took it to be real. Born in Sialkot,

Chandragupta's family—Kashmiri Pandits—shifted to Srinagar when he was a boy and did his schooling in this city. He was inspired to take on art by Subho Tagore, who he befriended in Srinagar. He passed away in New York in 1981.

Celluloid Man

It is a classic documentary on P.K. Nair. P.K. Nair is the (retired) Founder-Director of the first and the largest cinema archive in India. He founded the National Film Archive, Pune in 1964 and is singularly responsible for restoring and rescuing films virtually lost to history over his long relationship with National Film Archive of India (NFAI) till 1991. Today, he finds it difficult to walk without his stick but is as passionate about cinema as he was when a kid. The 164-minute long *Celluloid Man* has travelled to many film festivals.

Shivendra Singh Dungarpur, an FTII graduate, committed to the preservation and restoration of films and himself has documented the life and work of P.K. Nair to sustain for posterity, the significance of building up an archive of films. Nair has made it

Image 2.1. *Celluloid Man*: P.K. Nair

Courtesy: Shivendra Singh Dungarpur

possible for us to know Dadasaheb Phalke through clips from films *Raja Harishchandra* (1913) and *Kalia Mardan* (1935). *Celluloid Man* charts the journey of this man who wandered through every corner of the country to find out three lost and almost very old clips from Imperial Films or Sohrab Modi's classic *Sikandar* (1941), Bombay Talkies' *Achhut Kanya* (1936) through *Chandralekha* to Ghatak's *Meghe Dhaka Tara* (2013). When he retired, he left behind a priceless treasure of 12,000 films of which 8,000 are Indian films he helped preserve and archive can by can, reel by reel.

The film unfolds the history of Indian cinema as it grew over time in terms of technology, time, space and genres. "I found the Archive orphaned after Nair's retirement in 1990. I saw rusting cans lying in the grass, thick cobwebs hanging from the shelves in the vaults and Mr Nair's old office turned into a junkyard. I thought about this remarkable man who had devoted his life to collecting and saving these films and I was determined that his legacy should not be forgotten," says Dungarpur. The film is dotted with scenes showing the old man leaning on his walking stick as he moves inside the narrow gaps between shelves that hold endless round tin boxes of reels of film, sometimes framed by overhanging celluloid strips here, there and everywhere.

The film begins with a statement that says that it took the filmmaker 11 trips to Pune to convince the authorities to let him shoot with Mr Nair inside the Archive. "I started the film two years ago and what a journey of discovery it has been. I learned about the lost heritage of Indian cinema and how important it is to preserve and restore our films before it is too late," he sums up.

Nair grew up watching his first film, a Tamil mythological made by K. Subramanian, in a tent theatre when he was seven or eight. He sat on a floor filled with white sand. He wanted to become a film-maker but became the country's first and, till now, only cinema archivist who built up an archive of 12,000 films of which 8,000 are Indian films. "The families of early film-makers like Ardeshir Irani, not knowing the value of the films they had inherited, sold the celluloid films away for their nitrate content from which silver could be extracted. The selling price of 1 kg of 35mm film was ₹100, and we lost a part of our cultural history," says Nair.

Celluloid Man defines an ideal marriage between form, technique and content. It is shot against a live backdrop of old film clips, with famous old songs, or dialogues from old films on the soundtrack sometimes punctured by the sound of a live projector, interspersed with comments from great personalities of Indian cinema from Mrinal Sen to Gulzar to Shyam Benegal and Girish Kasaravalli extending to capture some famous FTII alumni. The cinematography is low key, alternating between monochrome and colour, never brightened with primary colours as it catches Nair in a long shot, sitting alone under the wisdom tree or zeroing on his hands as he ties a knot at different points on a film reel. "He is the only person I know who can tell you exactly in which reel of a film a particular scene can be found," sums up Dungarpur.

An American in Madras

Few film critics, scholars and film-makers outside the southern states have heard of Ellis Roderick Dungan, a film-maker and photographer who came to India from America and stayed back for 15 years to make some outstanding box office hits in different south Indian languages though he did not speak or understand a single word of the local lingo. Karan Bali, an FTII graduate in film direction (1993 batch), made a documentary on this man called *An American in Madras* (2013) and made the film fit for the film archives. Bali is also the Co-founder and Content-in-Charge of www.upperstall.com, a serious and analytical portal on Indian cinema.

"I was researching material for a luminary piece on Ellis R. Dungan for my cinema portal, I founded way back in 2000. I was amazed when I discovered his amazing contribution to Indian cinema in general and South Indian films in particular within a short span of 15 years. That is what made me decide to make an entire documentary on this great film-maker," says Karan Bali who created, with his stellar technical team, one of the most outstanding biographical documentaries that would become an integral part in the archive of Indian cinema.

"I began to think of making a documentary on Dungan but had precious little knowledge about this man. The material I had till then was not enough to make a full-fledged documentary. I met noted Tamil film historian, S. Theodore Baskaran, who gave me a lead to *A Guide to Adventure,* Dungan's autobiography co-written with Barbara Smik, published in 2001, the year Dungan died. Shivendra Singh Dungarpur, who shares a fascination for Indian cinema

Image 2.2. A Poster of *An American in Madras*

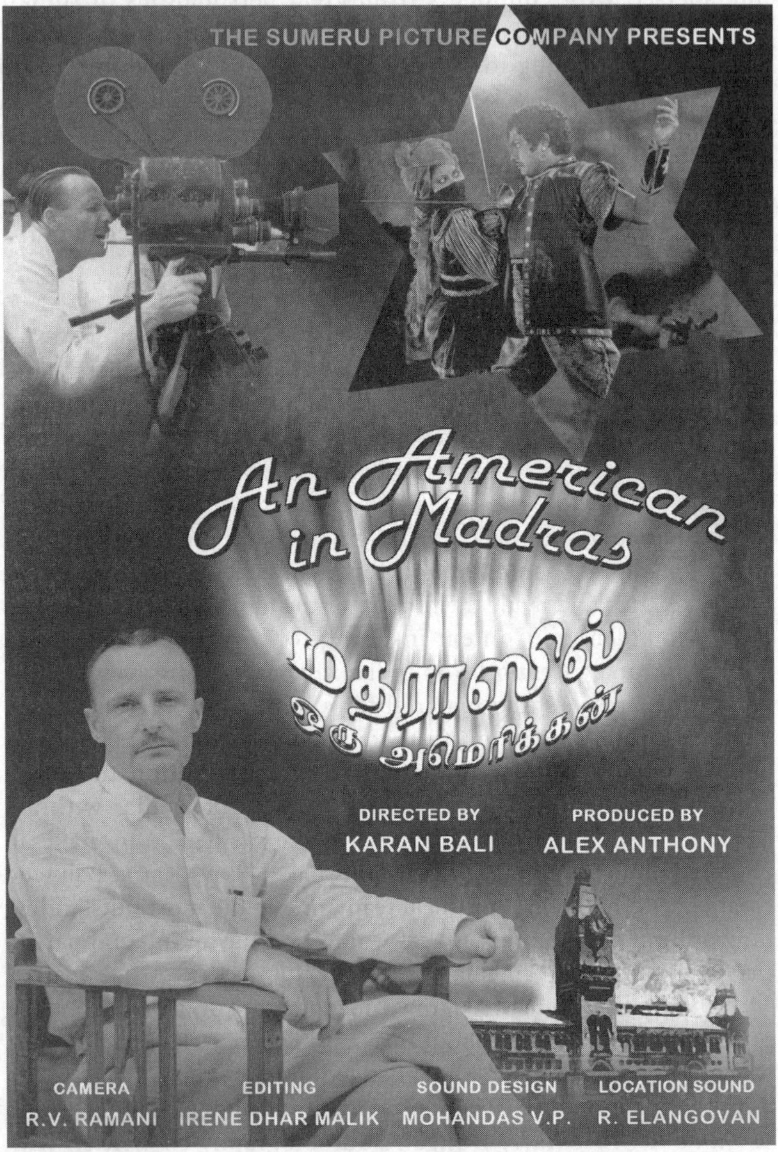

Courtesy: Karan Bali

history, had a copy of the book and this became a good source of information on the man," said Bali.

An American in Madras, while essaying the life of an American still photographer and film-maker who lived and worked in India to make brilliantly successful films, itself evolves into a moving celluloid statement on the creative challenges this man took. Bali has designed the graphics against the backdrop of what looks like ancient parchment paper to underscore the archival quality of its subject.

Ellis R. Dungan, commonly known as Dungan Aiyya in Madras, was an American cinematographer, born in Ohio on 11 May, 1909. An alumnus of University of Southern California's (USC) first batch of film students, Dungan came to India on the invite of a fellow USC mate—M.L. Tandon—in 1935 to see what he could do in the Indian film industry. His initial plan was to stay for around a year. However, he stayed on and made several Tamil films. He introduced Marudhur Gopalan Ramachandran (MGR) as an actor and directed M.S. Subbulakshmi's most celebrated film, *Meera* (1945), and the seminal MGR hit *Manthiri Kumari* (1950) among others, before returning to the USA.

Dungan first came to Madras for the premiere of *Bhakt Nandanan* (1923) directed by his friend Tandon. Tandon suggested Dungan get his feet wet in Madras. This triggered a journey that mapped the history of 15 stellar years in Dungan's life and for Tamil cinema. His first directorial work was *Sathi Leelavathi* (1936) produced under the banner of Manorama Films that marked the debut of MGR.

The documentary charts Dungan's contributions to technical innovation in those fledgling years of the Tamil talkie. Among other things, the 'Dungan track' and the 'Dungan trolley' were so called for more than a decade after he left India.

"He converted the carrier of his Dodge car to a platform so he could mount the camera on it and take moving shots! He had the script translated into English, divided into two halves, one side for the dialogue and the other for action. He would use that to break that down into shots and then shoot only after proper planning, extensive rehearsals and blocking of scenes. In *Meera*, regarded by Dungan as his finest film, he got a bust of its star, M.S. Subbulakshmi made, and he and cinematographer Jiten Banerjee did elaborate lighting tests on it to device a lighting scheme for her to look ethereal in the film. And boy, does she look it!" says Bali.

The documentary has rounded up scholars, historians, film-makers, even Muthu—a make-up man—who worked with Dungan when he was 14—to talk about the film-maker. Clips from old films such as *Sathi Leelavati*, *Two Brothers*, which he edited himself; *Ambikapathy* (1957), *Sakuntalai*, *Meera*, also made in Hindi later; *Ponmudi* (1949) and *Manthiri Kumari* are so lucid and clear that they appear to have been shot and developed yesterday!

"He gave Indian folk traditions and rituals a Western perspective and though some sections of the Tamil cinema audience were shocked, it widened the canvas of his films," says Hariharan, a film-maker and film scholar. "He tried to take away the theatricality that was a characteristic feature of old Tamil films," says Theodore Baskaran. Film actor and film historian Mohan V. Raman says that the colour of his skin and the 'Hollywood' tag gave him an edge in the industry helping him to overcome blocks.

"He refused to be studio bound and moved the camera as much as he could, and mixed image sizes and camera angles in direct contrast to many of the more static films of the period. One found the 'gora' or white man inside him offering a broader perspective to gender equations," says Bali. "His love scenes were very heavy and intimate and he did not balk from capturing kissing scenes," says the now-old Muthu with a naughty smile. "His women were very bold and pro-active and willing to go through rather intimate secrets. Unlike women in other Indian films whose destiny was decided by others, his celluloid women seized control of their own fates," says Vangal.

Hariharan points out the parallel dynamics between Shakespeare's *Romeo and Juliet* and Dungan's *Ambikapathy*, with the balcony scene showing the difference in class through spatial dynamics, the heroine standing on the balcony above depicting her higher class and the hero, down below. Dungan took advantage of the similarities between the two classics. Hariharan adds that since his films were flushed with many songs and a good musical score, he chose actors based on their singing talent and not on their acting talents. "He made love scenes seem very natural, unlike the awkwardness seen in other Indian films," said Hariharan. *Ambikapathy* was the then Tamil superstar M.K. Thyagaraja Bhagawathar (MKT)'s biggest hit that ran for a year,

Archivist and film historian, P.K. Nair, says that he was a school kid in 1941-42 when *Sakuntalai* was released. "Its beauty was comparable to any Hollywood film," he says. Nair also says how the theatres in which *Meera* was being screened would start playing the songs at least 45 minutes before the 6.30 pm show started in order to pull in the crowds.

An American in Madras is enriched through a collage of film clips collected from the archive, from collectors and archivists, stills and posters from Dungan's films, interviews and the most outstanding feature—Ellis R. Dungan himself—narrating his initial problems of shooting a Tamil film in Madras and how he overcame them. Thanks to Karan and his creative team for giving us such a wonderful film.

In the Land of Chhinnopatro

Saibal Mitra has one obsession—Rabindranath Tagore. Two films have resulted from this overwhelming desire to bring out little-known facets of the poet's life. One is his first film, *The Pilgrimage*. Mitra sheds light on the sociopolitical backdrop of the time, investing his new documentary, *In the Land of Chhinnopatro* (2003) with layered meanings through subtle tones hinting at a past when Bengal was more united, democratic and secular than it now is. The film is the first of a two-part film project based on Rabindranath Tagore's collection of letters, which he wrote during his days as a zamindar in the eastern parts of undivided Bengal (now Bangladesh.)

These letters were addressed to Indira Devi Chaudhurani. Tagore was then strikingly handsome, 29 and filled with creative passion and dreams. For Tagore, the period between 1889 and 1900 was formative, like a twilight zone before the dazzling break of dawn. Tagore would sail across the rivers of Bangladesh in a boat called the Padma, to visit the districts of Kushtia, Rajshahi and Pabna, the journeys offering him his first insight into life and people in rural Bengal, his touch with the soil that defined his roots and shaped his creativity. "I wanted to capture the landscape that created Tagore. It is true for all great men; they are the sons of a particular soil. This soil manifests itself in many ways through and in their creations. One can think of Stratford-upon-Avon for Shakespeare or Lake District for Wordsworth etc. The film is basically a journey through that Tagore landscape. I call it the 'Tagore Zone' of Bengal," recalls Mitra.[1]

It took almost three years of research into the film. "But it began even before that when I was making *The Pilgrimage* between 1986 and 1990. Poet Sankha Ghosh showed us a film, *Dear Theo* by Paul Cox, in Santiniketan. It was based on letters penned by Vincent Van Gogh to his brother Theo. Sankha-da was there all along, egging me to keep going. Then I went to Bangladesh to assist Goutam Ghosh for *Padma Nadir Majhi* (1993). I saw the river Padma in all her glory for the first time. I realised that life in rural Bengal had changed little since Tagore's time. After getting the funds from the Ministry of External Affairs, I wrote a script and gave it to Sankha-da. Once he okayed it, I went for location hunting. This was an eye-opener. I can now make another film on our journey looking for Tagore in the nooks and corners of those specific corners of Bangladesh. *In the Land of Chhinnopatro* is the first part of a two-part project on *Chhinnopatro*," sums up Saibal.

"Visva Bharati published *Chinnopatraboli* after Tagore had passed away. In *Chinnopatraboli*, one can get the full text of the letters. But the blackened lines are still there in the original manuscript. *Chinnopatro* and *Chinnopatraboli* are two different books altogether. It is difficult to say who blackened those lines out. Tagore's son Rathindranath drew public attention to these two notebooks for the first time. He had read the full text versions when he was young, before *Chinnopatro* was published. Tagore would never have done it himself. It is hard to believe that Indira Devi who considered Tagore sacrosanct would spoil these priceless documents. There was possibly a third person who either tried to protect the image of Tagore or, tried to veil his relationship with Indira. One cannot rule out the possibility of Pramatha Choudhury—husband of Indira—from this scenario of mystery," Mitra elucidates.

Images Unbound—The Life and Times of Rabindranath Tagore

It is a 90 minute documentary on Tagore, brings in a breeze of fresh air. It is a rare example of a biographical documentary that scans the littérateur's life and works principally through the results of painstaking research over three long years. Mujibur Rahman, an experienced documentary film-maker who has honed his skills with brief

Image 2.3. Tagore behind the Window

Courtesy: Mujibur Rehman

biopics on Munshi Premchand and Begum Rokeya says, "The film is an intimate kaleidoscopic journey into Tagore's oeuvre of life and art. I planned the film on Tagore to come out as a simple but grand bi-lingual documentary for the uninitiated mainly as an informative and educational exercise. So, I relied more on research and very little on fictionalization." He has also made a series of short films on legends of Indian classical music and on famous personalities from different fields.

When he heard about the Nobel Prize being bestowed on him, he wrote the famous song "e monihaar amaye nahi shaaje". The same man gave up his knighthood after the massacre in Jallianwala Bagh. The film covers almost everything you ever wanted to know about Tagore but were afraid to ask. Photographs of Tagore with Roman Rolland, Albert Einstein, Rothenberg, Mahatma Gandhi, Pandit Jawaharlal Nehru are rare archival documentations one does not easily get to see. His friendship with Victoria Ocampo and Rothenstein are referred to. One can glimpse a very young Indira Gandhi among the crowd celebrating the poet's birthday at Santiniketan.

Rahman has made imaginative and aesthetic use of different voices for the narration. Soumitra Chatterjee lends 'voice' to Rabindranath Tagore while the voice-over narrations are by Ananda Lal and Debashish Bose, respectively. One can also get to hear the real voices of the poet himself other than W.B. Yeats, Satyendranath Dutta—a renowned poet—and others. We have seen most of the photographic reproductions in publications of and on Tagore before. However, placed within a chronological narrative on his life and works is a different experience.

The only glitch is in Rahman's decision to use real actors to portray some of the characters with special reference to the little boy who plays the child Tagore, the young, bearded actor mainly shown in profile, who enacts the young Tagore and the young girl who plays Kadambari. They stick out like sore thumbs in an otherwise excellent film. The opening frame depicting an elderly woman painting out the poet's name on a wooden plaque is another anomaly. The image of the woman simply does not belong there. The happy news is that this film has been selected as part of their academic syllabus by the Rabindranath Tagore Center of Jadavpur University.

Rituparno Ghosh's ***Jeevan Smriti*** (2013) produced by the Ministry of Information and Broadcasting was premiered in different Indian cities as part of the 72nd tribute to Rabindranath Tagore's passing away. *Jeevan Smriti* is Rituparno Ghosh's first full-length documentary in his 20-year span of making feature films. Sandwiched between Satyajit Ray and Rabindranath Tagore, Ghosh had a tough task placing Tagore in perspective for himself and his audience today. However, his approach was different.

"I did not want the film to be limited within the achievements of the Nobel Laureate. My primary aim was to project the real personality of Tagore as a human being. My main focus has been on Tagore's international spirit. He was a global citizen much before the term 'globalization' came into being. He believed that loving one's homeland did not translate into hating other nations. For me, he remains the one and only global icon," he said.

"I have steered clear of Ray's interpretation of the poet's life. My emphasis, treatment and approach are different and they are my own. Ray made it biographical. My attraction is the flesh-and-blood persona of Tagore rather than in the larger-than-life figure of a great creative talent. He was a person with the instincts of a normal person, yet was way ahead of the others. The inconsistency in Tagore will be a point I will try and highlight," he said.

Has he really been able to mark *Jeebon Smriti* with his distinct, individual signature the way he did his feature films? Does *Jeebon Smriti* tell a different story? The 'story' cannot be 'different' because the subject—Tagore—is the same. His universal status of being one of the greatest intellectuals of the 20th century makes it a challenge to create an individualistic statement on Tagore even for Rituparno Ghosh. However, Ghosh was never afraid of challenges. His three films adapted, sometimes closer to the text and sometimes as an 'inspiration'—*Chokher Bali* (2003), *Noukadubi* (2011) and *Chitrangada—The Crowning Wish* have already proved this.

However, *Jeevan Smriti* falls short of expectations for a director who has created his own measuring rod of excellence to be judged by smaller humans like yours truly. It begins well with the Rituparno Ghosh signature, a powerful presence in the film. For the first 27 years of the poet's life, Rituparno has ingenuously created a string of brilliant images that are visualizations of lines picked from Tagore's autobiography *Jeebon Smriti* (1913), a rambling, unconventional and free-flowing reminiscences of the poet's life till he was 27. The images are intercut with sepia-toned and B&W photographs drawn from the archives with a voice-over— often Rituparno's himself— reading out the lines from the text as the visuals strike us in their aesthetic richness.

However, *Jeevan Smriti* has one black spot that assumes the shape and appearance of an ugly, big scar on a beautiful face. Ghosh's decision to be the anchor of the film and intercut the main script with his own entry into the frame along with his unit members as the film was being made, or when they were on a trip to Bolpur the second time, or praying in front of Tagore's garlanded portrait in the end, was a wrong and absolutely unwarranted decision. One has to concede that somewhere, this intrusion into Tagore's life is rather self-indulgent and narcissistic. As the voice-over narrates lines from Tagore's life, the continuity breaks jarringly as Ghosh steps into the setting with his crew and interacts with them silently or reads out to them from his laptop while they listen like school students! This is incredulous and demeaning to the subject of the film—Rabindranath Tagore.

The Loom

The Loom (2001), jointly directed by Anjali Monteiro and K.P. Jayasankar of the Tata Institute of Social Sciences (TISS), Mumbai, is the story of a poet, a painter and a city—Mumbai. The film offers an aesthetically composed insight into the seamier side of Mumbai, offering multiple perspectives of the city as viewed by the film-makers, the poet—Narayan Surve and the painter—Sudhir Patwardhan, stripping it of the glamour and the awe it is normally associated with. Titled *Saacha* in Hindi, the film focusses on the two creative artists who evolved and grew up in the city of Mumbai (Bombay when the film was made) and were part of the left cultural movement besides their roots in the working class. Much like a weaver's loom, the film is scripted, so that it weaves poetry and painting together with nostalgic stories from the artist and the poet who dot their narratives with their personal memories of the city. "We have tried to explore the modes and politics of representation and the relevance of art in the contemporary social milieu, alongside the decline of the urban working class in an age of structural adjustments, the dilemma of the left and the trade union movement and changing face of the huge metropolis."

"The first thing one notices about *Saacha* is the sensory qualities of the image. In a musical montage of rhythms the relentless churning of machinery in the textile mills frames coils of cotton that unwind languorously onto a spindle and workers' faces are masked by twisting strands of thread like enormous cats' cradles. The film captures and releases fleeting moments of sensory intensity; light passes across piles of coloured jujubes glistening in a glass case in a cafe, drops of water light up momentarily on a table, reflecting passing traffic, deep red tomatoes and baskets of green chillies shine in the sunlit street market, baroque gargoyles keep silent watch as endless feet stream up a staircase behind elaborate brass balustrades out of the railway station. The life of the city is built up out of a multitude of small fragments, intimate moments, glimpses and moments of sensory experience. The film weaves a fabric that has the texture and the rhythm of the city. Saacha is experienced as much as a love affair with the city as a documentary about the city."[2]

The opening frames close in on flax of wool being sifted in the textile mills of Bombay, which forms the backdrop of the film. The background music floats over with chants of a Powada folk number cutting into refrains from the *Pyaasa* (1957) song, "ae dil hai mushkil jeena yahan", elaborating on the crisis the city presents for people who live and work in it. The Powada[3] refrain functions like a punctuation mark over the footage of the film, establishing its grass roots Bombay identity.

Narayan Surve recounts how his mother abandoned him as a three-month-old baby in a dustbin on the streets. He grew up right in the midst of the working class and did every kind of work to keep his body and soul together while the soundtrack carries lines of his poetry in his own voice. He openly condemns the demand for a so-called socialist society of right-wing thinkers for their demand for what they call 'cultural nationalism'. Surve interprets this as 'casteist and Hindu nationalism' that seeks to destroy all minorities. Sudhir Patwardhan talks about how his early years of painting with oils on canvas focussed on the working-class milieu of the city soon after he migrated from Pune, his home town. His early paintings—*Screaming Woman, Train, May Day Accident, Street Play*, a scene from an Irani Hotel—cut into his monologues about his evolution as an artist. "I did some paintings with multiple perspectives where two or three scenes would appear in the same frame at the same time. Through these multiple perspectives, I was trying to organize my space so that my human subjects could seek their autonomy within that context to establish their relationship with their surroundings."

The Salt Stories

Lalit Vachani's ***The Salt Stories*** falls somewhere along the line of the historical and the political, where history is revoked in the present to find out how the present generation looks back on Gandhi's famous Dandi March. Nearly eight decades after the Dandi March, filmmaker Lalit Vachani made an interesting documentary raising questions about the contemporary relevance of the Salt March. *The Salt Stories* places the historic Dandi March in perspective by juxtaposing it against the reality of the poor where they are deprived of their basic freedom through needs such as food, clothing and shelter. Has Gandhi's non-violent means to attain a political end for the benefit of the entire country really brought freedom to their descendants, the poor and the oppressed? Or, has the Dandi March been reduced to a token for non-violence to be relegated to history textbooks? *The Salt Stories*, an 84-minute documentary, is a road movie set in modern India that follows the trail of Mahatma Gandhi's Salt March of 1930.

The film introduces the viewers to Mohammed bhai, standing in what remains of his bangle factory, where the number of workers had dwindled to a handful because his machines and his workshop were destroyed by Hindu fundamentalists during the riots. The team then sets off on their journey on the rickety road to Dandi via small towns on the way, talking to people to find out whether they knew who Gandhi was, whether they knew about the Dandi March. We meet Ketanbhai—Dalit leader of the Navagam village—who was forced to resign later because high-caste members would not allow him to go on. Gordhanbhai Bakhta, the 102-year-old sole living survivor of the Dandi March, who passed away soon after, recalls his experience.

Seventy-seven years later, Vachani and his Wide Eye Film team followed the trail of the famous Dandi March, in search of Gandhi's legacy. Set against the backdrop of Gandhi's original journey, this road movie makes caustic comments, simply through telling visuals and direct one-to-one interviews with a cross section of people, on how globalization of Gujarat equates Gandhi's 'salt' to a metaphor on poverty, forced migration, joblessness and injustice. Secularism, the film clearly points out, is conspicuous by its absence. Not one person from the majority community had a kind or unbiased word to say about the minorities.

"I was shocked by the anti-Muslim rant of the 'fake Gandhian' at Navagam village. I was also thrilled when I saw that in a village like Napa, Gandhian ideals are lived and cherished and there is no caste or communal conflict. Encountering this peaceful enclave in Gujarat seemed to make our journey that much more worthwhile," sums up Vachani.

The Saroj Khan Story

Saroj Khan has broken every rule in the choreography book. She is far from a visual beauty. She does not care about glamour. She can never be defined as a fashion statement. She is brazen, bold, uncompromising and, often, quite rude and ruthless. She is fat and quite masculine. She has been a single mother for most of her life. However, she is also famous, successful and rich in the cut-throat, male-dominated world of Indian cinema.

Image 2.4. The Saroj Khan Story

Courtesy: Nidhi Tuli

A young woman decided to pick slices of her life and present it as a documentary tribute. Never before in the history of Indian cinema has tribute been paid to a choreographer in Indian cinema in the shape of a documentary. *The Saroj Khan Story* is Nidhi Tuli's 57-minute celluloid tribute to Saroj Khan. The two women who made it possible are Nidhi Tuli and Saroj Khan. The film was screened in the documentary section of the International Film Festival of India (IFFI) in Goa.

Saroj Khan's career kicked off in the early 1950s. She began as a child artist with dancing as the talent she was gifted in. The upward climb was difficult but it happened ultimately. She began as a member of the background chorus and graduated as an assistant to the choreographer which brought her in contact with accomplished dancer-actresses like Vyjayantimala. By the time she became an independent choroegrapher, the prima donna she choreographed was the legendary Madhuri Dixit. Today, she continues to create, compose and choreograph dance numbers for Aishwarya Rai and Sonakshi Sinha.

Says Nidhi in response to her motivation to choose this subject, "The Saroj Khan Story began as a search for the genius behind one of the greatest choreographers Indian cinema has ever produced. What remains is a deeply personal story of determination, passion, extraordinary skill and the sheer will to survive that is both intimate and inspiring," explains the very young Nidhi, adding, "I was a fan of hers like most people who know about her choreography are, but it was during the making of the film that I discovered that she is a genius and she wears that so lightly; she is a perfectionist and a very passionate dancer."

Nidhi's career is marked with a Masters in Screenwriting from the Royal Holloway, University of London in 2003–04 under the Charles Wallace India Trust Scholarships. This was capped by her win at the Raindance Film Pitch Competition at the Edinburgh Film Festival in UK in 2004. Her first documentary, *Ladies Special*, bagged the John Abraham National Award in 2005 followed by the 'George Ragot love the train' award at the Cine Rail Paris in 2009. Her filmography includes *Art in Exile*, *TIPA*, *Of Friendship*, *Films and Swords* and *The Saint of Chitrakoot*.

The camera focusses on Saroj Khan as she narrates her slow but rickety rise in filmdom from a chorus dancer in the back row to a leading choreographer, who composed and directed every other leading lady, from Madhuri Dixit to Aishwarya Rai to Kareena Kapoor to the young Sonakshi Sinha. The film opens on Saroj Khan riding in her car, talking into her cell phone till it cuts to a close-up of the lady at home with walls filled with photographs and portraits of herself and family members. She looks back wistfully into her past that includes the unceasing sickness of a daughter who passed away later. However, Saroj-ji refuses to be bogged down by or gather sympathy from her private grief.

"It has been a long struggle with many ups and downs in my personal life," she says as she looks back wistfully into her past. "The dances I compose and direct do not show the tears and the heart-breaks in my life," she adds. She was betrayed in love by her mentor and guru who left her when she became pregnant. However, she carried the emotional, financial and professional burden singly on her bold shoulders and continues to do it till today. Her repertoire of having choreographed in more than 200 films ranges from the purely classical numbers in the Tamil film *Shringaram—Dance of Love* (2005) through the beautifully graceful numbers executed by Aishwarya Rai in Subhash Ghai's *Taal* (1999), to the sizzling duet performed by the lead pair in *Rowdy Rathore* (2012).

Shringaram (2007) was directed by a noted dancer Saradha Ramanathan, produced by Padmini Ravi—a classical dancer—and was a period film set in the 19th century on the life of a *devadasi* (In south India, the term *devadasi* is a conjoined noun composed of two words—*dev* meaning god and *dasi* meaning servant or slave). Aditi Rao Hydari, a talented Bharatanatyam dancer, played the role of the devadasi. Though the producer and director were both celebrated dancers, they chose Saroj Khan for the choreography. She won the National Award for Best Choreography, one of her string of three National Awards.

"The Madhuri Dixit number in the song "maar dala" in Sanjay Leela Bhansali's *Devdas* (2002) had the refrain maar dala four times in each stanza. I convinced and taught Madhuri to execute each refrain differently for each of the four times. This spread over to three or four stanzas and each time, she expressed this refrain differently," explains Khan. This choreography got for Saroj the National Award preceded by another National Award for the dance numbers in Hemant Gowarikar's *Lagaan* (2001) alongside the Filmfare Award. One similar milestone is Bhansali's *Hum Dil De Chuke Sanam*(1999), which brought her a string of awards and which also got her the Best American Choreography Award. Saroj Khan—the person—however, reaches far beyond the documentary.

Pancham Unmixed: Mujhe Chalte Jaana Hai (an unending journey)

Directed by Brahmanand Singh, the film takes an incisive look into R.D. Burman's (RDB) reflective artistry and buoyant but lonely inner being. It unfolds the voices of RDB's friends, colleagues and admirers trying to bring across the awe, the admiration and nostalgia that the film evokes. Singh is not a die-hard fan of RDB but grew up listening to his music. RDB, on the other hand, listened to his mother's melodious voice. The film-maker Brahmanand was influenced by the musical genius, RDB, and his creations like "piya tu ab to aaja" and "mehbooba mehbooba" and dreamt of making a film on this musical genius. These numbers still remain cult songs in the minds of music lovers.

One day, after his documentary *Ragpickers* was screened in Karachi, he heard a Sufi band playing "musafir hu yaaron", which set the gathered crowds on fire—such was the charisma of the music composer even in Pakistan. That fired in him the passionate desire to make a documentary on R.D. Burman. The film had a world premiere at Arclight, Hollywood in 2008. Singh admits that making a film on his musical hero, just to be able to watch him on screen, has been a rather expensive experience. At the same time, the accolades and the cheers the film collected at every screening, he feels has been well worth the long journey. Nostalgia is the bottom line in documentaries on music makers who are no more but live on through their musical creations.

With an image in mind, he worked around the figment, speaking to RDB's or Pancham's colleagues and contemporaries who shared space with him in daily life. These conversations revealed new and fascinating aspects of the man. He explored the music through these nuggets of information, and finally what emerged was quite exceptional. The narrative threw up a poignant story of prodigious talent, of emerging from the shadows of a luminary father, of soaring success and heartless desertion.

"People could empathise with the fact that such a great maestro was deserted by the industry at some point, the same industry which once thrived on him," says Singh. It took him 2,500 hours of editing after having sifted through collated and collected materials during his research, because he had to streamline and edit it to make it fit into the normal viewable footage, in order to cater to the niche audience for this kind of film. The film has been shown at 40 international film festivals and has received two national awards.

A sensitive tribute needs more than simple veneration, perhaps a deeper connect. The film-maker revealed a common root, of an ancestral musical bonding between S.D. Burman and Singh's granduncle. The two shared the same ustad—Bheeshma Deb Chatterjee.

Regretfully, RDB never won a national award. Singh says that Gulzar put it aptly when he said lyrically, *"kheer Pancham banata hai aur khaate hum sab hai"* (Pancham prepares the pudding and we all savour the sweetness).

The film is dotted with talking heads of about three dozen people, both associates and admirers, of Pancham along with close friends and relatives. Among them are Asha Bhonsle, Manna Dey, Gulzar, Javed Akhtar, Shammi Kapoor, Rishi Kapoor, Vinod Chopra, Vishal Bhardwaj, Shankar-Ehsaan-Loy, Louis Banks, Pt Shiv Kumar Sharma, Pt Hari Prasad Chaurasia, Ameen Sayani, Gautam Rajadhyaksha and Taufeeq Quereshi.

LIVES: LESSER KNOWN

From Shyamal Karmakar's irreverent—bordering on the indulgent—narrative of a bar singer in Mumbai in *I'm The Very Beautiful*, to Avijit Mukul Kishore's sensitive portrayal of his relationship with his mother in *Snapshots From A Family Album*, to Supriyo Sen's film *Way Back Home*, detailing his parents' first journey to their homeland in Bangladesh since the Partition, what these films share is that the personal often draws from the political, but the political also becomes the personal. Saba Dewan's *The Other Song* (2009) is a kind of search for the figure of the *tawaif* (courtesan) as a performer of Hindustani classical music, negotiating the past and the present as part of the journey. The need to represent alternative and transgressive histories and memories posed newer questions of form and narrative.

The Other Song (2009) focusses on Rasoolan Bai, well-known tawaif and *thumri* (common genre of semi-classical Indian music with romantic or devotional lyrics generally focusing on love. The lyrics are usually in Uttar Pradeshi dialect of Hindi called Awadhi and Brij Bhasha) singer from Varanasi. It explores a range of issues relevant to the politics of popular culture, female sexuality and the growth of communalism. Rasoolan Bai was born in 1902 and grew up at a time when the tawaif tradition was flourishing in north India. The film journeys through Varanasi, Lucknow and Muzaffarpur searching for memories of this dying tradition. Dewan pursues clues on Rasoolan Bai and other well-known singers of yesteryear, meets a few surviving singers and puts together the pieces to build up a fairly complex historical account.

The film-maker zeroes in on two versions of a thumri sung by Rasoolan Bai. The first version, hardly known today (although in 1935, Rasoolan Bai recorded it on gramophone) goes "Laagat jobanwa mein chot, phool gendwa na maar" (my breasts are wounded, don't throw flowers at me); the second version, extremely well-known, replaces *jobanwa* (breast) with the word *karejwa* (heart). This is no innocent replacement. As the film indicates, it is part of an effort to 'sanitise' culture, to obliterate sexually explicit messages and, thus, symbolically, purify the arts. In the process, the enigmatic figure of the tawaif is also virtually obliterated.[4]

The film introduces viewers to a number of living thumri singers. Saira Begum and her elder sister Rani Begum have an extensive repertoire and beautiful voices, yet are barely able to survive as professional singers. While Rani stopped performing 30 years ago, Saira still performs but is not considered respectable enough by AIR or Doordarshan—though experts acknowledge the depth and finesse of her singing. She sings at a concert or two, and teaches a few select students. Saira 'married' a wealthy businessman, but after he died, she was left penniless. She brought up her son and three daughters, educating them and teaching them simple trades such as stitching. Two daughters are married, the youngest engaged. She says she loves her mother's singing but never learnt it; nor did the others. Whatever remains of the tawaif's musical lineage will die out within a generation or two.

The film-maker's own voice is present throughout the film—candid, anguished, angry and analytical. Yet, at several points, the viewer is left dissatisfied—perhaps because so many issues are taken up that they cannot be dealt with in sufficient detail or depth. Tighter editing would have helped make the links clearer and more explicit. All the same, this is an important film with enormous archival value.

Jill Misquitta's **The Clap Trap** is a moving documentary captured from two first-person accounts, a story of the 'extras' or 'junior artistes' in Mumbai's film industry. It is at once a human-interest story, an investigative story and an ethnographic film. It is a politically powerful statement as well, because the director takes open potshots at the dehumanization of human beings in an industry where stars, directors, choreographers and technicians earn in eight to 10 figures but where these 'junior artistes' are victims of economic, emotional and sexual exploitation.

The film features the life stories of two major junior artistes in Mumbai, one a man with a hero-like body and the other a woman. Both of them confessed that they had entered into films with dreams of making it big. The man had also landed himself the role of a hero in his first film. "But the film was never made and after waiting for another dream role for some months, I began to accept bit roles in big films," he says. He is one among the higher hierarchy of extras and maintains a telephone in his small flat where he lives with his wife and children. "It was destiny that came in my way and who can I blame for it, tell me?" he asks, philosophically. The film shows how while 'selecting' females for a certain scene, the agent or his crew ignore the older women in favour of the younger ones even when older women are called for. "It's because we cannot give it to them," says one brutally candid old woman into the camera. And this is a pointer to the bed-hopping which the girls have to do in order to get that 'bit' role.

Zafar Hai's *Hyderabad: A Place in the Heart* (1993) sounds like a blend of history and geography. It is indeed both. However, it pushes its borders to reach out beyond history and geography. Says Hai, "It is a cinematic tribute to the Nawabi culture of Hyderabad, evoking the grand lifestyle they led a century ago." The magic of the camera evokes, through photographs, the flavour of things that are past. Nostalgia carries the tragic reality of decay and alienation. Centuries of Moghul traditions that have filtered down from the north to the south have been subtly hinted at. What genre would this film fall within?

Sherna Dastur's *Manjuben Truck Driver* (2002) is about a woman who broke gender stereotypes with her profession, her lifestyle and her approach to life. Her identity is in spite of the social, cultural and economic odds she was pitted against within the social landscape she belongs to and commands respects from her peers. She has deliberately assumed a 'male' identity of a macho trucker drawn from several popular notions of maleness. She dresses up like a male trucker, speaks like a local goon, gets herself photographed in typical movie-star clothes and blends totally into the masculine world of truckers. She also seems to share most of the patriarchal values she imbibed from her childhood. Therefore, in her own house, she eats before the men and the other women eat last. She is not a crusader for women's causes but is an enigma unto herself. The film is silent about her sexual orientation, though.

Pala, directed by Gurvinder Singh, is the profile of Pala, a storyteller from Punjab. The film explores the diversity of centuries-old storytelling and musical tradition of which Pala is an integral part. He travels across the length and breadth of Punjab with his group of musicians, performing at Hindu temples, Sikh gurdwaras, mosques, shrines of Sufi saints and at various fairs, highlighting the plurality of the religious and cultural fabric of Punjab. He claims to belong to no faith and easily transforms himself and his musical talent to suit the needs of the space where he is performing. He is a microcosm of folk religion that assimilates the traits of the three principal faiths of Punjab—Hinduism, Sikhism and Islam.

Says Singh, "The camera had to concern itself with his mind. At times, it watched from a distance, at times it participated with equal vigour, at times just listened (closing the camera's eyes), and at times wandered off into its own imaginary landscape. The movement in the film is a movement through Pala's minds and thoughts. Such a movement was possible because there was no predetermined thought to begin with."

The Bioscopewallah (2007) directed by Prashant Kadam is a brief encounter with an entertainer, Rau Kisan Waghmare, who is also an agency that brings pure and simple joy to children. They enjoy the show for a few minutes, but are left with memories of it forever.

A Dalit folk artist hit by an unfortunate drought, Rau narrates in colloquial Marathi the story of his struggle for survival in the face of a natural calamity and migration. Rau's cheerful singing and gestures, his unconditional pride in the bioscope, stand in stark contrast to the lurking shadows of poverty and failing health. There were a number of bioscopewallahs in India before the advent of television. Now they have become sporadic and are confined mostly to the villages. Rau was born in a Dalit family in Dev Dhanora, a remote village in the Osmanabad district, in Maharashtra, India. He played *songadya* (refers to the clown in any *Tamasha* performance. Tamasha is a folk performance form traced back to Maharashtra. The Songadya is one of the four major characters in the dholki-bari school) in a tamasha theatre company before he became a bioscopewallah.

Webster's dictionary describes the 'bioscope' as a kind of an early movie projector. In India, it is popularly referred to as a wooden box containing pictures and having four circular peeping holes. Bioscopewallahs are people who operate the box accompanied by songs, stories and jokes. They usually wander carrying a bioscope on their back and a tripod under the arm. *The Bioscopewallah*, Prashant's debut independent documentary, was shot entirely in natural and available light, sans crew.

Lakshmi Srinivasan of Wellesley College, USA, writes, "This charming story links past and present as it brings together film history and folk performance, revealing how an otherwise obsolete piece of film equipment likely to be found only in museums is part of a lived culture form in India. However, as film-maker Kadam notes, it is a vanishing form with fewer bioscopewallahs after television gained wide popularity with village audiences and the urban poor. The film is also an important instance of traveling culture residing in the mobility of the bioscopewallah himself as folk artist as well as in the mobility of images, characteristic of early cinema with itinerant exhibitors who were also performers."

Performing the Goddess—Chapal Bhaduri's Story

Performing the Goddess—Chapal Bhaduri's Story is the title of a 44-minute video film shot on Betacam and directed by Navin Kishore of Seagull Books, Kolkata, in 2002. The video film brings us face-to-face with the classic story of a single man who fought all the battles of life alone, but does not drown himself in the deep and wide ocean called self-pity or agrees to live off charity. In-depth interviews on the life of a *jatra* (a popular folk theatre form within the world of Bengali theatre. It is spread across Bengali-speaking areas of India in West Bengal, Bihar, Odisha and Tripura and across Bangladesh) actor, extracts from milestone fragments of jatra plays, the make-up process that transforms a man into a goddess and documentation of the play on the goddess provide the viewers a rare entry into an unusual world, and a close look at Chapal Bhaduri's life and work.

The film opens with a middle shot of the actor saying a silent prayer to the goddess whose role he is about to play. Then through a series of shots, most of them in extremely tight close-up, we are shown the actor applying make-up on his face. With make-up complete, the saree draped around his middle-aged male body, the wig secured, the tiara fixed, he stands in front of the camera and says, "Now, I'm Chapal Rani. Not Chapal Bhaduri."[5]

Chapal Bhaduri is 70 plus today. He lives alone in Kolkata, cooks his own food, keeps body and soul together by dressing up and performing the role of the Goddess Shitala in different temples and street corners of the city. Chapal Bhaduri, alias Chapal Rani or Queen Chapal, leading lady of Bengal's traditional, travelling folk theatre-in-the-round, the jatra, spent his life playing female roles. He feels, thinks and speaks like a woman today. To outward appearances, he remains a man. When history changed tradition, women stepped out onto the stage, they began to play female roles themselves. Actors such as Chapal Bhaduri, who were confined to playing women's roles, found themselves at the wrong end of the bread–butter problem. Out of work, Chapal Bhaduri turned a new page in the book of his life. He started playing Shitala, the poor person's dreaded Goddess of pox and disease in dramatized performances of the Goddess' sacred saga.

Since 1995, he turned into Goddess Shitala and began to slip under the Goddess' role—complete with costume, make-up and jewellery—to make the performance as credible and realistic as possible. Shitala's worship was widespread with the incidence of smallpox in the 18th century. Today, as there is no small pox, Shitala continues to be worshipped only for marriage. In West Bengal, she is still worshipped for fertility by women who believe that they are infertile.

Chapal offers us a fascinating insight into the milieu of the professional jatra that is still an integral part of the people's culture in Bengal. "I was in a bad way, so to survive, to save myself...those who organize this came to me and asked me to do this (the Shitala role.) I told them that there is no play in this, no script, nothing to show scene by scene, and the way one is used to in jatra or amateur (urban) theatre. They said, 'we'll tell you the story of the goddess, and you can take it from there.' From this, I understood that they would give me the outline, but the details, the character, arrangement, fleshing out, I would have to create myself. Even the dialogue I would have to do myself," says Bhaduri.

Bhaduri speaks of the way in which he was asked to play the role of Marzeenā in return for a job with the Eastern Railways. He describes the way he was made up for his role. He was hailed as a female impersonator—just as Leslie Cheung's character is assigned a female role as a young boy in the Chinese opera in Cheng Kaige's film *Farewell My Concubine* (1993)—and that, in Althusserian terms, is what he became.[6]

Naveen Kishore's camera holds Chapal mostly in tight close-ups except for the times when he is performing Maa Shitala, but sustains control in respecting the privacy and dignity of this courageous man. Shot in B&W, the film invests in nostalgia while in the present with the flashbacks heard directly from Bhaduri in his narrations.

His effeminate bearing, voice, pitch and throw of lines bears out his inborn genius for female impersonation. "I began this from the outset of my career on stage, opening with the promise that this would land me a job with the Eastern Railways. Miraculously, it did!

I was reluctant to don female costume and gear to begin with. But when I look back in retrospect, I feel that I really had more of the feminine than the masculine in me," he says.

Making the Face

Making the Face by Joshy Joseph explores the identity of a little-known make-up artiste in Imphal, the capital of Manipur in the north-east, a state where like the other north-eastern states, gender equity is rooted in the culture and the identity of everyone who lives here. The central subject, Tom Sharma, is a transgender. Joseph's film offers a unique analysis of identity formation of the Imphal-rooted Sharma who belongs to the Meitei tribe on one hand and his integrity into his transgender on the other, weaving all this with his passionate desire to be accepted not just for his alternative sexual identity and orientation but also as an individual in his own right. Sharma presents a cheerful, happy face who is in great demand for his skills in the art of make-up and is forever flooded with independent assignments. Women and girls who form his clientele feel comfortable and free in his company and some of them use him as a shoulder to weep on and a confidante.

Image 2.5. Tom Sharma in Film: *Making the Face*

Courtesy: Joshy Joseph

Produced by the PSBT, *Making the Face* won the National Award for the Best Film on Family Welfare in 2011. It takes the audience on a journey along with the protagonist Tom and the citation gives the jury's reason for awarding the film. It stated, "It is a multi-layered exploration of the issue of alternative sexuality in the politically-troubled state of Manipur." It is an extremely challenging journey by film-makers Joseph and Suvendu Chatterjee also because just to shoot a documentary in the disturbed area of Imphal and Manipur is itself an extremely difficult journey. Joshy's very discovery of his subject reveals his unceasing effort to discover unknown territories and people for his films.

Says Joshy, "The visibility of transgender people in the otherwise strictly traditional Meitei society has increased only during the last decade or so. Many of them are professionals in beauty related saloons. Tom Sharma earns around ₹2,000 per day during the wedding season. Transgender people learn to live in their own circles, even as they remain within the rigid framework of traditional Meitei society. They cannot live separately in exclusive communes. So they learn to create their own microcosm within the wider macrocosm of society at large."

The play on the film's title, the multiple layers of meaning, expressed or implied, *Making the Face* is a telling account of Sharma's struggles—inner and outer. The inner struggle is to 'hide' his transgender identity instilled by the hidden fear of rejection by the conservative Metei society that runs alongside the contradictory desperation of acceptance and the outer struggle of using his talent to 'make up the faces' of dancers and artists, mostly female. This constant tug of war between the 'concealed' and the 'revealed' in a politically and ethnically conflict area such as Manipur makes the film outstanding. The physical journey the directors take, following Tom from one place to the next is also the film-maker's journey. It guides him to decide which line to take or whether to take several lines without detracting from the identity formation of the subject, Tom Sharma.

The marriage of Tom's partner has not affected his professionalism or his hectic pace of work on fashion shows and the make-up classes he gives, or even in the chores at home that he shares with his former partner and wife. Tom displays an apparent ability to accept life as it comes. He seems to be able to smile at the world, and even laugh at himself. But perhaps, the casualness of his moods and the flippancy is indicative of other deeper and darker emotions that remain hidden inside. Being different is not easy anywhere. However, in Manipur the problems are compounded in many more ways, because a turbulent social and political ambience wrests away the private space that could have created the space to allow Tom Sharma to be the way he is. And yet, he is at an obvious level free to live his life the way he wants to. The problem begins when others are included into his growing community. The increase in the sheer visibility of alternate sexuality today disturbs society, though the dichotomy remains. His parents find it impossible to accept that he is different from the others," sums up Joshy.

CONCLUSION

What significance does the biographical documentary have within the wider canvas of documentary film-making in India? The answers are obvious. They are very positive and inspirational because they inspire us to go ahead, give us the space to dream and reach a definite destination. They are also one of the most outstanding ways of archiving audiovisual lives of great men and women for posterity that will not be limited by time, space, culture and language. Biographical documentaries of little-known and unknown men, women and groups give the audience a learning experience from their lives about how struggles are sometimes worth going through to attain and achieve some definite goals or even how struggles can sometimes change the course of one's journey, or destination.

Biographical documentaries also flesh out, frame by slow frame, how a celebrity's identity formation takes place whether one has attained recognition in the performing arts, or in the field of literature or fine arts or social work. It places the person in perspective, tracing the evolution and growth of the person through geography, history, form, content and attainments. 'Attainment' is a fluid word that can apply equally to the great as it can to the small and the anonymous because each attainment is subjective and conditioned to the time and the place it takes place in a given individual.

It would be pertinent to close with what S. Priyadarshini writes about this subject,[7] "Biography on celluloid invariably makes a good watch, especially if the figure is from the public domain. The handling of such a retrospective is often tricky because the film-maker, in most cases, suffers either from overwhelming adulation, which may be the reason for the production, or sometimes in anticipation of such a bias remains sadly detached. In both cases objectivity is at risk."

NOTES
1. Interview with the author, published in SCREEN in June 2003.
2. Anne Rutherford, "Buddhas Made of Ice and Butter: Mimetic Visuality, Transience and the Documentary Image," *Third Text* 20, no. 1 (2006), 27–40.
3. The powada is a genre of Marathi poetry that emerged during the late 17th century. The powadas are a kind of ballad written in an exciting style and narrate historical events in an inspiring manner. The composer-cum-singers of the powadas are known as shahirs. The early powadas are mostly composed by the eyewitnesses of the great events celebrated in these ballads. (Source: http://en.wikipedia.org/wiki/Powada)
4. For this film, the author is indebted to the insightful review of the film by Priua Deepti Malhotra's *The Politics of Popular Culture, Infochange News and Features*, April 2009.
5. Niladri R Chatterjee, "'Now I'm Chapal Rani': Chapal Bhaduri's Hyperformative Female Impersonation," *Intersections: Gender and Sexuality in Asia and the Pacific* (October 2009), no. 22.
6. Louis Althusser, "Ideology and Ideological State Apparatuses," in *The Norton Anthology of Theory and Criticism*, ed. Vincent B. Leitch, trans. Ben Brewster (New York and London: W.W. Norton & Co., 2001), 1483–1509.
7. S. Priyadarshini, "Celluloid Biographies," *Hindu*, 22 February 2012.

3
THE ETHNOGRAPHICAL FILM
A Cinema for the People, by the People

After hundreds of years, anthropology has tried to perfect a way to accurately record and make an adequate translation of a culture as heritage for future years, and yet we find to date, that perhaps, it is the humanist, the novelist or the feature filmmaker, and not the anthropologist who has made the best translation of culture.

Timothy Ash

BACKGROUND[1]

An ethnographical film is a bit complex to define. It is basically linked to anthropology and deals with a study and interpretation of the social and economic behaviour of little-known ethnic groups. But it goes further than that. The ethnographical filmmaker captures these groups on film for record, for posterity, for research, or purely for the love of people and in quest of knowledge for its own sake. But to do this with honesty and integrity, he like his anthropologist brother, must commit himself to what is known as participant observation. This is also called cinéma vérité, where interpretation follows filming. The purpose of it is to let people being filmed express and explain themselves through their own words and action. In cinéma vérité, the film-maker does not tell his subjects what to say or do. He is aware of the fact that before actual shooting begins, he does not quite know where his camera should be or how it should move. He tries to film his subjects as thoroughly as he can with minimum interference. He lives for long periods with the people he is going to film, learns or tries to learn the language if he does not know it. He ensures the participation of the camera in events as they unfold through the people featuring in the film.

There is a major ethical consideration involved in the making of ethno-documentary. It is necessary for the film-maker to let the people he films know why he is filming them, what his specific purpose is and how he plans to use the footage he films. Another ethical question relates to showing the film to the people it talks about and then asking them to react to it. This is precisely why an ethno-documentary film-maker keeps showing his subjects what he has shot between shootings, so that he stands corrected by them if he has gone wrong, or if a certain camera angle has changed the perspective of a shot so much that it means something totally different from what was actually intended to be shown.

INTRODUCTION[2]

The birth of the ethno-documentary in India could probably be credited to Paul Zils—the German prisoner of war (POW)—who came to India in 1945 and was asked by the British India Government to head the external unit of their Information Films of India. He made several films for the Shell Film Unit of London. Among these, the two ethnographic films are the *Oraons of Bihar* (1955) and *The Martial Dances of Malabar* (1958). In the mid-1950s, a Russian documentary film-maker Roman Karmen and a Swede called Arne Sucksdorff came to India to make documentary films. The term 'ethno-documentary' was unknown then but Arne's film, *The Flute and the Arrow* (1957), could be called the truest ethnographical documentary made in India. The film is about a Bastar tribe known as Murias whose lifestyle remained unchanged for thousands of years. Sucksdorff went to Bastar in Madhya Pradesh, lived with the tribe for 18 months weathering the inclemency of the tropical climate and reportedly exposed 120,000 feet of film.

Paul Zils' *The Vanishing Tribe* (1959) remains a milestone in the history of ethnographical documentaries. Within 19 minutes, Zils introduces his audience to the Todas of the Nilgiris through the oldest woman in the settlement, Bjak and her grandson Pliyanersh. The film clearly brings across their cultural identity, their pride in their customs and rituals and mores. Incidentally, the first Indian documentary to win an international award was an ethnographic film. Made under the banner of Information Films of India (IFI) between 1943 and 1956 during the tenure of Ezra Mir, *Tree of Wealth* was directed by Bhaskar Rao. Through varied uses of the coconut as his main theme, Rao unfolded the lifestyle of the people of Kerala. It won an award at the Edinburgh Festival. During the late 1960s, Shyam Benegal made a documentary called *Close to Nature* (1967). The film covered some tribal pockets of Madhya Pradesh, exploring lifestyles of people through their gods, songs and dances, their food, and their love life. Within the parameters of the narrative, he included the internationally famous Ghotuls where young boys and girls are initiated into sex without the trappings of marriage.

Mani Kaul made some few interesting documentaries that could be called ethnographic in terms of covering folk artistes and the people who were the subjects of the films. For *The Nomad Puppeteers* (1953), Kaul followed a group of traditional puppeteers from Rajasthan who kept travelling to keep body and soul together, fight as they must, but gradually lose out to alternative forms of modern entertainment. The film also covered the loss of integrity among the puppeteers as they were forced by market conditions to compromise to commercial demands by using puppets to perform film dances and songs. Kaul's 20-minute documentary, *Chitrakathi* (1977), was produced by Films Division. The film is about folk artistes of western India who narrate religious stories with the help of leather puppets. Mani steps right into a Konkan coastal village home where the family managed to preserve this ancient art for centuries. Kaul touches upon the tragedy of the art being wiped out in course of time since the younger generation sought a more economically secure life in the city.

GATHERING MOMENTUM

From the 1990s, the ethnographical documentary has evolved into a 'given' among hoards of young film-makers and the practice sustains till this day, imbibing and creating new forms, new content to open windows to the audience to unknown worlds, unknown heritages and unknown people. Charu Kamal Hazarika's *Main-Taris of Assam* is a 20-minute documentary which studies the lives of the tribe in Assam. M.A. Rahman's *Gothrasmriti* is at once a straightforward documentation and an anthropological-political interpretation of the traditional enactment of Thaiyyam rituals among the Thaiyya community of north Malabar in Kerala. "In ancient times," says Rahman, "this community migrated from the hills to the lowlands, making the transition from a hunting-and-food-gathering existence to the margins of agriculture. The spectacular Thaiyyam performance is for them, a means of celebrating the memory of their earlier culture and collective history."

Sudhanshu Mishra's *Mithak Bhan* (The Disappearing Poem) is an ethnographic documentary because it traces the lifestyle of the Agarias, a group of tribal iron smelters living in the forests along the margins of the Kanha National Park in Madhya Pradesh. As one uncovers the surface to reveal the layers underneath, the film becomes one of social concern. The film changes direction to question the rising economic desperation of these people, pushing them to social disintegration. This is heightened by the growing economic relevance of their traditional craft created out of iron smelting. From this point of view, it is a film of social concern and communication. Looked at from a different perspective, it emerges as documentary that determinedly digs into a remote, unknown part of the country's indigenous culture through the group's rituals, performed through song, dance and music. How would one slot this kind of film?

Gautam Bora's *Songs of Abitani: The Missings* (1990) portrays the life of the Missings, a large tribe in Assam who live on the banks of the Brahmaputra. Once prosperous people, they have now been reduced to penury by reason of natural calamities like floods and earthquakes, and man-made disasters like urbanization and technological progress. Nilita Vachani's lovely film *Sabzi Mandi Ke Heere* (1993)—financed by a German television company—offers a unique insight into the conditions of interstate bus travel in north India. It highlights the manner and attitudes of the vendors who hawk their wares in these buses during the journey. If one is a hakim, selling anonymous pain balms and indigenous ointments, another is a *surma* (an ancient eye cosmetic) seller who confesses that he would have loved to sing *quawallis* (a form of Sufi devotional music) for a living if he had the opportunity. Another is a self-styled magician who clubs his show with an offer of a book that explains the tricks he has shown. The film is shot entirely in the cinéma vérité style, without the help of a script or preschooling the performers for the camera.

Balaka Ghosh's *Vehicle with the Soul of a Man* (2000) is a telling documentary that 'tells' nothing, but only shows. Sans commentary or dialogue, the film is a pictorial documentation on the *pithoos*—porters who come down from Nepal to carry pilgrims to

Kedarnath on their backs. Thousands of pilgrims embark on this journey to the heavenly abode of Lord Shiva located at a height of 12,000 feet. The silent question the film raises is—what meaning does a 'pilgrimage' have when it is achieved by one human being who violates the rights of a fellow human by riding on his back? It is an ethnographic film by rigid categorization. But it is also a human interest story that makes an acidic comment on the gross violation of human rights, simply through visuals and a completely silent soundtrack.

Alok Das' *Lyrics of Life* (1995) looks at the huge city of Calcutta viewed through its huge slum population. Most of the slums of the city are peopled with immigrants from other parts of the country, though they learnt to imbibe Calcutta into their system. The film captures the common rhythm that flows through their lives filled with poverty and despair driven to the edge of the basic needs of life—food, clothing and shelter. The film also explores their trying to seek temporary pleasure through drinking, drugs, gambling and so on. Yet, the rising sun instils hope in them and life goes on.

Buddha Weeps in Jadugoda (1999), directed by Sri Prakash, is an attempt to record how the lives of people in Jadugoda turned into a veritable hell by the Uranium Corporation of India Limited (UCIL). Made right in the middle of threats and harassment by authorities at the UCIL and the district administration, the film demonstrates the gross misuse of power that has displaced its original inhabitants, showing utter disregard to the effect of mining on the local environment and its effects on the health of the people. Backed by official support, UCIL does not bother to follow internationally accepted norms and safety precautions in the handling of uranium. The victims are the tribals living near Jadugoda, located in East Singhbhum district of Jharkhand. They are aware of the danger they are being exposed to, but they are helpless.

Colours Black (2001), by Mamta Murthy, is beautifully structured around four children, now adults in different stages of life—recounting mainly off camera—their experience of child abuse and the silence they were coerced into which continued till they grew up. Murthy counters the voice-overs with visuals that do not belong to the voices, yet evolve into telling narratives of private pain. *Jari Mari: Of Cloth and Other Stories* (2001), by Surabhi Sharma, weaves its way through the narrowest of narrow bylanes of the Jari Mari slum in Bombay where men and women eke out a living, further weakened by their lack of power to organize and their supposedly 'illegal' status as residents.

CASE STUDIES

Two Ethnographic Films Set in Sikkim

In 1999, Nilanjan Bhattacharya was commissioned by Anthropological Society of India to make a documentary, *In The Land of Hidden Treasure* (1999), on monastery crafts and arts in Sikkim. It was a very low-budget film and he, along with his small team, could manage only a single trip to Sikkim. They shot in three monasteries there—Inchey, Phodong and Labrong. He visited Dorji Bhutia, a respected mask maker at his Timchim house in north Sikkim. He interviewed Bhutia on his work that involved mask-making rituals, traditions, techniques. More important was Nilanjan's interest in finding out if and how he had transferred the art of his craft to his son, Duduk.

Image 3.1. *If It Rains*

Courtesy: Nilanjan Bhattacharya

THE ETHNOGRAPHICAL FILM

"Duduk's son was then only ten years old and went to the village school. We spent some time with Dorji and his family and discovered that he was famous for his power to stop or bring rain. I made up my mind to come back and make a longer film later on to explore the character in detail. I went back in 2001. Dorji had passed away, leaving behind stories about how he had willed his own death. So, I changed tracks and decided to follow the lives and dreams of Dorji's son Duduk and grandson Sonam," said Nilanjan, explaining the source of his two films *In The Land of Hidden Treasure* and *Jodi Bristi Ashey* (If It Rains, 2001) that were screened at Kolkata's Goethe-Institut's Max Mueller Bhavan recently. The second film has been jointly produced by Nippon Hoso Kyokai (NHK), Japan and Streamline Stories, India.

In The Land of Hidden Treasure, traces the lives and lifestyles of three members of a family— father, son and grandson— who live in Timchim in Sikkim. The father, Dorji Bhutia—now deceased— was a maker of masks and could also manipulate the rains for the welfare of the people with his meditative powers. His son, Duduk Bhutia, learnt the craft of mask making from his father, though this is not a hereditary but a traditional art.

Jodi Bristi Ashey was triggered when Nilanjan heard that the old mask maker had passed away. He wished to find out whether this simple man with great spiritual powers had had a natural death or whether he had willed his death. The director continued to frequent the father-son duo for the next eight years and then began to make the second film with his own funding till NHK— a Japanese television channel— stepped in with funding. He grew close to the family and discovered that Sonam had opted out of the Lama training school at Deorali, where the family had sent him to become a Lama, and had chosen to study in Benares. His father, a lottery addict and also a master at mask making, confessed that he did not have the power to manipulate the rains like his father did and went on to tell Nilanjan that his father had indeed willed his own death.

Both films are shot straight from the shoulder in a no-nonsense manner, spilling over with candidly shot frames of the hillscapes, the countryside, the people and the three men spanning three generations of the same family. There is no artifice, no pretensions, and therefore, no picture-postcard-kind gloss one sees in a touristic film, but is honest precisely because these things are not there in both films. The films were shot with a gap between the first and the second, but the common ground is the place—Sikkim as seen through the eyes of the director and his interactions with real-life characters he came to know during the making of the first film.

Ranu Ghosh cinematographed both films and also did the sound design for the first one. Dibyendu Porel and Indrajit Das edited the first and second films, respectively. Partha Barman designed the sound for the second film, more poetic and lyrical than the first one. "This long journey with this family in the lap of Himalayas made me richer in many senses. It was fascinating to see and record the growing up of a young boy. In the course of nine years, I could also understand the changing society, the impact of modernization and the conflicts of contemporary living. I am planning a longer film because I have more than 100 hours of footage spread over 9 years. I continue shooting Sonam and plan to shoot this family at least for another five years till Sonam comes out of that Sanskrit college. Then maybe I could come out with another film," Nilanjan sums up.

How did Duduk and Sonam react when they saw the films? "They reacted very positively when they saw the first one for the first time. Even while I was shooting, I used to show them and other members of their family the rushes sometimes. Their reactions were emotional whenever they saw grandfather's footage. I once showed these footages to their extended family in their village. The reaction was really moving as people cried and thanked me profusely for having documented the grandfather on film for posterity," says Nilanjan.

Khepar Mon Brindabon

Khepar Mon Brindabon (2014) is an intriguing documentary produced and directed by Ladly Mukhopadhyay. It is a film that condenses the director's 35-year-long journey with his subject—Gour Khepa—that resulted in 300 feet of film shot over 12 years, slashed to 90 minutes of screening time. Ladly honed his skills with documentary films on the Nandigram and Singur upheavals followed by bio-documentaries on Sambhu Mitra and Subal Gosain who were Gour Khepa's mentor and guru, respectively. Gour Khepa, who passed away tragically in a car crash in January 2013, is perhaps the

Image 3.2. Gour Khepa Lost in His World

Courtesy: Ladly Mukhopadhyay

last of the genuine Bauls who lived, thought and ideologized the principles of Baul philosophy and was proud of being a Baul.

Many documentary films have been made on Bauls and the Baul community. In 1979, George Luneau made a documentary on Bauls when they were already established in the European cultural landscape as accomplished performing artists. Ladly had helped Luneau when he made this film. Gautam Ghosh made a fictionalized feature film *Moner Manush* (2010) on Lalon, perhaps one of the earliest Bauls in history some years ago. But *Khepar Mon Brindabon* makes a distinct, individual and subjective statement, that is, the viewpoint of Gour Khepa as seen and projected by a film-maker who journeyed with him for 35 long years.

Khepar Mon Brindabon is an ethnographical film as it traces the anthropological and cultural history of this ethnic sect of wandering minstrels—the Bauls of Bengal—who spread their progressive and secular faith through their song and music. It is a biographical film on a Baul performer who left his footprints on the sand of time with his courage, his forthrightness, his philosophy and his caustic comments on the modern and the postmodern. It is also informative and educational because it sheds light on a talented artist who died unsung and unwept. *Khepar Mon Brindabon* is a journey film because the director and his crew travels the landscape of Baul territory across West Bengal, covering every single Baul fair where Bauls from all corners travel to perform and to watch others perform.

The suffix *khepa* attached to Gour and other leading Bauls suggests that the Baul is wild (khepa) who lives life on his own terms, lives together with his partner minus wedding rituals, never believes in being rooted to a single place and funds his life through alms he collects from his music. "The word Khepa also means 'wise'" explains the 69-year-old Gour Khepa in the beginning of this film, smiling widely. In fact, he is ever smiling even when he is making an oral mincemeat of what has come to be termed as the Bangla Band—a new class of fusion music created in the late 1990s by young and trained singers who perform in groups (bands), write lyrics themselves, compose the music and also sing these songs. Gour does not like their music at all because he feels the bands are not dedicated to music.

"Gour was a Baul maestro who redefined the word *Khyapa*. All I have done is capture as many moments as possible," says Ladly who directed the film. Every frame of this 90-minute narrative is filled with Gour Khepa in his varied moods, talking to the director and to others present, making no bones about his comments on the world of the Internet and the computer and social media networks underscoring his information map, suggesting that though immersed in his music and song, he is not ignorant of the dramatic changes taking place in the world of communication. Even at 69, he sings beautifully, without a single note going out of tune or a pitch missing, despite being addicted to hemp and bidis he smokes right through the film. The film belongs entirely to Gour Khepa and is his point of view on life, sex, addiction, god and one's attachment to god, music, musicians and performers and on his experience of interacting with noted music personalities abroad.

Gour Khepa was worldly wise and travelled widely but this experience did not impact on his music or on his lifestyle. He performed with Bob Dylan and was invited by Peter Brooke to perform in his Mahabharat. He declined the offer when told in no uncertain terms that he would not be legally permitted to carry hemp with him to the USA! In the film, he points out the difference between a genuine Baul and a fake one. He emphasizes again and again that

Baul is not just a folk performance but an entire philosophy, a way of life and an ideology all Bauls live up to and music is just a part. Candid and caustic, he points out that he liked some of Bob Dylan's music but not all. He worked with Jerzy Grotowski. He had a clear-cut take on traditional folk versus Westernized urban music. He also had close links with the urban elite, littérateurs, singers and men of culture.

The film opens on Gour belting out *Baul Howa Sohoj Katha Noy*. Translated, it reads, "It is not easy to become a Baul." Sometime later, as the film journeys with him and the audience learns to look at his philosophy through his eyes, he says, "Dive deep. Go to the deep, and then you can become history!" Ladly adds, "Gour was a Baul maestro who defined the word '*khepa*' in the truest sense, an advocate for 'natural' against 'artificial' and pretentious ways." Bubbling with electric energy and ready wit, he is shown to be a person who loved to attract and surprise people with his performance. He enjoyed baffling people with his comments on social situations and life in general, speaking about true and false, natural and artificial, good and bad, purity and pollution.

When asked what drew him to the Baul culture though he was brought up in mainstream Kolkata, Ladly says that he was interested in folk culture from a very young age. He won a senior fellowship from the Indian Council of Cultural Research. This resulted in two books. One was entitled *Kholamelar Mela Khela* and the other was *Udashi Babar Akhda*, both on Bauls. During his field research, he happened to meet Gour Khepa and says, "It is as if my life, touched by a magic wand, changed forever. This was my dream project. The only regret I have is that I could not show it to Gour Khepa."

Gour Khepa, as the film unfolds, amazes us with his awareness about the changes happening around him though he is not a part of those changes. He talks about the environment, pokes fun at the Internet and social networking sites, talks about how the philosophy of the body is important to transcend into the philosophy of the mind and the spirit. His companion sits beside him echoing his comments like repeating question tags. His listeners echo everything he says. He ends his one-liners with a question tag, and when this tag is repeated by his audience, it is as if he needs affirmation of what he has just said or asked.

The film travels to many Baul fairs such as the Pathorchakuri in Birbhum, the Tonkaitola Mela in Birbhum, the Poush Mela in Santiniketan and to Nadia district, the central hub of Baul culture and Baul practice founded by none other than Sri Sri Chaitanya Mahaprabhu and so on. Many of these melas are now commercialized while the Jaydev Kenduli Mela in Birbhum is now dominated by Keertaniyas, a different group of folk performers renowned for their *keertans*—spiritual songs dedicated to different gods from the Hindu pantheon.

Khepar Mon Brindabon is almost like a musical because it is dotted with songs rendered by Gour Khepa and his chorus group that often stands and dances to the songs, *ektara* (Indian one-stringed musical instrument) in one hand, perhaps a *dugdugi* (Hindi/Urdu word which refers to a musical instrument) in the other and dancing bells tied to their ankles. It is a total performance and not just music. The lyrics spill over with their philosophy and with comments on life—funny, sarcastic, caustic and critical— and Gour Khepa spins them out so beautifully that seeing the same person in every frame for 90 long minutes neither bore the viewer for a single minute nor takes his/her attention away from the screen. It also offers an insight on one true Baul and the ideologies he believes in and lives by. He is not afraid of speaking his mind. In spite of his unkempt hair, his dirty robes that need a wash, his constant use of hemp (cannabis), his speech filled with four-letter words and other colourful vocabulary decent civilians scoff at, as the film goes along, you not only begin to look at him with reverence and respect but also look at life differently—albeit the film continues to haunt you. Sadly, since documentaries do not have the space for public viewing in our country, few filmbuffs will have the opportunity of watching *Khepar Mon Brindabon*.

Bottle Masala in Moile

One of the strangest ironies of life is that we do not know about small ethnic groups living in our city of birth and growth though they have lived here for hundreds of years. One such ethnic minority group is the east-Indian community in Mumbai. Today, their existence stands threatened as *Bottle Masala in Moile* (2013), a 38-minute documentary by Vaidehi Chitre on the community, sets out to show. The east Indians, all Catholics, originated from diverse

Image 3.3. A Production Still of *Bottle Masala in Moile*

Courtesy: Vaidehi Chitre

local groups such as farmers, fishing people, toddy tappers, salt-pan workers and others. Several of them were agriculturalists working on the land that they also owned.

Bottle masala, as all fish-eating non-vegetarians must know, is a unique brand of home-made mixture of 22 grains and spices that works like magic in east-Indian dishes and is now used right across Mumbai by the mainstream population too. Moile is a unique fish curry that cannot be made without this masala. Chitre uses these two common words for the title of her film. It begins with the white-haired, Marathi-speaking Cecilia Gonsalves, who makes and sells bottle masala through retail shops in Bandra. Then the film reaches out to become a metaphor for the displacement that threatens their lives.

"Today, as owners of ancestral property in a city that is developing at an aggressive pace, the community finds itself rapidly losing land to government and corporate forces. For the community as a whole, this has meant losing a valuable connection with the soil to which their culture is tied—the 'story of us'. But for many, especially those in the rural areas, this has also meant a threat to livelihood and consequently, as a small community, a threat to their very existence," explains Chitre.

The film is divided into two thematically interconnected but dramatically discrete chapters. 'Belly of the Whale', based in mainland Mumbai, is a collection of individual stories loosely held together by a common thread of the experience of loss. 'Eye of the Storm' is set in Dharavi Island and is driven by the narrative of the community's resistance movement against land acquisition. The main thrust of the film is a step-by-step revelation of how this ethnic group's very existence is threatened by the state government's lop-sided and partisan 'development' projects.

Francisca Falcon recalls when, as a child, she saw a whale land up on the beaches of the sea near where they still live. "This resulted in a flood of sardines in the sea and everyone feasted on them. Farmers would tell us to collect the dried up sardines in sacks and give it to them for which they would pay us," she says. Later, she says, "People living in *Gaothans* (village or hamlet) were not allowed to build beyond two storeys. But now, MMRDA (Mumbai Metropolitan Region Development Authority) is allowing the big construction houses, promoters and builders to build multi-storied constructions. They are forcing us to sell our ancestral land. One fine morning, they simply picked up our gate and took it away. This was daylight robbery but who is listening?"

Fr Larry Pereira, a church historian, says, "The word East Indian was officially adopted by the community elders way back in 1887 during the Golden Jubilee of Queen Victoria. Interestingly, though their origins are traced back to the Portuguese, they decided to throw their lot with the British rather than the Portuguese whose importance had faded by that time." He adds that the original inhabitants were from north Mumbai, Vasai and the Mumbai region, but later on other people of the Catholic faith who had embraced it from the Portuguese came from north Konkan and Goa.

Prem Moraes says that all the land they own have been acquired through land reclaimed from the sea. He even began a website on east Indians in 2004. "You will not find any mention of the east Indian Catholic community in any history or geography book brought out by official publications of the government and quasi governmental bodies. It is as if we do not exist. So, I began this website so that our existence is established, recognized and sustained."

Another belt of east Indians live along the Dharavi Islands in Gorai, Uttan and Bhayander where the population is around 150,000. Walter Murzello informs us that they are the last bastion of the east Indian population in Mumbai. The lives of the east Indians began to change when in March 2006, the Government of India granted, 'in principle of approval' 1,000 hectares (2,471 acres) of land in Dharavi Island to PIPL (Pan India Paryatan Pvt. Ltd)—owners of EsselWorld amusement park—for the development of a special economic zone (SEZ). Later the same year, the state government agreed to a total of 5,740 hectares (14,183 acres) for eventual acquisition.

This led to collective and strong resistance from the east-Indian community. Protest bodies were formed because according to Lourdes D'Souza, Secretary, Dharavi Bet Bachao Sangharsha Samiti, 10 villages would be swallowed by this so-called development project. These are—Marve, Gorai, Chowk, Culvem, Marve, Uttan, Tarodi, Dongri, Rai and Murdha. This happened way back in 1997–98.

The movement gained momentum and strength over time with fishermen and women, local residents, farmers and everyone else from six villages voicing their protest against SEZ. Finally, on 22nd September, 2008, the SEZ was cut down to 110 hectares (271 acres). But Walter Murzello adds a point of dissent. "The 110 hectares are mangrove land. Mangroves protect the environment and also the lives of the locals by stopping tidal waves from entering into living areas. Besides, we will lose all the land where fish come to lay eggs, which will directly impact the production of fish and on the livelihoods of the fisher folk."

Again in November 2009, newspaper reports announced that bids were invited for an INR 200-crore bridge at Manori Creek on grounds that this "will help improve connectivity of Manori, Gorai and Bhayander areas." But villagers believe that the proposed sea link will cause damage to marine ecology and will have an impact on the livelihood of the east Indians who live and work there. A group of fishermen complained to the MMRDA and also filed RTI query, demanding an explanation about the need for the project. Lourdes D'Souza says, "We will go into litigation if the officials plan to go ahead with the project. There is hardly any traffic here and we did not even demand any such bridge. Why does MMRDA need to spend such a huge sum of money on this project?"

Francis Pereira, member, Manori Gramastha Bikas Mandal said, "It is ironic that our villages lack basic facilities like roads and hospitals, but the authorities plan to spend such a huge amount on this bridge. The MMRDA has not even taken us into confidence."

Bottle Masala in Moile won the Best Short Documentary Award at the 10th Jeevika Asia Livelihood Documentary Festival, 2013 and Bronze Remi Award at the Houston International Film Festival, 2013 besides being screened at the Ladakh International Film Festival's Competition Section, 2013 and International Documentary and Short Film Festival of Kerala's Competition Section, 2013 (World Premiere).

Dancing for Themselves

Dancing for Themselves is a documentary directed jointly by Jiban Saha, Arun Halder and Siddhartha Samadder. Shot totally on location in colour and in 16 mm, over its 52-minute span, *Dancing for Themselves* traces the aesthetic underpinnings of this dance form, performed often in the shape of a dance-drama or a ballet, yet underscoring the grace, the skill and the talent of individual performers. The film opens at the daybreak, marking the last day of the Bangla calendar which coincides with the Charak fair in Laharia. The Sun God has completed yet another annual circle. This fair heralds the beginning of the Chhau season because performed only in an open-air ambience, Chhau can be performed in dry seasons alone. As crowds converge onto the fair grounds, praying for a good harvest in the coming year, the Chhau dancers perform to a happy audience, celebrating the rites of spring. Charak itself is defined as a call of rites for spring, of which the chhau dance is merely an extension. There are debates about the origin of the word Chhau. Some say it derives from the word *chhaya*, meaning shadow, whereas there are others who say that it comes from *chhauni* or barracks. There is another school of thought which maintains that the word originates from *chhadma* or disguise. No one really knows the truth and the practitioners do not care. They are too busy trying to practise this very skilled form of dance-drama on the open grounds of their villages or trying to sustain this art by training their young, since this is mainly hereditary in nature and performed only by men.

There are three different styles or gharanas of Chhau, the Purulia gharanas, the Seraikela gharanas and the Mayurbhanj gharanas. The audience sits around a central space which forms the performing space. Performed mainly through acrobatic movements that include graceful pirouettes, somersaults, jumps and leg throws, the Chhau—in all three styles—commands a complete mastery over the body and mind, because such tremendous command over body does demand equal control over the mind. The very lives of Chhau dancers and gurus are imbued with the form of Chhau, with Chhau thoughts, Chhau wisdom, Chhau rhythm, Chhau faces and Chhau masks. The main musical support comes from percussion instruments such as the dhol and the dhamsa with melody flowing from the flute. The beat is more important than the music because perfect timing must be maintained, as evinced in this film through the group and individual rehearsals conducted in an open air ambience for want of proper and permanent rehearsing space.

The camera takes us along to Chorida village in West Bengal's Purulia district which is chock-full of gods and goddesses around every road corner; all of them mask makers or chhau dancers themselves, and one easily bumps into a *nara-rakshasa* or a Hanuman. Funny though it may seem to the city tourist, the village folk take it in their stride because it forms part of their lifestyle. For these village youngsters, collecting clay is a thrilling experience. Without structured apprenticeship to back them, they grow into mask makers par excellence. Their fathers and grandfathers educate them about the mythology of the faces they are sculpting into the masks, with facts, with deities and demons they will learn to handle in time to come. Chorida forms the main source of supply of masks. Mask makers hang their masks framed in tinsel and silver foil on the handles of their bicycles and ride away to performing villages to provide the artistes with masks. Chhau basically is a mask dance. The interplay of masks and movements is spectacular because there is interplay between the face and the mask; the mask metamorphosing into the face and the face transforming into the mask. This is specific to the Purulia and Seraikela styles because the Mayurbhanj style does not have masks at all. But does the mask really hide the face? asks the voice-over. Apart from using the mask as an integral part of the performance, the mask offers him the veil of covering the mystique of his life, his triumphs and his failures, his sadness and his mirth.

Behind the mask, the dancer laughs and cries, his feelings flow out of his body movements.

The film has shot a complete Ratri dance that forms the highlight of many chhau performances. The choreography of the concept of Ratri germinated in the Ratri Sukta of the Rig Veda. The mask of Ratri acquires a mysterious quality as the choreography takes inspiration from the rhythm of the night. This is a beautifully shot scene in a simulated natural lighting.

"It took us two years to complete the research, one year for documented research and another for locational research in the areas we were to shoot the film. Then, as we began shooting, the rains came and with it, one more year of waiting for the next spring to come on," says Jiban, one of the three directors of the film. Incidentally, this is the first directorial effort of all the three young men. One classic characteristic of chhau is that except in Mayurbhanj district in Orissa, it is performed with masks. The film beautifully highlights the painstaking and creatively artistic process of mask making, which the performers themselves have learnt to create. However, there are specialized craftsmen who have mastered the art of mask making. "The subjects differ from region to region," informs Jiban, adding, "While the Purulia masks define mythological characters like Durga, Shiva, Parasuram, the Seraikela masks depict abstract forms of nature and moods like storm, rain, ocean, night, peacock, monsoon, etc."

The film reveals one such peacock performance in rehearsal without costume or mask, in effect, underscoring the elasticity and grace of the traditional chhau performer who has imbibed the art from his father. Interviews with the doyens of the chhau form such as Guru Gambhir Singh Mura, Guru Sudhendra Narayan Singhdeo and Guru Kedarnath talk about the lack of state patronage without which it is difficult to sustain this rich aesthetic form of creative expression through the human body. The Purulia chhau is oppressed for want of funds while the Seraikela chhau is comparatively in a better position because the royal family has always patronized these dancers. For the last three generations, the royal family has been actively participating in the dance, devising new compositions and creating new masks. Sudhendra Narayan Singhdeo is probably the last dancer of this royal family. Most of them have received awards but it does not make them happy because the state has done nothing to sustain or promote the art form. Yet, they keep on dancing for themselves. In terms of film technique and aesthetics too, the film scores in cinematography (Madhu Shi), in editing (Mahadev Shi), haunting background score (Gautam Chatterjee) and imaginative graphics (Hiran Mitra.) What marks this documentary is not so much its focus on the dance as on the lifestyle and the philosophy of those who practise it.

Nee Engey (Where are You, 2003)

R.V. Ramani, an FTII graduate in cinematography, has made a documentary in Tamil entitled *Nee Engey* (2003). The film highlights the pathetic condition of shadow puppetry and shadow puppet artists of south India made with two research grants, one from the South Zone Culture Centre and another from India Foundation for the Arts, Bangalore. The film was completed in 2003. A graduate in cinematography from the FTII (1985 batch), since 1989, Ramani has made more than 15 independent documentaries and short films. He has established his individually distinctive style and considers his works an exploration into the various facets of expression. MIFF 2002 honoured him with a retrospective of his works. His retrospectives were also held at the International Documentary Film Festival at Neubrandenburg, Germany, in 1999 and at the Asia Pacific Triennale in Australia in 2000.

"I made the film to celebrate the dedication of these performers to their art form, the art of moving images. I have tried to create an impressionistic ethnography, reflecting on shadow puppet theatre, its history, mythology, and its intersections with contemporary cinema and with our lives. The making of the film has been a journey in search of the missing link common to all communities, cultures, traditions and artistic expressions."

"I noticed that all the puppeteers I met were Marathi speakers. Marathi culture, and in particular, theatrical genres have had a profound influence upon south Indian and Telugu performing traditions. The presence of Marathi speaking puppeteers suggests the influence of Marathi theatre conventions," informs Ramani who also cinematographed and edited the film.

Shadow Puppet Theatre is a puppet tradition found in the Telugu-speaking areas of south India—Andhra Pradesh and in parts of Karnataka and Tamil Nadu. It dates back to 700 years, yet little is known of its form or its practitioners prior to the late 1950s, when scholars first began to scrutinize it and publish their findings. These puppets—often life size or larger—are made from the dried skins of goats. The skins, once dried, are translucent. This feature is exploited in the process of making the puppets. Once they have been trimmed to size and the desired figures have been cut out and elaborately incised, they are dyed rather than painted. This permits light to pass through the puppets. As a result, when the puppets are placed against a white screen and lit from behind, the light passes through the puppets making them appear in full colour on screen, an illumination rather than a shadow.

"Before cinema, shadow puppetry was one of the most popular forms of performance entertainment in India. The shadow puppeteers are 'original film-makers' who created moving images on screen. They led a nomadic life—travelling, camping, setting up screens and performing the story of the Ramayana—adapting local languages and flavours as they moved from place to place. There are few puppeteers left, and their lives have changed along with their performance," says Ramani.

Traditionally, episodes from pan-Indian epics, the Ramayana and the Mahabharata, were set within an outer frame that followed a set sequence of events, starting with a prayer for the puppets and the puppeteers' ancestors. Then came the invocation of Ganapati and Sarasvati who would appear and dance on screen in puppet form. After they left, the *bhagavatar* (stage manager/narrator) and the puppet clowns would present a series of dialogues that entertained the audience through comedy and introduced the evening's production and epic episode. "Puppeteers have adapted their art to changing tastes. One troupe made new puppets by redesigning the traditional patterns for the clowns, demons, and women. This ability to adapt extends to shortening their performance from six hours to two or three to suit the demands of the urban audience," explains Ramani. Yet, as the film reveals, the performers suffer. One of them needs INR 150 to put up each performance and has a family of seven. Another says INR 20,000 could take his performance to five villages. Subba Rao, in his mid-80s, sang the Ramayana in one single song right into the camera. He performed for 40 long years, but today only one of his sons carries on the family profession. There are no patrons and hardly any audience to speak of. The sheer economics of their livelihood is appalling. Ramani deserves credit for shedding light on these forgotten artists. It is a travelogue, which, apart from being a documentary film, is a metaphorical and physical journey through the ethnographic history of a performing art and of its performers who will soon fade away from the pages of our cultural history.

Today, the community is dying for want of a paying audience because of television and cinema. A few like Lakshmanan Rao have innovated their performance. Rao has brought his five children and wife into the act. He has trained his children to perform brief skits, picked from popular Tamil films, before the shadow puppet performance begins. These are elements that find vivid and candid expression in Ramani's film.

Divine Drums

Against the backdrop of Sealdah station in Kolkata, shimmering in the glow of small lights adorning the brick-red-and-cream building as its way of celebrating the festive mood of Durga puja, a drummer

Image 3.4. *Divine Drums*

Courtesy: Biplov Majumder

on stilts plays on his drum. A juggler juggles hats in front of the *dhaki* (drummers who play on the specific kind of drum played during Durga Puja and other pujas). They are giving an impromptu performance to the audience that has gathered around. It is Durga Puja in Kolkata. This is a scene from *Divine Drums* (2010), a 67-minute documentary by Viplob Majumder, an FTII alumnus. These drummers or dhakis arrive from their original habitats in villages of Murshidabad and Behrampur to look for work. The film charts the difficult lives of one of the most creative performers of the dhak, a traditional percussion instrument mandatory for every religious festival among Bengalis across the world. These dhakis arrive at Sealdah station just before the Durga puja. With modernity and for lack of government assistance of any kind, their lives and their music stand threatened by extinction. This too, is portrayed in the film through an exploration of their sad lives behind and beyond the festival and the music.

The film explores the lives of the dhakis and their insight on the art of playing dhaks that is gradually dying a slow death. It deals with the socio-economic conditions of these artists, their philosophy and their beliefs. Nikhil Rabi Das is a wandering performer who travels in his bicycle from place to place. He lives in Gulzarbagh in Murshidabad district. He is a traditional drummer but he makes a living out of mending shoes and repairing umbrellas. "I play on the drum as and when work comes. I cannot give it up as it is a compulsory ritual of worship, is sacred and is our own tribute to the Mother Goddess." The camera captures him on a brown, rough roadside where he sits with his cobbler's tools and his cycle-repairing kit. His cycle rests on a fence on the side while his drum is beside him. He picks up the drum and begins to play to the camera. But he does not want his children to learn the drum because, "the money is very little compared to the labour we put in." Viplab adds that some of the women roll bidis to support the family while a few are driven to prostitution.

Lolit Mohan Das, an ace drummer with shoulder-length hair who performs with his troupe dressed in shimmering yellow silk costumes, was invited to Russia in 1987. "Our lives have pleasure and pain that go side by side," he says philosophically, adding that he used to peddle a rickshaw earlier and his brothers still do. His performance blends imaginative acrobatic movements, often playing at two or three drums at the same time, holding one by his teeth and two hanging from each shoulder. His drums are aesthetically decorated with floral cloth frilled at the edges and adorned with feathers. Has the Russian trip changed his financial status quo? Not really because it began and ended with the trip and it was back to square one—driven to the edges of poverty.

The soundtrack in the opening frames is filled with the chanting of the *Chandipath*, a ritualistic recitation that takes place every year at daybreak on Pitri Amavasya, which Bengalis call Mahalaya. The voice is that of the late Birendra Krishna Bhadra who charmed generations of Bengalis with his chanting of Durga's names and paths on All India Radio (AIR)'s Calcutta station. Visuals of beautiful white *kash* flowers blowing in the wind immortalized in Satyajit Ray's *Pather Panchali* overlap the chant. A little girl draped in a red-bordered white sari wanders across the fields filled with blades of tall grass, a metaphor for Durga, the little girl in Ray's film. *Divine Drums* travels across Murshidabad through places like Pasthhubhi, Andiron, Kandi, Beldanga, Gulzarbagh, Jojaan, through parts of Behrampur to Horpur in Birbhum drawing colourful portraits of their grey lives committed to the sacred rhythms of the dhak. The camera dwells on the browns and the ambers of the landscape, dotted with the smiling faces of the dhakis and their family.

We see quick cuts of trains rushing into Sealdah, the river Ganges with a glimpse of the Dakshineshwar temple across, men dipping into the holy river on Mahalaya to pay their respects to their late parents and so on. Durga idols in different stages of completion, idols being bought, installed and worshipped are intercut with comments by eminent musicians and scholars. The film ends with *sindoor khela* (married women in West Bengal smear each other with vermillion powder after touching the feet of Goddess Durga and her two daughters), *dhunuchi naach* (dance with a kind of handheld earthen instrument with one handle and an open top which can hold coal) and *bisarjan* (equivalent of the English word immersion specifically applied only to the immersion of gods and goddesses after their worship is over), to zero in on Sealdah, as the dhakis make their way back home. The sound of drumbeats and the drummers' performances make a background score redundant. The film throbs with the pulse of the people in the city and villages with smiling and cheerful faces of a little girl or an infant boy peeping from one corner of the frame. The late Dhanapat Das, one of the most learned players of the drum, details the scientific technique with detailed notations. Dinabandhu Das of Pastubhi in Kandi says that there are 12 kinds of percussion instruments and he can play them all. He manufactures drums with his son helping him and learnt manufacturing from his father who was a master craftsman. He makes drums by hollowing out the trunk of mango, neem, *babla* and *shirish* trees. The ends are made of goat skin. "Different kinds of wood produce different kinds of music and sing different tunes," says Bidhan Das. Six students of Andiron in Beldanga explain how different rhythm compositions are used for different occasions even during Durga puja—one when the goddess is being taken to the *mandap* (a raised platform permanent in aristocratic homes and temporary in make-shift local pujas constructed to place the goddess with space for actual rituals to be performed), one when she is welcomed and one when she is being worshipped, varying during the puja from morning to night.

Just as calypso beats are unique to the West Indies, the sound of Bagpipes makes one imagine Scotland, so does the sound of dhak paint a picture of Bengal, covered with the lush green carpet of enchantment that does not reach out to these drummers. This film is dedicated to the fledgling breed of dhakis, without whom the autumn in Bengal is never the same. The film is not pessimistic or dark because it is brightened with the smiling faces of the dhakis who do not wear their sad story on their faces and beat on, when it is festival season.

The Shillong Chamber Choir and the Little Home School

In a world where cut-throat competition is a way of life, Neil Nongkynrih stands out as an exception. He is not a social activist. Nor does he represent any NGO. He does not hold flags aloft or circulate slogans for the welfare of the masses. Then, what does he do? He has collected a bunch of children to build up a choir. He started the choir, "just to gather some people around and sing a variety of songs." The choir has tasted success, and now performs all over the world. *The Shillong Chamber Choir and the Little Home School* (2008) is a documentary made by Mumbai-based film-maker Urmi Juvekar that was screened as part of a film festival in Kolkata recently.

THE ETHNOGRAPHICAL FILM

The Shillong Chamber Choir and the Little Home School captures a series of impressions about a choir, in the remote north-east state of India, as they prepare for a concert. The film follows Neil Nongkynrih, a concert pianist, as he struggles to find a balance between his music and purpose of his life; to look after underprivileged children. The film is about his effort to create and maintain his little home school, an ideal world where he and his wards can live, practise music and pray together. It is a world where music is only a means to achieve the bigger end.

The film is a series of impressions about this choir located amidst the steep hilly greenery in Meghalaya a remote state in the north-east, as they prepare for a concert.

The little home school Neil has founded has around 16 members and an equal number forms the choir. Not all the children live with Neil but they spend their days there. The film opens with two girls hanging the washing on the clothes line while they are also belting out lines from one of their repertory in perfect harmony and synchronization without musical accompaniment. It is as if music is not external to their lives and to their daily chores. It is a part of their bodies, souls and minds. As Neil talks in the film, one discovers that not everyone who is there is musically gifted. But that is precisely the idea. The kids are English-speaking Christians. Most of the parents are poor or troubled so they prefer to let their children be with him and visit the natal home at intervals. It is more like sending your child to live with an uncle.

Most of the songs are hymns and psalms in English. Neil has himself composed the Sohlyngem Opera which they performed only in Shillong. It is a very secular and socially relevant story of a rich boy marrying a poor girl. Neil is also working on one composition called Sati. In the film, they also sing a Khasi opera composed by Neil. Iba, the soprano, sings a Mozart composition in German. Neil founded the choir in 2002. It has performed in London, Poland, Switzerland, Colombo, Milan, Bengaluru, Mumbai, New Delhi and Guwahati. Kohung Chiang and Sachin Gandankush shared the cinematography, Arindam Ghatak has edited the film and Indrajit Neogi has taken care of the sound. The film has been produced by the Public Diplomacy Division, Ministry of External Affairs, Government of India.

Urmi showed the film to Neil and the kids and they loved it. "He was worried at first that I might make mistakes in cutting and editing his music. But after seeing the film he told me that his worries were baseless. He has many copies of the film so that he can gift them to his friends. Neil is regularly in touch with me and we speak to each other at least once a month. He feels that I have shown the true sense of the place," explains Urmi.

In today's India, the emerging super power, where success and material wealth are the only yardsticks of existence, Neil is chasing something else. Reminisces Urmi, "in the evenings, we would argue over what he is doing and the reasons behind it. The pianist and musician in him have taken a backseat. It is not easy to look after sixteen children and create music as well. Many consider him unfair to Ibarisha, the high soprano in the choir, who studies music with him because he makes sure that she remains unaffected by her talent. He has dreams for her but they are not about fame and money."

Little Magaziner Katha (The Tale of Little Magazines)
The history of literature for public consumption in the shape of magazines, newspapers and so on has a place for a different genre of publications—little magazines. Little magazines, often called "small magazines," are literary magazines that publish experimental and nonconformist writings of relatively unknown writers. Their agenda is free of profit motives and depends on a loyal readership. West Bengal is noted for its great volume of little magazines spread across the entire state. Two committed film-makers, Abhijoy Karlekar and Utpal Basu made a documentary called *Little Magaziner Katha* (2014).

The Little Magazine Movement originated in the 1950s and the 1960s in many Indian languages like Bengali, Tamil, Marathi, Hindi, Malayalam and Gujarati, as it did in the West, in the early part of the 20th century. But West Bengal tells a different story full of colour, music, sound, and three back-to-back book fairs (*boi melas*) that happen annually in December.

This film produced by Shape captures the contemporary history of the little magazine. The film encompasses every genre of literature, "poetry, short stories, cultural investigation, society and politics, linguistics, environment, public health and science—a live sample of the astonishing variety of the little magazine oeuvre that is impossible to render in any single account," says Karlekar.

Image 3.5. Little Magazines Stall at the Kolkata Book Fair

Courtesy: Abhijoy Karlekar

Sandip Dutta, Librarian of Little Magazines Library and Research Centre located in the northern parts of Kolkata where all the intellectual writings are said to have taken birth, traces the history of little magazines in Bengal to literary magazines to around 1818 when, between two magazines *Digdarshan* and *Bangadarshan*, around 172 small and big magazines were being published. "Not all of them were centred on literature. There were magazines focussed on religion, on philosophy, politics and that era could be defined as the era of creation and construction—meaning, giving shape to the individual, creating the individual—or that is how one feels about this. The 19th century was the age when the individual was taking shape," says Datta.

Anindyo Bhattacharjee, a graphic designer and illustrator dedicated to his little magazine that is now modernized to fit into the computer age and the age of the Internet, says, "The 1990s has perhaps seen the dramatic metamorphosis of the world. The Soviet Union collapsed. The Tiananmen Square tragedy redefined the language and expression of students' revolt; socialism had brought in its share of disillusionment. Along with that, Indians ushered in the era of economic liberalization. But the biggest event that changed the entire dynamics of communication between and among people, the give-and-take between one individual and another was the Internet in 1995. This has been a revolutionary change. Looking back, one can perceive that the 1990s decade is a decade of tremendous change not only across the world but also in India. The little magazine is no exception," he says as he works on his computer editing or drafting or redrafting a new article for his next issue.

Shankar Prasad Dnere brings out a little magazine from Akrur Dutta Lane in the northern extremes of Kolkata. The magazine is called *Jele Padar Shong*. *Shong* suggests the artist who performs a comic routine of skits and small pieces dressed up in different disguises or *vesh* for a rural audience as a unique form of entertainment. *Jele Pada* means a neighbourhood of fishermen. "In the city of Kolkata also, each neighbourhood has its own *shong* such as the Taaltala Shong, the Kansaripada Shong, the Kidderpore Shong and so on." Folk poets like Rupchand Pakshi and Gopal Ude began to compose rhymes on these performers. "We have given this name to our magazine to pay tribute to the marginal people in our society such as the sweeper, the travelling salesman, the street sweet vendor who sing along as they work. They project a completely unique and different culture and we are trying to bring out and sustain their culture for our readers," says Dnere.

Why are they called 'little magazines?' Some little magazines on poetry that came out in the 1970s were little in size and volume. 'Little' therefore is more metaphorical than literal. Most little magazines have a normal format that do not draw revenue from advertisements, do not run on profit, do not pay its contributors and the staff works out of a sense of commitment and not commerce. Its founders and functionaries have a regular source of income from other sources and work on the magazine after working hours. "It (little magazines) observes a culture of intellectual creativity and curiosity allied to disciplined, voluntary and collaborative work in a mode where commercial reward is not the goal. It is a 'life of the mind' flowing outside the banks of media and mainstream publishing," say Karlekar and Basu.

The countdown to an issue printed on schedule, or in time for the Boi Mela provides a framework for portraying the love for literature and ideas, the sociocultural commitment, the stretching of limited resources and the last-minute tensions that go into bringing out little magazines—year after year, month after month for years together. Most of the men and women who bring out these magazines are at regular jobs to keep body and soul together. The running of the little magazine is a labour of love, passion and a positive obsession kept alive by its loyal and committed readership.

Little Magaziner Katha strips itself of the need for a commentary or an anchor person to hold the many strands of the story together. It is also a journey film as the camera journeys into different spaces and places in Kolkata and across West Bengal, opening up a world we know little about. The camera travels from the College Street Boi Para—the hub of books—through Patiram Book Stall, Little Magazine Library, Ultadanga Hudco, Sunil Babu's Book Stall, Kalyan Ghosh's Book Stall, Akrur Dutta Lane, Barisha Art Studio, Roy Bagan Street, office of Saptarshi Publication, The Cybergraphics Studio, Badartala Market and so on, scanning the wide expanse of little magazines that are alive and kicking. The directors have only focussed on ambient sound to give the film a real feel.

"Though a majority of featured magazines in the film are from Kolkata, the story travels to events, publications and personalities in Purulia, Bardhaman, Medinipur and Jalpaiguiri and we have spoken to around 80 people ranging from writers through readers to illustrators, publishers and printers to make *Little Magaziner Katha* a live experience seen through celluloid," Karlekar sums up.

WHEN DOES AN ETHNOGRAPHICAL FILM BECOME AN INVESTIGATIVE FILM OR A POLITICAL STATEMENT?

This is a question that defies answers because the answers are inherent in the question itself. When a film-maker sets out to make an ethnographical documentary, he/she encounters questions of ethics, conflict, social justice, violation of human rights and so on that the film-maker did not conceive of when he first thought of making the film. Once the idea is mooted, accepted and the funds organized, as research and field work begin, questions crop up. Some film-makers steer away from addressing these questions or offering suggested resolutions and continue with the purely ethnographical aspect of the film. This could be due to commercial compromise with the funding agency, or prompted by possible censorship issues in future that could lead to blocking public screenings or litigation or both. Other film-makers get so involved in the project they are working on at a given point of time, that they turn themselves into celluloid activists participating in people's movement against social injustice, or trying to delve into an investigative exploration of issues that were not apparent at the conceptual stage but began to emerge as film-making actually began.

When a film-maker becomes an activist is something perhaps even the film-maker cannot state with precision or knowledge. The film-maker goes back again and again to explore the same condition of the same people again and again which turns the entire subject of the film into a politically investigative documentary. In this sense, most ethnographical documentaries tend to have some stories of conflict, social injustice or ethical questions involving human rights violations. It is left entirely to the film-maker to decide whether he/she wishes to seriously step into the delicate domains of investigation or whether he/she would prefer to go on with the informative, educative and aesthetics form and content of the documentary film without getting into these in-depth questions that dog investigations and political comments.

The films chosen for discussion below are ethnographical and also investigative, sometimes by design and intent and sometimes by coincidence. But even so, the choice itself was problematic because these two genres are so overwhelmingly overlapping that it is difficult to label them separately. For example, Saurav Sarangi's *Bilal* (2008) might not be considered 'ethnographic' in the popularly understood concept of the term. But the fact that this sighted boy Bilal lives with his blind parents in an impoverished, neglected slum within the minority group of Muslims he belongs to, makes him also a microcosm of an ethnographically categorized community. The social and financial history of his existence groups him within a specific community that lends itself to ethnographic readings on celluloid.

Some films chosen in this section, on the other hand, are investigative first and ethnographic afterwards. For example, *Ab Aur Waqt Nahin* set out to make a political statement on the conditions of adivasis after the formation of the state of Jharkhand. But since adivasis are the central concern of the film, and they represent specific ethnographical cultures and lifestyles, the film opens itself to its reading into the victimization of given ethnographical groups and how the formation of the new state has victimized them in many ways. This makes it an ethnographical film also. Debananda Sengupta's *Maatir Bhaanr* on girls who work as domestic maids in urban Kolkata automatically gets slotted into the ethnographical group of deprived girls who are denied education, information and are forced to work as domestics in urban cities. As they are indigenous workers, they can be defined as an ethnographical group.

Ab Aur Waqt Nahin (2006), a 108-minute documentary directed by Abhijoy Karlekar, explores the history of Jharkhand adivasis and takes the viewer across the length and breadth of this state to point out the complete unaccountability of the establishment to the constitutional rights of the adivasis. The film locates the crisis of adivasi agriculture in the larger context of Jharkhand's political and economic history, placing the indigenous adivasi people and their ecosystem against overwhelming national interventions that have forcibly imposed urbanization and industrialization in Jharkhand. This led to dramatic mutations in its inherent and naturally rich environment and demography. Around 40 lakh adivasis have been forced to migrate to other places in search of work distanced from their traditional occupation—agriculture. Forty lakh non-adivasis have stepped in to gain ground here, toppling the demographic ratio in favour of the latter while displacing the former only to push them into dire economic uncertainty and desperation. The film shows how the formation of the state of Jharkhand has had no positive sociopolitical significance for the adivasis at all.

As the film traverses the countryside, the camera closes in on a rippled up hillside with its fragmented limbs lying helter-skelter and a stone quarry where women and children of Bargutu, a village of adivasis, work as coolies. The voice-over continues to narrate the history of past invasions into adivasi lives, the visuals telescope into different pictures of the present—interviewing medicine man Ghanshyam Munda or talking to Birhan Kui, who says that she barely manages to eat in exchange for looking after other people's cattle as "there is no work even to dig soil or break stones." The viewer slowly gets sucked into this tragic reality of some of our own people.

The film raises questions like—"Is it really too late to rescue the tribal communities of Jharkhand from moving towards extinction in terms of culture, ethnography, lifestyles and livelihood?" "Is the birth of Jharkhand as an independent state comprised of 18 southern districts of Bihar squarely responsible for the death-like mutations in the lives of its adivasis?" Shape, a communications design and production company, has produced *Ab Aur Waqt Nahin*, which raises many questions like these. *WAQT*, an acronym for the longer title of the film, offers some answers that are an indictment to the statehood of Jharkhand, acquired at the expense of the livelihoods and lifestyles of what once formed the major slice of the population—the adivasis. Produced by Ahmed Hussain and directed by Abhijoy Karlekar, with brilliant cinematography by Ranajit Ray, *WAQT*, spans the roots of the adivasis through history, portraying their self-sufficient economic system based basically on agriculture, intercutting the commentary with glimpses into the sad present, talking to people involved in the movement to sustain and reclaim the rights of the adivasis, juxtaposed against the lop-sided projects in industrializing the state under the thin veil of 'development.'

It took 70 long years of struggle for a separate statehood that finally resulted in the formation of Jharkhand. The struggle was fought and led entirely by the adivasis. The names of those who laid down their lives during the long struggle are engraved on a rough plaque, unlike the memorial plaques of famous people set out on marble with letters engraved in gold that one comes across in Indian towns and cities. Yet, now that statehood has been achieved with effect from 15 January, 2000, these very adivasis have been marginalized, oppressed, humiliated and, in other words, told to mind their own business in their own way.

"There is this growing feeling among the adivasis of Jharkhand that in this newly created state, given to them only in name, they stand at the crossroads," says the commentary. The Mundas, the Hos, the Santhals and the Oraons are the four major adivasi tribes who came to settle in these areas about 2,500 years ago. They were not artisans but were cultivators, harvesters of the forest produce and hunters. Their traditional tools were the axe, the plough, the bow and the arrow. The tradesmen who later stepped in to complement their livelihoods were welcomed to share their environment.

What happened to these happy people content within a world they created themselves, filled with their personal knowledge of medicine through minerals and medicinal plants? What happened to the adivasis who now constitute only 26 per cent of the population of Jharkhand with four million of them having left Jharkhand to migrate as wage labourers across the Indian subcontinent, replaced by an equal number of non-adivasis from Bihar and Uttar Pradesh who came to Jharkhand all within the 30-year span from 1970 to 2000?

Though the sale of adivasi land to non-adivasis remains prohibited under the 5th Schedule of the Indian Constitution, the film points out that in the 14 scheduled area districts of Jharkhand, it is common to find that adivasis' lands have been transferred in the names of non-adivasis, never mind the lifetime of legal disputes the adivasis have to spend over inherited land that legally belongs to them. In the opening lines of the commentary, the film points out that under Schedule V and VI of the Indian Constitution, it is the responsibility of the Indian State to protect the environment, economy and culture of the country's indigenous adivasi communities that form eight per cent of the national population and who live within traditional ecosystems across the country. These constitutional rights have been maintained more in the breach than to the letter as *WAQT* details over its 104 minutes of running time.

One hundred years of change has created two Jharkhands, one comprised of Chaas—the boomtown that grew along with Bokaro Steel—and the other consisting of adivasis desperately trying to eke out a livelihood, where virtually none seem to exist. So they are forced to leave home and hearth to seek food elsewhere. The people of Chaas are hardly aware of the Adivasi Jharkhand. Lalpur Chowk in Ranchi has become the meeting place for two kinds of people— the non-adivasi labour contractors and the cultivators from the hinterland, mostly consisting of adivasis looking for work as labourers in the capital city of the state.

By the mid-1960s, a network of six dams and seven power stations were created in accordance with India's agenda for industrial development as spelt out in the 2nd and 3rd National Five-year Plans which set about the designed wreckage of the Chhotanagpur Plateau and its river valleys. The Damodar Valley Project was initiated for industrial and urban development of eastern India. But what it actually achieved through the dams and power stations was to displace 100,000 cultivator families from their natural habitat with a token compensation that is more an insult to their dignity to live a life of respect than compensation.

The centre of the project was the two million tonne integrated steel plant at Bokaro. But the final nail on the coffin for the adivasis came with the nationalization of the coal industry in 1972, introducing open-cast mining that changed the scale and cost of mining and increased its impact on the environment. By 2000, 206 mines had begun to function, of which 140 are open-cast mines accounting for 80 per cent of the coal production in Jharkhand. No individual or political party, even the opposition, ever cared to find out the human cost of uprooting traditional cultivators. No group within the state and the Centre cared to pay attention to the massive state-sponsored ecocide that began with the command of the coal belt over the economics and politics of the state. Damodar, the life-thread of Jharkhand, continues to get polluted by coal washeries and power stations. Over 150 km through the coal belt, the Damodar River is absolutely free of fish. The adivasi woman, who was once equal decision-maker within her society, has now been reduced to a coolie in the labour market. Not one legal action has been taken against the 82 cases of rape of adivasi women by non-adivasis in 2000 even after six years.

Why are the adivasis not fighting back? They are, in their own small way. Through collective groups joined in solidarity against any violation of their rights. In the 1990s for instance, the government of Bihar sought to take-over 1,471 km^2 of land near Netarhat. The purpose of the take-over was to offer space for a field-firing range for the heavy artillery of the Indian Army. This would have displaced people from 245 villages. They all united to resist the army and stopped their convoys from entering the notified area.

They are trying to reclaim control over what was once theirs by right, by occupation, by culture and by demographic majority, by seeking to control their local environment. An example of this is their reclaiming hold and control over Barambe Haat, a thriving vegetable market for many years. Till 1999, non-adivasi traders and their touts—forever trying to cheat and exploit the adivasis of their rightful share and ownership—controlled the Haat. In 1997, local villages organized themselves and demanded their right to run the market as per the rules pertaining to scheduled areas. This led to a killing, but it forced the government to hand over the market to an adivasi-organized Bazar Samity, according to Bandhan Tigga, one of the crusaders of the movement.

They are also struggling to enforce the customary powers of the Gram Sabha. One of these Gram Sabhas formed a Forest Protection Committee in Kundrijhoor in west Singhbhum district. This was to rebel against a timber mafia, which in league with the employees of the Forest Department, was plundering their forests, thus threatening their income and their consumption from these forests. In October 2001, members of the Forest Protection Committee fought off the mafia and took over 1,500 acres of forestland which was once their own. They grew the forests back within the next four years and the Forest Department was forced to surrender to their claim.

Today, Jharkhand adivasis are comprised of 31 active groups in seven districts controlling 100,000 acres of reclaimed forests. The state government is trying its best to contain this movement by trying to form Village Forest Committees. But no one is willing to join or work for these committees. 'Self-Rule through Direct Action' seems to be the bottom line for the victimized and vandalized adivasis of Jharkhand. All the same, one cannot either deny or defy the claim of this film its right to the title—*Ab Aur Waqt Nahin*—time is running out.

Despite its footage, slightly lengthy in documentary terms, *WAQT* manages to sustain interest and attention mainly due to its no-nonsense, no-holds-barred approach to the issues raised within the film but not necessarily resolved. It is not the task of the documentary film-maker to offer solutions since the makers are distanced from the issues themselves. They have worked out a balanced blend of form and content, straightforward yet aesthetic, with a melodious musical score by Dr Ram Dayal Munda that adds to the authenticity of the film and takes it closer to the audience at the same time. Anup Mukhopadhyay's sound mixing is just right as is Utpal Basu's editing. Even to the uninitiated, WAQT is informative, educative and enlightening. It succeeds in raising moral questions about justice and fair play in a world with a spillover of injustice and corruption. John Grierson once said, "Documentary is the creative treatment of actuality." *WAQT* reminds us of this classic definition of the documentary.

The Conflict—Who's Loss, Who's Gain

Debranjan Sarangi's *The Conflict—Who's Loss, Who's Gain* (2010) is a 90-minute film in Oriya subtitled in English, produced by Pedestrian Pictures, explores through the lives of a tribal community in Orissa that seems to be on the wrong end of India's progress. Mass movements towards globalization and industrialization have placed their lives and livelihoods at a greater disadvantage than ever before.

The film also focusses on the communal violence in Kandha following the murder of Swamy Laxmananda, unfolding the sad tale of scarring violence inflicted on converts from lower castes by the upper castes in the area.

"The violence in Kandha forced me to re-analyse the situation. I wanted to know why it happened and was left searching for answers. The film was what I learnt from my searching and hence I would like the world to see it," says Debaranjan. "People need to know that such things happen. We can't keep ignoring how adivasis are treated in this country," he adds. Sarangi is an Orissa-based anti-mining activist and a writer who has dedicated a decade with the anti-mining movement of adivasis in Kashipur. He is also involved in anti-communal struggles. *The Conflict* is his first independent documentary as a director.

The Conflict is a courageous and painstaking coverage and investigation through real time about the lives of a tribal community in Orissa that offers a completely different perspective on the 'development' model India tries to present across the media and in the public domain. It unfolds a tragic story of the misfortune of adivasis who are losing and will continue to lose land, their homes and their indigenous culture. Tribals in Kandha and Kashipur have been suffering untold miseries, thanks to a government that revels in playing the ignorant onlooker. The film also speaks about the adivasi community 'Kondh' with whom Sarangi has been working for eight years before he made this film.

In 1993, Utkal Alumina International Limited (UAIL), earlier a joint venture of four multinational companies (MNCs), arrived at the Kashipur block of southern Orissa to mine bauxite, the raw material for aluminium, found from Baphlimali bauxite mines, and to set up an alumina plant at the Kucheipadar/Doraguda site. This was after India embarked on economic reforms, inviting more MNCs into the mining sector. Because of people's resistance, big companies like Tata (India), Alcan (Canada) and Hydro (Norway) left Kashipur, except Aditya Birla (India), who adopted fraudulent means and was determined to proceed. For the company, the project spelled out market and profit. For the government, it was all about getting royalty from the MNCs. But for the Kondh adivasis of Kashipur—it meant loss of land, livelihood, forest and food, their streams and rivers, their culture and ancestry. By 2006, many villagers in the 24 villages of Kashipur block left their land, including three villages that were evacuated for the company.

Swamy Laxmananda was killed on 23rd August 2008 at his Jaleshpeta ashram. The Maoists immediately claimed that they had killed him. But anti-Christian violence began from the very next day. Sangh Parivar and Laxmananda had converted many Christians into Hindus (it was nearly 18,000 by 1987 as per the People's Union for Civil Liberties (PUCL) report.). The government of Orissa admits that the communal violence resulted in a shocking statistics of 38 dead, 3 missing, 415 villages affected, 3,226 houses destroyed, 195 church and prayer houses damaged and 25,122 forced to take shelter in government-run relief camps. Nobody knows how many thousands more fled to other districts of Orissa and other parts of India. Adivasis Hinduized by the Sangh Parivar participated in large numbers in the violence against Christians.

Had the government really taken interest in the development of adivasis, would adivasis been influenced and exploited by others? Are adivasis becoming sacrificial goats by corporate globalization and communalism? This film is the director's journey with three tribal leaders to Kandhamal and Kashipur, soon after the violence in Kandhamal broke out in August–September 2009.

Apna Aloo Bazaar Becha

What happens when remote, isolated mountain communities come face-to-face with globalization? Jardhar Gaon, a typical village in the Hemval valley of Garhwal, led an isolated, egalitarian existence until just 30 years ago. A series of events forced it into joining the market economy. This short documentary, based entirely on local perspectives, reflects on this process of change—what triggers the shift to modernization and what impacts it has on the personal, social and environmental spaces.

Pankaj Gupta, who directed the film with a grant from the PSBT, says, "Two factors personally motivated me. One was my obsession with subsistence cultures and second was my interest in organic or natural farming. As Jardhargaon was one of the last living examples of subsistence culture, I was very keen to make a film on it. The place was also famous for its Beej Bachao Andolan, a movement to resist changes to their unique brand of farming. I had first visited Jardhargaon in 2000, and it took me 6 years to get funding for

Image 3.6. *Apna Aloo Bazar Becha*

Courtesy: Pankaj Gupta

this film, and by the time I got there with my camera, the old way of living and farming had already changed!"

Gupta is a documentary film-maker and sustainability researcher. He has worked on several documentaries with organizations such as The Energy and Resources Institute (TERI), Centre for Science and Environment (CSE), and PSBT, and conducted research and training programmes for International Fund for Agricultural Development (IFAD) and International Development Research Centre (IDRC). He has produced and directed several factual series for television, including *Artscan* and *Youthquake*. At present, he is Visiting Fellow at the Centre for Interdisciplinary Studies in Environment and Development, Bangalore. About the target audience for this film, he says, "I believe it has a universal theme...of migration, separation, rapid social change... Some professors here in Bangalore have cried during the filming because their own sons have gone abroad, and left them all alone...some others have found in it a 'microcosm' of the state of our economy...so it should appeal to a range of audiences."

Bilal

Saurabh Sarangi's *Bilal*, an 88-minute documentary film shot in one of the darkest slum pockets in Kolkata, has won awards at 14 film festivals in India and abroad. Strange but true that this film was rejected by the selection panel for the MIFF of documentary, short and animations films in February 2010. Kuldip Sinha, Director, Films Division and MIFF, could not give any reason for the exclusion of this film along with four other documentaries from Kolkata. *Bilal* is an India-Finland co-production with support from Jan Vrijman Fund, Amsterdam, official development aid from the Ministry of Foreign Affairs, Finland and in association with Yle, Finland.

This movie is about a three-year-old boy named Bilal who is born to blind parents but has normal vision himself. It is a simple, but very dark film—visually, literally, and metaphorically, because the 8×10 feet partitioned room he lives in, with parents Shamim and Jharna and little brother Hamza, is almost completely dark. Bilal lives in Taltala, a low-working-class neighbourhood in Kolkata where the rains flood the streets and children play around freely in the flooded bylanes, where the sun does not care to shed its brightness, where the yellow shop-sign of Bilal's father Shamim's once-upon-a-time subscriber trunk dialling (STD) booth stands as a silent

Image 3.7. *Bilal*

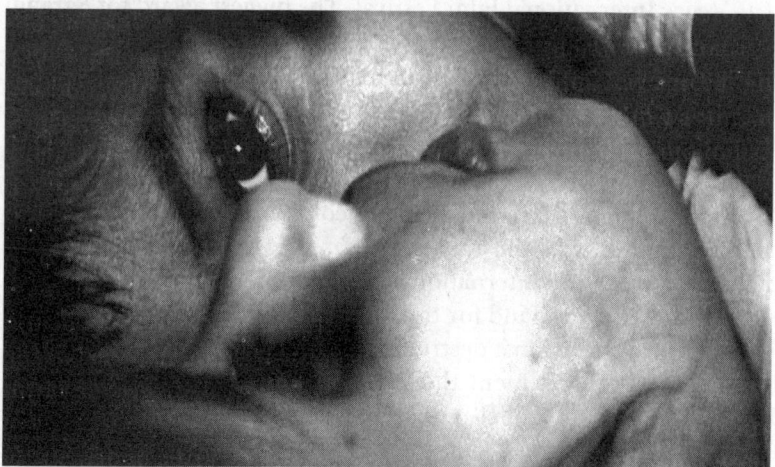

Courtesy: Sourav Sarangi

signifier of somewhat better days, where there is no milk left for tea because Bilal finished it all. Hamza also has normal sight.

The film is visually dark because there is hardly any light and the filming team organizes some temporary lighting with the help of Shamim to get things going. It is literally dark because the audience too has to cope with the dark and is challenged to keep their eyes glued to the screen which often goes pitch black or is very dimly lit with the street lights streaming in, or sometimes brightened by the bright lights of the film's lighting equipment. The only scenes that are bright are the ones shot on the streets outside. The film, though it revolves around a bright little boy called Bilal, is dark because it reveals to us one of the darkest underbellies of Kolkata where humans are forced to eke out an apology of existence in subhuman conditions. The film stands out as a critique on the documentary form itself through the absence of the hierarchical relationship that evolves between the director and his subject. It is difficult to merge with one's subject and yet retain one's objectivity, especially when there are such stark differences between the film-maker and his subject.

Bilal won the Aljazeera Golden Award at the Aljazeera International Documentary Festival, the Award for Best Documentary at Festival de Cine de Pobre Humberto Solas in Cuba, the Silver Palm at the Mexican Film Festival and the Silver Ace Award at the Las Vegas International Film Festival. The biggest award for Sarangi however remains a Christmas gift for little Bilal and his brother from an elderly couple, following the film's first screening in Amsterdam.

Loha Garam Hai (Iron is Hot)

Bijoo Toppo is one of the first adivasi film-makers who has effectively used the medium of cinema to counter the misrepresentation of his community by the 'mainstream' media. His films have bagged national awards and international recognition. Meghnath is an activist working in Jharkhand for the past 30 years. He has been with the people's struggle against destructive development. As a film-maker, he has tried to document the voice of the section of people who remain unheard of and also unseen. He makes films with Bijoo and also teaches in the Mass Communication Department of St Xavier's College, Ranchi. The organization that they founded together in

Image 3.8. *Loha Garam Hai*

Courtesy: Meghnath and Biju Toppo (Akhra)

the beginning of the 1990s with some committed youngsters is called Akhra.

Over the past 20 years, Akhra has made around a dozen documentary films on various issues directly linked to adivasis in different pockets of Jharkhand. Some of them have won National Awards. Akhra also makes communication films to spread information, education and awareness among the adivasis. One of its films, *Loha Garam Hai* (2008), won the Best Environmental Film Award from Indian Documentary Producers Association (IDPA), Mumbai, in 2009. *Loha Garam Hai* is the story of people surviving within the sponge iron industry. Sponge iron is made out of iron ore used for making steel. India began producing sponge iron just 20 years ago. Today, it is the largest sponge iron manufacturer in the world. India had only three sponge iron factories in 1985. The number rose to 23 in 2001 and multiplied to become 206 in 2005. Today, reportedly, 225 factories are under construction and the number is anticipated to reach 450 very soon, though the unofficial figures may be much higher. The sponge iron industry is spread over Orissa, Chhatisgarh,

Jharkhand and West Bengal and is found in Goa, Maharashtra and Karnataka in small numbers.

Loha Garam Hai, within 43 minutes, presents a holistic picture of an industry allowed to grow, oblivious of its effects on the lives of the people, in violation of every law in the book with help from the powers that be at the administrative level. Through graphics, title cards, data and interviews with people of Sundargarh, Rajgangpur in Orissa, Siltara, and so on. The film is a scathing comment on the lopsided concept of industrialization gained at the cost of human lives, environment, agriculture and livestock. It includes interviews with some victims, a few experts and some angry men and women who are staunchly against this industrial growth. The film opens a world of information and education on a little-known industry that is endangering the environment and is also posing a threat to the lives of livestock and human beings. Few Indians are even aware that there is sponge iron manufacture in the country. We learn about it through this film. The film won the National Award in 2011 for the Best Film on Environment in the non-fiction category. Directed jointly by Meghnath Bhattacharya and Biju Toppo, the film has been produced by Akhra, a cultural organization based in Ranchi, Jharkhand, comprised of young adivasi youth who makes documentary films on violation of human rights, environmental pollution and other socially relevant issues that affect indigenous tribes.

So what is wrong with an employment-generating industry that generates huge profits? *Loha Garam Hai* tells us what is wrong. Beginning with figures and estimates about the industry that generates very high levels of pollution in the area where it exists, the film goes on to capture the people's movement against these factories and their perpetuation. Through interviews of local adivasis, ordinary men and women, pictures of the smoke that emits from the factories to the surrounding areas offer a graphic glimpse of the damage to the environment and to the people living within that environment.

In other parts of the world, sponge iron is produced in gas-based plants that are smokeless and less polluting. In India, however, 80 per cent of the sponge iron factories are coal based that emit heavy smoke notorious for generating pollution. "A 100 tonnes/ day plant produces 250 tons of garbage every day. No pollution control body keeps any account where this garbage is disposed. They are dumped near agriculture field, by the side of highway or at the bank of rivers which then ultimately flows in the stream. The plants emit poisonous gas and heavy metals like cadmium, nickel, manganese which are harmful for human beings. Due to soil and water pollution agricultural activities within the 5 km radius of sponge iron plants is seriously effect and there is drastic reduction of the agricultural yield," say some of the local people.

The directors have not identified any of the locals by name or designation because, says Meghnath, "they are a microcosm of the victims and the 'voices' of the many. We did not feel it necessary to put names to the faces we used." A 100-tonne capacity plant needs daily 160 tonnes of iron ore, 125 tons of coal, 3.5 tons of dolomite and 150 tonnes water. This means that an input of 350 tonnes of raw material will produce 100 tonnes of sponge iron and generate 250 tonnes of waste material daily. A 100-tonne capacity plant needs an investment ranging between INR 7 and 12 crores, yielding a monthly profit of around INR 60 lakhs, and the investment comes back within a year and a half. "It is this quick rate of return that defines the biggest attraction for entrepreneurs and the fast mushrooming of new factories within the industry," says a local in the film.

The local inhabitants are aware of everything that is happening in the industry and the repercussions on the environment and on their health and well-being. A woman says, "The solid waste such as dust, coal, and other waste are dumped on the roadsides, in farming fields and on the banks of the river. In some places, they are dumped directly into the river. The main emissions that pollute the air are carbon dioxide, nitrogen oxide and particles of heavy metals like cadmium, lead, zinc, mercury, manganese, nickel, chromium and arsenic."

There is a direct reference to the London Smog Disaster of 1952 considered to be one of the ten major environmental disasters of the world. The tragedy took a toll of 4,000 lives within the first five days of the incident and another 8,000 in the next three months taking the total toll to 12,000. "What you see here is not London, but Rajgangpur in Sundargarh district. We see the same kind of smog in winter in Raipur and are afraid of a similar tragedy happening any time."

But, the film shows that the immediate tragedy is no less. Land areas where sponge factories have been installed are noted for their production of paddy. But any agricultural activity within a radius of 5 km of a sponge iron factory affects the fertility of the soil due to pollution of air, water and earth. One woman cites a finding of the Agricultural University of Raipur that points out that around 25,000 hectares of land in the vicinity of Siltara near Raipur has turned barren because of sponge iron production. People forced to subsist on this rice are falling ill. The milk yield of cattle has come down and so have their lives been shortened because they survive on leaves and grass thickly covered with black dust from these factories.

Diseases that can affect the local people include silicosis and cancer. Mercury and lead particles affect brains of little children. Mercury particles cause wounds in kidneys and damage the digestive system. Particles of heavy metal can lead to skin diseases. Sulphur dioxide and nitrogen oxide cause cough, bronchitis, asthma, inflammation in the eyes and throat infections.

The legalities are practised in the breach with impunity, thanks to the corruption that has eroded the Pollution Control Board, which the local people have dubbed as the "Pay and Pollute Board." Due to soil and water pollution, agricultural activities within 5 km radius of sponge iron plants are seriously affected and there is drastic reduction of agricultural yield. But Siltara, 10 km away from Raipur, has 30 sponge factories jostling with each other. The factory must maintain a minimum distance of 1 km from the nearest village. Reality shows that the factories are installed very close to residential areas.

A significant Panchayat Extension in Scheduled Area (PESA) Act in 1996 was passed in the interest of the tribal communities. According to this Act, consent of the Gram Sabhas is essential before installing any factory in the scheduled area. This Act is being openly violated everywhere within the sponge iron manufacturing fields.

The film captures how government machinery is tilted towards the industry. The administration organizes 'public hearings' where though the majority opposes the construction of the plant, the government report shows 'people have agreed' in gross violation of human rights and environmental regulations.

But not all is lost yet. People's protests in Chouranga village near Raipur in Chhattisgarh has successfully stopped production in a plant. In Palakkad district of Kerala, where there was a sponge iron factory located in Malampuzha, the local panchayat objected and the state government backed this objection. In November 2006, the

Goa government passed a stay order on some sponge iron plants in the state. There is a saying, "strike when the iron is hot." The heat of people's anger in these areas keeps rising. Today there is opposition everywhere.

Crosswinds Over Ichamati

The international protocol requires that 150 yards on both sides of the international border are left fallow. But this has not been possible on the Indo-Bangladesh border. So the poor farmer whose farms fall on the so-called No Man's Land has to sign a register every day before he crosses the fence to till his land. The 4,000 km-long Indo-Bangladesh border meanders through paddy fields, marshes, villages and even backyards of homes. The last 148 km of the river is fluid, formed by the river Ichamati. The first border post on land is near a village called Panitar. It is a neglected village with about 30 families, almost outside the folds of the country's administration. All this comes across beautifully in a blend of the emotional, the documented and the informative in *Crosswinds over Ichamati* (2012), a moving documentary. Subha Das Mullick who has more than 50 documentaries on different issues and subjects to her credit, has made the film.

Image 3.9. On Location of *Crosswinds Over Ichamati*

Courtesy: Subha Das Mullick

"I happened to read The Final Cut, an article in special issue of *Time Magazine* (August 1997) brought out on the occasion of 50 years of India's independence. It was about how Cyril Radcliffe was forced to divide the country within six weeks. This triggered my interest in the entire saga on Partition. That was the beginning of my research and my visits to the border," explains Subha.

Das Mullick narrates the story of her film through the personal accounts of several eyewitnesses and direct victims of this Partition. Among them is 95-year-old Mani Mohan Sardar who has seen the cross migration after the Partition; the slow but sure way in which the border began to get tightened that brought about a marked change in the demography in the neighbourhood in which he lived. He just cannot understand why the country needed to be sliced into two pieces, who did it and who benefited from this division. The 16,000 inhabitants of the village are comprised of 80 per cent Muslim and 20 per cent Hindu who live in harmony, but are now forced to face the everyday problem of an excuse to defy the borders. Das Mullick talks to some important people of the village, explores the gateway on this side of the border where cattle, dogs and fish, which have to be cleared by the border police along with humans and often, are smuggled across only to be caught. The cinematography explores boats sailing across the Ichamati filled with people in wide-angle long shots adding aesthetic finesse to an investigative documentary. The scenes of the Durga immersion are beautiful.

This Land Is Mine and Whose Land Is It Anyway: Two films on Singur and Nandigram

The term 'eviction' usually applies to 'people'—driving people away from their lands and homes, against their wishes, forcibly. Eviction is not just the physical displacement of a few persons. It signifies destruction of society, livelihoods, lifestyles, cultures, the interdependence of human life and nature. In West Bengal, forcible eviction or attempts to do so is not a new phenomenon anymore. It is undertaken in the name of industrialization, globalization and progress. Both Singur and Nandigram in West Bengal have become vulnerable spaces for a spate of senseless torture, rape and killing of innocents.

The violence and repression in Singur and Nandigram in West Bengal caused large-scale loss of lives and displacement marking perhaps, for the first time in the history of state politics, the direct

Image 3.10. *Whose Land Is It Anyway*: The Director and His Crew on Location

Courtesy: Ladly Mukhopadhyay

involvement and participation of the government in this gross violation of human rights. Among significant spillovers comprising massive resistance, one may mention the names of intellectuals and scholars like Sumit and Tanika Sirkar who gave away their prize money as part of their Rabindra Puraskars (awarded by the state government in 1998 and 2004, respectively) to the Nandigram Relief Fund, is the active participation of documentary film-makers rushing in to Singur and Nandigram to capture actual footage of police repression on the one hand, and public outcry, mainly from women, on the other.

Free Bird Productions, a Calcutta-based documentary unit involved in cultural, ethnographic and documentary films, made two films in two places—Singur and Nandigram. The first is *Whose Land Is It Anyway* (2007) on the Singur tragedy and *This Land Is Mine* on the Nandigram crisis. Ladly Mukhopadhyay directed both the films.

"Beat up that girl," one can hear a policeman with a baton shout in *Whose Land Is It Anyway?*, the film on Singur. The visuals show a posse of policemen drags a young woman along the fields. "They have not spared the women and the children," shouts a local woman. "On September 25, 2006, they stepped into our houses and used tear gas on us, making our children almost choke and used abusive words to malign us in every which way," she adds angrily. The West Bengal Government handed the Tata Group a plot of 997 acres to establish an automobile factory. This not only affected the 5,000 strong peasant population of Singur but also endangered the lives of their wives and families, the working peasants who come from neighbouring villages every day, small tradesmen, shopkeepers, hawkers and everyone, amounting to a staggering figure of 50,000. How many of these 50,000 would the Tata automobile factory employ? Not more than 800–1,000 people said the Tatas themselves. Did the state government prepare any alternative channels of employment for the 49,000 who would lose their livelihoods in the process? Mukhopadhyay raised these very pertinent and uncomfortable questions through visuals, comments and some authoritative opinions given by experts from different fields.

The farmlands of Singur are cultivated right round the year. The state government cannot raise any question about the fertility of these lands. These are lands that produce four kinds of farm produce such as paddy, jute, potato and vegetables, among the best the state. These are lands where the current market price is somewhere between INR 25,000 and INR 35,000 per *cottah* (a unit of measurement) of land. But the peasants are paid a paltry INR 10,000 per cottah of land as compensation. "We don't want compensation. We want our livelihoods back. We don't want to work in factories. We want to remain peasants," says another angry young peasant woman. Why should a simple process of shifting from farming to industry need lathi charges by the police, the release of tear gas in peasant homes or the imposition of Section 144?

This Land Is Mine, shot and edited almost immediately following the March 14 carnage, begins with the statement, "This ballad is dedicated to the spirit of the people fighting against forcible acquisition of their house and hearth in the name of industrialization all over the world."Nandigram, located in east Medinipur district in West Bengal, has a population of 185,000 of which 60 per cent are Muslim and 30 per cent are BCs. The place is conspicuous more by the facilities it lacks than those that it has. It has no electricity, no safe drinking water, no paved roads, no basic health care and sanitation. Yet, this place is earmarked as the subject for acquisition of land for the setting up of a chemical hub by the Salim Group and SEZ.

The film records the argument presented by Buddhadeb Bhattacharya, the then chief minister (CM) of West Bengal. He says that agricultural land comprises of 62 per cent of the total land in West Bengal. Of this, 1 per cent is fallow land as against the standard 17 per cent in India, forest cover is 13 per cent as against the standard 18 per cent in India, while urban and industrial land make up for 24 per cent. Disregarding the statistical anomaly of his data, he adds, "Income from agriculture is reducing so we cannot stop growth because over the years, the population has increased several times over," in justification of his decision that brazenly evaded the responsibility of taking the local people into confidence.

Another shot focusses on an elderly woman who repeatedly says, "we will give our blood, we will give our lives, but we will not give our land". Maulana Siddiqullah Chowdhury, a local political leader indignantly asks, "How many lies will you tell? Stop your lies," following the report about the people who died in Nandigram in the police firing on March 14. All semblance of humanity vanished on that day. A woman says that the police began to lathi charge the crowds and fired at them within 15 minutes of its arrival. "I was trying to help my injured husband and the police began firing on me too. Women who locked themselves in a room were subjected to unimaginable torture as the police broke down the doors, dragged them out, pushed guns into their private parts, pulled at their breasts and tried to strip them down." Another woman says that they are not able to go to the market for their daily supplies. "We hide in the fields all night. They use filthy and abusive language. One girl was raped by eight policemen and later slaughtered. Some families have lost six to seven members and 35 bodies have been cremated," says another woman. The anger of the masses was so great that 3,000 party workers at Nandigram were forced to take shelter in Calcutta. The film captures Bibhash Ranjan Chakrabarty, a committed theatre activist, as he says, "I feel hopeful that the people of West Bengal have finally awoken from their sleep to realize that we are wrong." Around 50,000 people gathered at a public meeting at Sonachura—an incredible example of public uprising against a government they had lost faith in.

The film is strung together with threads of an old folk song that runs through the narrative like a comment, a character and a metaphor. "Don't kill me please," says a cringing and frightened young girl to theatre person Saoli Mitra who visits her at the hospital, offering just a glimpse of the fear psychosis that grips them, but that has failed to kill their fighting spirit. Each of around 40 minutes duration, *Whose Land Is It Anyway* and *This Land Is Mine*, through telling graphics, first-person interviews with intellectuals, social activists, and the common man, and the actual footage of the topography on the aftermath offer strong indictments on the state government's industrial policy. The nagging question that remains is—why should beautifully enunciated commentaries in impeccable English (byAnanya Biswas) be used for films with a human rights agenda that is culture specific and ethnographic at the same time? Does not the use of English as a power language and a language of the global and liberalized world for a commentary on these Third World human rights' violation films in some way smack of the complicity with the concept of globalization and industrialization in a larger sense?

Yet, the films succeed in carrying their united message across. Time does not stand still. A new era replaces the old one. No one wishes to debate these truths. But no plan for a shift from agriculture to industry can ethically, politically and economically justify itself if the peasants involved are not taken into confidence.

Chena Kintu Ajana (Known Strangers)

Chena Kintu Ajana (2014) is a documentary film that traces the contribution of 15 female impersonators of the jatra dating back to the beginning of the 20th century. Three surviving female impersonators, one of them having passed yonder during the making of the film, feature as their real selves. Chapal Rani and Janardhan perform extracts from their famous characters.

The film opens with a performance by Chapal Rani portraying an abstract of Kaikeyi from Ramayana. Prof. Ananda Lal, playwright and theatre historian, elaborates on how the suffix 'Rani' to the name of the actor who portrayed female roles became a signifier of his identity as man playing the role of a female character. Most of them entered the profession driven by extreme poverty especially during the famine in the 1950s.

"Rani, Rani, Rani, who is this Rani? Where did she come from? Whose 'rani' is she? She is our very own Bibhuti Rani. Why is she referred to as 'rani'? Because she was bestowed the title of Rani by a

Image 3.11. *Known Strangers*: Janardhan Rani and Chapal Rani

Courtesy: Debojit Majumder

king enchanted by her looks and her performance," says Janardhan now in his 90s filled with nostalgia about the golden days of the jatra. Bibhuti Rani's son Babulal Ganguly says, "Bibhuti Rani was fifteen when she joined professional jatra. My grandfather Rajani Ganguly was a jatra performer and an avid lover of music and art. Bibhuti Rani was charmed by the art form and decided to become a jatra artist and since he had long hair, was fair and good-looking and no one could guess unless told that it was a man disguised as a woman. He had a huge fan following. People would sit happily for hours watching her perform. I feel honoured when I recall that I had the opportunity to perform as a child artist alongside Upen Rani in the play *Bir Puja*."

The film traces the cultural iconography of female jatra impersonators like Nitai Rani, Upen Rani, Kanai Rani, Rakhal Rani, Harigopal Rani, Haripada Rani, Bonophool Rani, Khsitish Rani, Phoni Rani, Chhobi Rani, Babli Rani, Satadal Rani, Chapal Rani, Jatin Rani and the very contemporary Bobby who is young, attractive and still performs female roles.

Of the 15 impersonators, two, namely Chapal Bhaduri in his 70s and Janardhan in his 90s, are still alive and talk about their work.

Chapal Rani (Bhaduri) says how the evolution of technology in terms of light arrangements changed the scenario to their disadvantage as even heavy make-up could not disguise actors playing female roles. Prabhat Das, a theatre researcher says, "They brought to life in front of thousands of viewers their characters in different hairstyles, make-up and ornamentation. They were the nucleus of every jatra company and their awe-inspiring performances are legendary. They were stars jatra companies vied for because in every aspect from voice modulation to change in pitch and depth in terms of stage presence they were outstanding." They were very good singers too as most jatra performances had many songs and around five to six female characters in each jatra.

Known Strangers has been extensively researched with the crew travelling beyond Kolkata to different parts of the state to meet families of those who are no more. Janardhan sings beautifully for the film as he performs an extract in the compound of the famous Shobhabazar Rajbari in Kolkata. The cinematography is brilliant and so is the music tracking songs from old jatra performances.

Jayashree Devi, the lone female voice in the film who stepped into jatra to perform female roles when women began to replace men as female impersonators, says, "Everything about them fascinated me. Their makeup, their costumes, they way they looked on stage... extraordinary! The power they infused into every performance is something I have tried to learn from them."

Debojit Majumdar who directed the film jointly with Dipankar Dutta says, "I was inspired to make this film after I saw two documentaries on two famous female impersonators of the past century. One of them was *Sundari—An Actor Prepares* (1998) on Jayshankar Sundari, by Madhusree Datta. While researching, I discovered an amazing world of facts, memories and research findings and decided to place this in a single film." Jayshankar Sundari was a popular female impersonator of the Gujarati stage in early 20th century in Bombay (now Mumbai).

Known Strangers elaborates on how female impersonators perhaps began in Bengal from the time of Sri Sri Chaitanya Mahaprabhu, propagator of the Vaishnava sect in Hinduism who portrayed the character of Rukmini in a play staged at Chandrashekar Bhavan in 1506. He was only 20 years old at the time. He also enacted the roles of Adya Shakti, Radharani and the Universal Mother during the evening and night.

Chapal Rani, who continues to give solo performances in temples in and around Kolkata, says, "I am deeply indebted to Banaphool Rani for initiating me into jatra. I met her during a performance at Deogarh. Banaphool saw my performance and suggested I begin essaying female characters. My first character was Anjana in *Raja Debidas* as professional jatra and for the next 30–35 years I never looked back till we were considered redundant when women came in and replaced us. I had the good fortune of watching the performances of most of the leading Ranis of the times. I learnt a lot from Phoni Rani and was astounded with the grace with which she performed varied roles. Her voice was a unique blend of power, pitch and sweetness. During the 1950s, jatra entered a new phase. And the credit for this can be attributed to Jyotsna Dutta. An insecure future lay ahead of actors like me who specialized in performing female roles. I soon realized that we were now a fallen lot," he sum up realistically. The film closes with the actors as they looked in normal lives juxtaposed against their female impersonations. *Known Strangers* is a film no one should miss.

Known Strangers has been extensively researched with the crew travelling beyond Kolkata to different parts of the state to meet families of those who are no more. Janardhan sings beautifully for the film as he performs an extract in the compound of the famous Sova Bazar Rajbari in Kolkata. The cinematography is brilliant and so is the music tracking songs from old jatra performances.

Sons and Daughters

Jyotsna Khatry's 38-minute documentary *Sons and Daughters* (2013) is a well-researched, painstaking exploration of child trafficking in Delhi for domestic service in upper-middle-class households in the capital city. "An unsuspecting employer often hires domestic help from a 'placement agency.' Most of these agents are traffickers. The children they hire are likely to have been tricked, kidnapped or forced into work and nearly every trafficked child undergoes physical and sexual abuse during this business transaction. While they work, their salaries are deposited directly to the agent which makes the child an operational slave. The employer is oblivious," says Jyotsna in her director's statement.

Image 3.12. A Poster of *Sons and Daughters*

Courtesy: Jyotsna Khatry

She started her career as a film-maker with Act Now for Harmony and Democracy (ANHAD), a non-profit organization where her role was to interview, conceptualize and edit films on Gujarat carnage victims and on ANHAD's work in livelihood and education in Kashmir. She later assisted Rakesh Sharma on projects—State of rehabilitation of Gujarat carnage victims, 2002; Emergence of Hindu Right wing in the country and farmer suicides in the state of Gujarat. Jyotsna won the national-level award for L.I.V.E (learn about options, implement a plan, voice your decisions, engage others) campaign, a *Times of India* initiative for her short film.

In November 2013, 35-year-old Rakhi Bhadra who worked as a domestic maid in Delhi, was reportedly tortured and murdered by Jagriti Singh, the dentist wife of the Bahujan Samaj Party (BSP) Member of Legislative Assembly (MLA) Dhananjay Singh. According to the autopsy report, the deceased 35-year-old Rakhi Bhadra, a native of West Bengal, had injury marks all over her body, from head to toe. Subsequently, she succumbed to the injuries inflicted on her by beating, due to "excessive bleeding." The post-mortem that took nearly four-and-a-half hours was conducted at Sucheta Kriplani Hospital.

Jagriti reportedly confessed to have beaten up Rakhi who was found dead in their apartment in Chankyapuri in Delhi. Rakhi had allegedly been burnt with hot iron rods and kicked repeatedly. She had burn marks all over her body and injuries on the chest, stomach, arms and legs. Her son, Shehzan, 21, reportedly fled from Chanakyapuri in Delhi for fear of his life and even refused to take custody of his mother's body.

On July 24, 2014 a Delhi court rejected the bail plea of a woman who was arrested for allegedly torturing and illegally confining her teenage domestic help in her house here in Vasant Kunj. Metropolitan Magistrate Gomati Manocha dismissed the bail plea of accused 50-year-old Vandana Dhir and directed the jail authorities to provide psychoanalysis therapy and counselling to her.

A 15-year-old domestic help, continuously tortured by her woman employer, was taken cognizance of by the Delhi government in October. Calling the incident "horrible, barbaric," Minister of Women and Child Development department Kiran Walia said the government would bear the medical expenses of the victim, who was rescued last evening from her employer's house in Vasant Kunj and admitted to hospital with knife injuries. Walia, who visited the girl in hospital, said, "She has various kinds of marks on her body and doctor would be able to tell whether these are dog bites or not. But apparently, somebody knifed her."

In keeping with the rulings in the Juvenile Justice Act, the names of the children in the film have been changed to conceal their identity. We learn with shock that Delhi has around 2,300 domestic work agencies. Each agency charges INR 25,000 from each client and even takes away the monthly salary of the domestic servant, girl or boy. The children have no clue about whether their families are receiving the money or not. A child goes missing in India every eight minutes. There is no law to prevent child trafficking for domestic servitude in the country which makes the problem more acute and insoluble.

Responding to what motivated her to make this film, Jyotsna says, "I was a film student at SAE Bangalore in 2007 when I read the story by Neha Dixit in Tehelka called *The Nowhere Children*. It talked about the different purposes for which kids were trafficked. I had no idea that kids were trafficked for domestic servitude too. That's when I decided to find these kids and do a film with them."

Then why did she base her film in Delhi? "I used to live in Bangalore in 2011 and after trying to find these children and talking to a lot of child rights activists, realized that Delhi is the best place to make this film. I moved to Delhi in 2011. I had no clue about how funds could be raised. I started looking for a job and found one in Times Foundation and funded the film with my savings. By the time the shoot got over, I had to leave the job to be able to sit with an editor and by then I had no money left, so friends started giving us money for editing. We used an online platform called Orangestreet. in where we uploaded the trailer of the film and people who did not know us gave us funds to finish the film."

Vinay, 13, works as a domestic help since eight years. He belongs to Barabanki in UP from a village called Dube Ka Purwa. He says he was beaten and bashed up mercilessly, but he internalized the beating as 'natural' between master and servant. He subsequently returned home with the help of one of the many NGOs Jyotsna interacted with during her research for this film. Sabina, a Bengali girl, says she had gone to Chapra market in December with Rocky, her boyfriend. "He gave me something sweet to ear and I really do not recollect clearly how I landed with the agent who placed me as a domestic in a Delhi home. She finally managed to escape."

Savitri, from Lodhma village in Jharkhand, has been missing since 2002. The last her family heard of her was when he got a letter from her stating that her salary was INR 2,050 per month. She wrote that Sameena Placement Agency (Registration No.1112001) had asked for her transfer certificate and caste certificate which her father provided, but the girl is untraceable. Pakur with a family of parents, brother and kid sister is from Loondry village in Khunty, Jharkhand. The parents when interviewed could not even say how many children they had! Jayram, an agent, reportedly took a bunch of girls to Delhi from Salepur village in Jharkhand.

Khatry used a hidden camera while interviewing Rihaan Khan who runs his agency at Tughlakabad Extension. The camera closes in on his expensive, gold-banded wristwatch. He says they get a one-time commission of INR 25,000 adding that most of the little girls and boys do not know their correct age. The camera moves into a high-end shopping mall asking questions to mothers about babies and nannies. A white lady says "Bengalis are good nannies and some of us take them along to England with us. They all come from West Bengal."

But they come from all over the place mainly from the eastern regions—Jharkhand, UP, West Bengal and Uttarakhand. Assam and the neighbouring states are also not exempted. The film also takes a close look at the notorious case that made national headlines. It is about the teenage girl employed as a domestic in an upper-class home in Delhi whose employers were both doctors. They locked her from outside and went away to holiday abroad without giving her enough food and even the water supply dried up. She was finally rescued by a fellow maid who came in part-time. This maid informed the police, the girl was rescued and the couple was arrested. The camera interviews this girl. The camera discretely keeps away from focussing on the full face and figure of the girl to protect their privacy and to refrain from any sensationalization of the subject.

"One thing we have badly missed is to be able to have a very open talk with the employer of such children on the whole issue of trafficking for domestic servitude and how even employers are being tricked by the agents, not treating them as culprits, but unfortunately no employer was ready to talk to us so we had to conceal our subject and interview them on a very superficial level which hasn't worked very well for the film," laments Jyotsna.

The father of a missing girl from Sundarkhali village in the Sundarbans in West Bengal says that he was deceived by an agent in the village who said the girl would be placed in the agent's sister's home in Delhi. Another mother of a girl from Sandeshkhali, Sundarbans in West Bengal complains that she was not allowed to speak to her daughter working in a home at Sangam Vihar. Many months later, the girl was brought back to her family. Another girl was brought back by her brother with the help of the police and is now reunited with her family.

"We did not have too many obstacles because everybody helped us in every way, be it the NGOs, Delhi Police, subjects and even the people who worked on this film. The biggest obstacle while making this film was my own attitude change on how footage hungry I had became but one of the subjects helped me tackle that," sums up Khatry.

Fortunately, there are many active NGOs who are totally committed to the rescue and rehabilitation of these children. Shots show a group of rescued girls being sworn in before training at the Kishori Niketan rehabilitation home in Ranchi, Jharkhand. Another shot shows some of the rescued girls singing and dancing at the Mahila Shikshan Kendra in Jhansi, Jharkhand. "Other organizations we would like to thank are Kishalay Bhattacharjee, Shakti Vahini, Delhi; Kamla Market Police Station, Don Bosco, HAQ Centre for Child Rights in Delhi; Shakti Vahini, Sister Seli—Sistrers of Mary Immaculate Krishnanagar; Chidline, Sandeshkhali, Dhangagia Social Welfare Society, Sandeshkhali in West Bengal; Save the Children, Bharatiya Kisan Sangh and Jharkhand Mahila Samakhya Society in Jharkhand. We got some additional footage from JMSS, Shakti Vahini and Tanveer Ahmed of NDTV, Delhi," says Jyotsna.

Yamuna Gently Weeps

Journalist-turned-author-turned documentary film-maker Ruzbeh N. Bharucha has made a 72-minute documentary *Yamuna Gently Weeps* (2006) that not only explores the history of the Yamuna along

Delhi and the politics of the establishment that triggered the demolitions in the first place but also goes on talk to the original inhabitants whose present state of rootlessness defines the horror of the death of a culture along with the social, political, moral and emotional death of a people. His work highlights the solid support system slum residents provide to all of us but remain deprived of these very basic amenities. Thanks to their below-subsistence standard of living. "It it is because of them that our quality of life is so greatly enhanced. Our cooks, maids, drivers, peons, clerks, garbage and rag pickers, road sweepers, electricians, plumbers live in slums or resettlement colonies that are bereft of basic amenities of life and where, most of us, wouldn't survive even for a few hours," says Bharucha. His earlier documentary, *I Believe I Can Fly* (2011), offers a glimpse into the lives of mothers and their children in Indian prisons and the role of the India Vision Foundation, an NGO, headed by Dr Kiran Bedi, which focuses mainly on prison reform.

The Yamuna Pushta is one of the oldest and biggest slums in the country. It was the permanent residence of 150,000 people nurturing 40,000 families. What kind of lives did the people live before the powers that be decided to re-write it mercilessly? What did these people do for a living? "It formed a complete world within itself, complete with self-help groups, medical and health care centres, shops, restaurants, creches, small businesses and various social organizations, defining a close-knit society looking forward to positive changes. And then, one fine day, the shanties were razed to the ground, reducing homes, schools and medical centres to rubble, robbing 120,000 people of their home, hearth and livelihood and relocating 20 per cent to a barren piece of land in Bawana, some 40 kilometers away from the main city, under the transparent 'guise' of 'resettlement'," elaborates Bharucha.

Mobile food stalls, selling food at modest prices, were a common sight in Yamuna Pushta. These eateries mushroomed after sunset. During the day, the stall owners and workers found out other ways of keeping body and soul together. Often, the entire family, including the kids, was involved in their running. The food was wholesome, the prices were low and the eateries were a blessing for those who worked hard, who often did not have the strength to prepare a meal at the end of the day. With schools in and around the Pushta and easy accessibility of livelihood and medical facilities close by, a world within a world existed and the families were taken care of. "The demolition of a slum does not only mean the demolition of bricks and belongings but it also means bulldozing of education, security and the chance of a decent future. Many children are forced to leave school and become full time rag pickers and get into odd jobs, very often injurious to life and health or even peddle drugs or indulge in prostitution. This is what I set out to point out," says Bharucha.

"When Yamuna Pushta was demolished, no laws were passed! No fuss created! The poor silently accepted their lot! Delhi, with its media, judiciary and its political parties, slept peacefully! No one then thought of, 'one-year moratorium from punitive actions'. No issues were raised in the Parliament by our leaders about, 'unnecessary hardship and harassment!' In India, there are two laws, two types of governance, and two roles of the media, one for the powerful—the affluent, or those in the government, or the middle class that constitutes a mass vote bank—and the other for the poor, deemed an evil necessity, invisibles suffering from financial leprosy," Bharucha sums up, the bitterness palpable in his voice.

CONCLUSION

In the circumstances, it would be in the fitness of things to club this movement as the movement for 'alternative' or 'counter cinema' because film-makers who people this movement are attempting to counter the masala that is dished out by the mainstream while they are, at the same time, having to counter all attempts to abort their mission in making socially relevant documentary films by that establishment called 'censorship'. They are also trying to redefine the term 'documentary' from the preconditioned understanding perpetuated by Films Division.

What are the characteristics of this 'socially relevant' cinema that defines alternative or counter cinema? Gaston Roberge[3] describes socially relevant cinema as follows:

- A film that raises the viewer's awareness about central issues even if the issues cannot be dealt with exhaustively.
- A film that educates the sensibilities of the viewer about these issues and suggests the possibility of different worlds.
- A film that gives some information about the actual mechanisms of alienation and oppression; however, an overload of

information might invite strong censorship by the powers that be.
- A film that features a hero who is imitable and rational in his approach to given problems not necessarily violent.
- A film that promotes human virtues that make life worth living, such as hope, recognition and compassion.

The first three characteristics mentioned above are viable and logical. But the fourth and fifth characteristics are so ambiguous and ambivalent that they may permit access to mainstream films and make the entire subject of social relevance a futile and meaningless argument. Who defines counter-cinema? Documentary film-maker Pankaj Butalia[4] places the credit for initiating this vibrant, angry, questioning and consciousness-raising movement squarely on the shoulders of Anand Patwardhan "for creating conditions in which such a climate could become respectable."

"The challenge of translating the lives of people in one culture to people in another can be creative and absorbing," writes John Marshall. "Participant observation and shooting cinéma vérité can be exciting," he adds. But he warns that this could often lead to appalling and even dangerous situations. The challenge multiplies when one considers the practicality of participant observers engaged in an open-ended enquiry that stops only when the time, the money or the film runs out. But the challenge remains and the film-maker sustains himself purely through this undying challenge that keeps haunting him till he has done what he sought to do.

NOTES
1. Shoma A. Chatterji, "The Ethnographical Documentary," *Spectrum India*, 4th ed. (Mumbai: International Film Festival for Documentary, Short and Animation Films, 29th January to 5th February, 1996), 11–13.
2. Ibid.
3. Gaston Roberge, "Problems and Prospects of Short Filmmaking in Third World Countries," *Deep Focus*.
4. Pankaj Butalia, "The Indian Documentary in the '80s" (paper presented on Tendencies of Development in the Three Continents, 1988).

4
THE RAY FACTOR

RAY'S DOCUMENTARY FILMS

No treatise on the documentary can be complete without a brief elaboration of Satyajit Ray who has gifted some of most outstanding ones in the history of documentary in India. This extends to *Ray* (1999), a documentary made on the film-maker by another film-maker, Goutam Ghose. This section will first explore Ray's contribution to the documentary and then move on to *Ray*, a film by Ghose.

"He could have created a storm even if he had made documentaries alone," said the late Harisadhan Dasgupta, friend of Ray and a brilliant documentary film-maker. If Ray's documentaries on Tagore and Binode Bihari Mukhopadhyay, his blind painter teacher from Santiniketan are examples, and if his short film *Two* (1964) for French television and *Teen Kanya* (Three Daughters) are illustrations, then Dasgupta's comment was simply a statement of fact without exaggeration.

Ray's 'feel' for the documentary format may perhaps be traced back to his work with Harisadhan Dasgupta, when Ray penned the screenplay for Dasgupta's *A Perfect Day* in 1948. This was an ad film shot in the documentary style. It unfolded a day in the life of a smoker who buys a pack of cigarettes in the morning. The camera follows him till the end of the day when the packet is empty. Ray's rapport with Dasgupta continued through a few more ads and corporate films. Ray scripted Dasgupta's *Tata Iron and Steel* and wrote the musical score of the latter's *Quest for Health* (1967) made for Sandoz. They produced two films jointly. One, made for the Dunlop group, was entitled *Our Children Will Know Each Other Better* (1960) and the other, *The Brave Never Die* (1978), was for the West Bengal state government on floods.

Dinkar Kaushik, one of Ray's oldest friends from his days at Santiniketan, who later headed Kala Bhavan, said that Ray once toyed with the idea of making a documentary on Pandit Ravi Shankar in 1948, much before Ravi Shankar became an internationally renowned celebrity. "He asked me to get back a sketch book of his from Ravi Shankar from Delhi. When I thumbed through its pages, its contents amazed me. It was filled with close-up sketches of Ravi Shankar at his Sitar, done from every imaginable angle, marking fade-outs, highlights, crisscross marks for shootings, detailed studies of the maestro's hands, fingers, everything. It was a collage of work that did not merely inspire, but evoked instant emotional response." Ray never got down making that documentary.

The Inner Eye was a title with a double meaning. It at once signifies the painter's 'inner' eye to denote his ability to visualize life and all that it stands for despite his disintegrating vision. It also symbolizes, in a manner of speaking, Ray's own 'inner' vision to see beyond the 'surface' story of the painter's childhood, training, and growth as a painter.

He met the painter's family to collect his childhood photographs, put all this together on the editing table and finally rounded this up with a running commentary in his own golden-honey voice and delivered in his impeccable diction. The film does not ever try to sentimentalize the painter's blindness. The film won the Swarna Kamal in the non-fiction category in the National Awards in 1972.

The painter Binode Bihari Mukhopadhyay's philosophy contained in his words, "I believe in live design" comes across with a strange vibrancy in Ray's *The Inner Eye*, the documentary on this blind painter. Ray was particularly sensitive to Mukhopadhyay's distinctive personality whose entire visualization came through his inner feelings while he was going completely blind. The painter's fascination for line to define and explain form inspired his one-time disciple Ray. It took Ray one full month in Santiniketan to shoot this film. Then he took his crew to Kathmandu, Patna, Mussoorie and other places.

Rabindranath Tagore (1961), Ray's first documentary with a running time of 54 minutes marks the film-maker's venture into composing the music for his films. It has been "the best biographical film yet made in India," wrote Chidananda Dasgupta.[1] "In a mélange of still photographs, live shooting of re-acted scenes from the poet's early life, newsreel clippings, drawings, shots of landscape, paintings, songs, evocation of political events, constantly moving by means of quick dissolves and held together by a narration written and read by Ray himself, Ray created a massive tribute."[2] The film is rich in its historical perspective and magnitude. Ray did not interpret Tagore in and through the film but took views from scholars and commentators, informed with narrative clarity and a quiet sense of reverence that was uniquely Ray's own. The film won the Swarna Kamal at the National Awards (1961) and the Golden Seal for the Best Documentary at the Locarno International Film Festival the same year.

Rabindranath Tagore, commissioned by Films Division in celebration of Tagore's centenary in 1960, is a milestone in the world of biographical documentaries across the world. It is amazing to discover that Ray shot this documentary simultaneously with *Teen Kanya*, made in the same year, which was a three-part feature film based on three short stories by Tagore—Postmaster, Monihara and Samapti. The film was premiered on 5 May, 1961 in Delhi. Ray said, "I put in as much work on it as I did on my three feature films. My approach to the biography was to stress Tagore as a human being and patriot."[3]

His painstaking research produced a wealth of material in the form of manuscripts, books, conventionally posed photographs, and Tagore's works of art and graphics. Tagore was no more, so the material was static. Ray's main issue was how to invest the documentary with fluid movement demanded by the audiovisual medium of cinema. He did not write a script but prepared a visual continuity plan that took him around a month. The opening voice-over says, "On 7th August, 1941…in the city of Calcutta….a man died. His mortal remains perished but he left behind him a heritage which no fire could consume," without naming the great man that was the subject of the film.

The newsreel archival footage revealed five shots of the expired Gurudev Rabindranath Tagore being borne through the streets of Calcutta in a hearse spilling over with white floral bouquets to the burning *ghat* (crematorium built along a river bank). Ray used 14 different songs composed by Tagore to fit into his conception and ideology of presenting Tagore as an institution and as history. The first song, "nobo arunodayo joyo hoke", is used on the soundtrack in chorus while the visuals depict a portrait of Tagore rising from the flames of the funeral pyre suggesting the rising of a new sun. The second song, "amar mukti aloye aloye ei akaashe", strongly suggests the claustrophobia of Tagore as a boy within the conventional rigidity and discipline in the Tagore home, learning by rote lessons taught within the four walls of the school classroom, from where Tagore as a boy wanders off with his father to Punjab and to the hills of Dalhousie while the skies resound with the echoes of 'freedom within light' investing the visuals with brilliant mood music created by the subject of the film.[4]

Each song has been selected with great care to punctuate the different phases and some memorable moments of the poet's life on the one hand, while on the other, taken together, the songs form a small microcosm of the versatility of Rabindra Sangeet. It ranges from a prayer song through a song from Balmiki Pratibha inspired by Western music composed in an early phase of his creative life, to a famous rain song "rimjhim ghono ghono re boroshe", bringing across the poet's nature (*prakriti*) songs, to the beautifully patriotic "amar shonar bangla ami tomaye bhalobashi", that was to become the national song of Bangladesh reflects the poet's creativity in music and lyrics in all its glory.

Ray could have easily extended the story of *Pikoo* made for French TV into a full-length feature film. It had elements of drama, conflict, and the scope for propounding Ray's own ideological stance, perhaps in greater detail. A lesser director would have easily fallen into the trap. But Ray did not need this. He had his craftsmanship, his artistic creativity, his aesthetic vision, and his ideology completely within his command for every film that he chose to make. In doing so, he honed and perfected the skill and the mastery of deciding the footage of his film without compromising on any of these things. The film won the Best Documentary Award at the 9th National Film Awards.

Sukumar Ray (1987) was a documentary by Ray, produced by the Government of West Bengal, as a celluloid tribute to his father—Sukumar Ray—a multi-talented person who was a London-educated printing technologist. Upon his return to Calcutta, he took over the reins of his father Upendra Kishore Roy Choudhury's children's magazine *Sandesh*. Till this day, Bengali literature is yet to find a parallel to the nonsense literature and rhyme compositions of Sukumar Ray published in book form as *Haw-Jaw-Baw-Raw-Law* and *Abol Tabol*, respectively, with graphic illustrations done by him. He also wrote intelligent, sharp and funny satires on formal school education and is famous for his series of stories under the title *Pagla Dashu*. The film carries all these. With the voice-over by Soumitra Chatterjee, the film turns information into education and entertainment. The music composed by Satyajit Ray is low key, melodious and beautiful. Ray has drawn generously from source materials such as archival B&W photographs, print fonts and graphics, cartoons and drawings by his father and a few dramatic reconstructions to bring across the satire in some of his creative works. Few have had the opportunity of watching this film because it remains in the cold storage of the archive. The film also touches upon the harmony in Sukumar's family when he grew up among five brothers who remained united till the end. His sisters Sukhalata and Purnalata were also noted writers. Within its 30-minute span, Sukumar Ray holds up a mirror to the historical evolution of the Bramho Samaj, the youth wing of which Sukumar Ray was the leader.

Sikkim (1971), Ray's most controversial documentary till date, was jointly commissioned by the then *Chogyal* (Sikkimese equivalent of the word ruler) of Sikkim and his American wife, Hope Cooke. It was more due to the enthusiasm of the latter to promote Sikkim as an attractive tourist spot to the world that Ray was asked to make the film. Ray agreed. The Chogyal is said to have felt that the sovereignty of Sikkim was threatened at the time he commissioned the film, both by China and India.

It is a pictorially beautiful film that not only scans the picturesque mountainscape of the land, its diverse orchids that carry its maker's inimitable signature, but also his command over holding a picture of its people, culture, poverty, music and dance. The filmmaker's son, Sandip Ray, says that the original 'rush' print of the film was screened to a very small audience at Kolkata's Indrapuri Studio's projection room. This 'rush' print footage ran for nearly 40,000 feet covering five hours of screening time. The film was processed at Mumbai's Film Center. The commentary was written by Ray himself and the voice-over is also Ray's.

Problems cropped up at Sikkim because the royal couple, the Chogyal and his wife, were not happy with the final film when they saw it. The objections, wrote Dilip Mukhopadhyay, were probably due to some scenes the king and his wife found unpalatable and unflattering to the royal family and the image of Sikkim. There is a scene of an open-air party thrown by the royal couple in the royal gardens where a grand royal table is laid out for the invitees comprised of aristocratic families of Sikkim and foreign guests. Ray is said to have juxtaposed these scenes with scenes of the poor and the starving, hunting crazily for the leftovers in the darkness outside the palace in the biting cold. Without articulating in words, Ray pointed out the contrast in the beautiful land ruled by a king who either did not care about the poverty his subjects reeled under or did not know. Chogyal asked for several cuts in the film and also some snipping of Ray's commentary. Ray was firm. He staunchly refused to make any changes to the original footage. By virtue of ownership rights, the film went back to Sikkim and according to reports, just 60 per cent of the Ray's original print remains.

Critic Andrew Robinson in *Satyajit Ray: The Inner Eye*, reprinted in *Chitrabhash*'s special issue on Ray, Bergman and Antonioni (Vols 42 and 43, 2008) wrote that Ray "was compelled to make about forty per cent of the film into something 'bureaucratic with statistical information' and a disproportionate emphasis on the Sikkimese population instead of the Nepalese, as would have been appropriate given the latter's actual preponderance in the state."

The story did not end there. Four years later, the Government of India banned the screening of the film when Sikkim was integrated into India in 1975. In 2000, the copyright of the film was transferred to The Art and Culture Trust of Sikkim. The ban was finally lifted by the Ministry of External Affairs (MEA) in September 2010. Which version—the one Ray originally made or the one edited by the Sikkim royalty—was screened at Nandan at the 16th Kolkata Film Festival in 2010? No one knows. Cinematographer Soumendu Roy said in his pre-screening speech at Nandan that this print had been reproduced from another print and is therefore a reproduction. Towards the end of the royal regime in Sikkim, reports were rife that all prints of the film were destroyed.

The screening of the version that was shown at Nandan in 2010 seems to have suffered from the ordeal of double censorship—from the commissioners at Sikkim and from the Government of India in 1975 when Sikkim became a part of the India. After this ban, reports were rife that the Government of India not only banned the screening of the film but also destroyed all known copies of the documentary. In January 2003, it was reported that a good quality print was kept at the British Film Institute in London. The Kolkata-based Satyajit Ray Society had tried to trace a print of the film with the Chogyal's family. But it was damaged beyond repair.

Angel Video succeeded in getting a copy from Sandip Ray who could access it from a friend of his father, a distributor based in London, "because the original negative is no longer available," says Ray. The print was restored by the Academy of Motion Picture Arts and Sciences in 2003. A restored version of the film was screened at a Ray retrospective at the Nantes Three Continents Festival in France in 2008.

Bala (1976), on danseuse T. Balasaraswathi is enriched more by the rich commentary written and voice-overed by Ray himself than by the subject of the film. Balasaraswati was a seventh-generation representative of a traditional matrilineal family of temple musicians and dancers. *Bala* was jointly produced by the National Center for Performing Arts, Bombay (now Mumbai) and the Government of Tamil Nadu. Two documentaries are said to have been made on Balasaraswathi. The first is a recording titled *Balasaraswathi* produced by Wesleyan University in the US. The second, called *Bala,* was directed by Satyajit Ray in 1976 when the dancer was 59 years of age.

The film fleshed out the history of classical dance styles through Bharata's *Natya Shastra* explaining that of the 27 chapters in the treatise, one was devoted entirely to classical dance forms. The opening frame defines a close-up of *hastra mudra's* (hand movements) executed by Balasaraswathi with her face captured in out-of-focus shot to stress on the hastra mudras. This sets the tone of the film tracing the family background of the danseuse whose roots are traced back to her great grandmother, grandmother and mother steeped in music that spurred her on to train in Bharatanatyam.

The command Ray had over aesthetics is subordinated to description, narration and the transcending of the dancer's performance from *nritta* (pure dance) to *nritya* (a combination of sentiments and moods. *Natya, Nritta and Nritya* are the three forms of *abhinaya*—techniques used to convey mood) which, considering Ray's technique, is a little unusual. There is one long scene of Balasaraswathi performing the famous "krishna nee begane vaaro" cinematographed against the picturesque backdrop of the waves of the sea where the dancer, also a singer of exceptional talent, sings the *padam* (form of musical composition in Carnatic music) herself. Minal, a blogger on the use of Indian dance in cinema, mentions[5] that in her paper, *Multiple Pleasures: Improvisation in Bharat Natyam*,[6] dance scholar Avanthi Meduri questions Ray's placement of the dance performance performed against a live backdrop of the ocean. Asks Avanthi, "Did the director situate Bala against this backdrop as a way to naturalize and essentialize the dance, to evoke notions of cosmic plenitude, timelessness and infinitude? Or did he desire to spiritualize and idealize both the dance and the dancer?" She feels that regardless of Ray's good intentions, the performance falls flat because Bala is "separated from immediate engagement with her musical ensemble, which had always supported and accompanied her live performances."

Private moments of the dancer with her daughter and disciple Lakshmi depict how fiercely she guarded her private life. There is a moving scene where Bala teaches her daughter to dance and another showing the two playing a game of dice where the senior dancer smiles perhaps for the first or the only time in the entire film.

The discomforting quality of the film is the lack of rapport between the subject and the director. The social and emotional gap that sustains between Balasaraswathi and Ray leads to a lack of resonance and rhythm in the aesthetics of the film. Though the dancer says in one scene how the time of her day is scheduled by the hour and the minute, the film fails to explore the psychological process of the artiste's coping with her mastery over abhinaya in Bharatnatyam, the form of her choice. There is no attempt to explore the power relationships that evolve over time between an artiste and her art, between the danseuse and her audience, between the guru and her disciples and between the dancer and her accompanists. These interactions play significant roles in the evolution of an artist from one among hundred performing artists and an icon to be worshipped, celebrated and imbibe from. One can only ask—*why*? And let the question hang in the air till eternity. For Ray is no longer around to answer it.

Even so, the intercutting of documented materials such as old photographs, newspaper clippings, brief interviews with cultural scholars such as Dr Narayana Menon offer the depth of information a biographical film on a great cultural icon demands. There is an archival B&W photograph of Uday Shankar standing in a group after Balasaraswathi's first performance in Kolkata. The voice-over informs us that Uday Shankar was so deeply impressed by her performance that he opened the gates of international recognition for her. The tremendous success of the dancer's performance at the Edinburgh Festival in the UK where her recitals drew a packed house each time is mentioned as a reference to her international acclaim.

In performance, Ray has placed the dancer against her immediate physical perspective by cinematographing her mainly in mid shots and long shots but rarely in close-up. Some veteran cultural scholars and film critics had suggested the possibility that Bala was publicity shy and did not cooperate with the film-maker over time. But there is no one to give the right answers anymore. Having said that, one must concede that *Bala* stands out as an example of how much of creative advantage a film-maker can take from his subject within limited circumstances where he does not know about the dance form, he does not know the language of the songs for the dance, and is unfamiliar with the language, geography and culture of the artist he is making the film on. In this sense, it is a learning platform for biographical documentarists.

FILMS ON RAY

Gautam Ghose's Ray

The relationship between the film-maker and his subject is a relationship of power. Everything in the film, every person, every event, is predicated to this relationship. This practicality of the documentary is questioned when the subject is Satyajit Ray and the film-maker is Gautam Ghose—one, an icon immortalized within and by his creations in multiple dimensions of art, and the other, much younger in age and experience, more a hero-worshipping fan looking upon his subject more as a role model than as a subject. Does Ghose live up to this challenge? He does. He almost takes a backseat and lets the genius do the talking, at times, literally. Ghose creates a collage of events, incidents, talents the master is known for, puts them together with a soundtrack filled with music picked up from Ray's own compositions for his films, and lends a commentary alternately voiced by Aparna Sen and Ray himself.

Ray turns out to be a documentary where form and content merge as one—the content in this instance deciding the form. It is more difficult than challenging to capture vignettes from the emotional, physical and creative growth of a thinker such as Ray, who balanced many talents within one of which, his film-making perhaps happened to take top priority in his life. Ray, the little boy who lost his father at two and a half years, who lived for another three years with his grandfather Upendra Kishore Roy Choudhury, who observed with the keen curiosity of a child, the printing press his grandfather ran, recalling the artistic innovations in printing the old man ventured into, are juxtaposed in the film against the alternate personas of Ray.

Ray's stint at Santiniketan, when he was not sure he was interested in becoming an artist, telescopes into clips from some of Ray's films. Archival stills reveal his short stint with Renoir when the latter was shooting for *The River* (1951) in India. The illustrations of frames, costumes and characters conceived by Ray, next to the script written in his beautiful handwriting, are frozen in time. His unique scripts written in those red notebooks that evolved into a sort of a diary-writing exercise in later years find place in the film. His book cover illustrations, his experimenting with graphics for the Bangla alphabet, his sketches of renowned personalities, and his evolving into the most successful writer in modern times seep into the narrative of this beautifully put together collage.

The critical point of the film is the intrigue it triggers off by shedding light repeatedly on a sentence Ray often marked his beautiful scripts with. "I don't know." These three words occur time and again, sometimes in the margin, at other times, right into the script, or below a dialogue, raising questions about a sense of uncertainty that seems to have dogged Ray along his journey towards greatness. The film closes with a translation of the poem Tagore wrote in seven-year-old Ray's autograph book left with the poet by Ray's mother the day before. While handing the book back to the little boy, Tagore had said that though he was too little to understand the words now, he would when he grew up. "I have travelled around the world to see the rivers and the mountains," wrote Tagore, "and

I have spent a lot of money. I have gone to great lengths. I have seen everything. But I forgot to see just outside my house, a dewdrop on a blade of grass." These lines marked much of Ray's philosophy in his later life and work.

Shyam Benegal's Satyajit Ray

Shyam Benegal made a documentary on Ray called *Satyajit Ray* in 1982. The film was shot by Govind Nihalani. Benegal captures Ray over a time when he was recovering from his first heart attack while he was shooting *Ghare-Baire* (1984) alternating with his telefilm *Sadgati* (1981) based on a short story by Premchand. Working clips from Ray's film shootings such as *Mahanagar* (1963) captured to offer a glimpse into his versatility as a film-maker of great merit. This gradually mutates to a long interview interspersed with clips from his earlier films and working footage. Subsequently, Seagull Books published a version of the film's script available for film buffs, students and teachers. Ray's rich voice embellished with his beginnings at Santiniketan where he states that though he went there to study art, it was never his intention to become a painter, moves over to the way he evolved in his working style, his approach and his treatment within film-making.

In an interview with Kushali Nag[7] about his experience of working with Satyajit Ray, Benegal says, "When I made *Satyajit Ray*—the documentary on Ray—there were no DVDs, so I sent him a cassette." He saw the film and made only one remark, "Too much Ray, too little Benegal." *(Laughs)* "But then I explained to him that it was a film about him and I didn't want anybody to give their opinion on him. In most documentaries, you ask different people what they think of the person. I didn't want that, I preferred to have him speak for himself." Benegal said that Ray was a very private person suggesting that he did not open out easily and he looked back on their relationship as one that sustained between a master and his pupil.

Ray's magnificent screen persona enriches the film and marks it for posterity. It also shows how he chose actors to act in his films, such as Victor Banerjee for *Ghare-Baire*, would report on the sets just to watch even on days when he did not have a call sheet for him. The film produced by FD bagged the National Award for the Best Biographical Film in 1985.

Shyam Benegal's documentary on Ray is from the perspective of one film-maker looking at the works and working style of another film-maker he considers much above him in achievement and mastery, and so captures the master mainly at work, intercutting it with Ray's personal takes on his life that led him to becoming a film-maker. Shots of the film-maker and his actors as he shot the final shots of *Mahanagar* are unforgettable.

The Music of Satyajit Ray

In 1983–84, when Ray was making *Ghare-Baire*, young film-maker Utpalendu Chakraborty made a 90-minute documentary on Ray's work as a music director. Unfortunately, for some unexplained reasons, this film has hardly been open to wide viewership. In this film, Ray traces his command over the art and craft of music to his family antecedents explaining that his grandfather Upendra Kishore Roy Choudhury was a composer and also played the violin, the flute and the *pakhawaj*, an Indian percussion instrument. Ray goes on to add that everyone from his mother's side were natural singers. His initiation into Western classical music came from a collection of gramophone records in his childhood residence. "My familiarity with Western composers like Bach, Beethoven, Tchaikovsky and Mozart began quite early when I was around 14 and had a friend from a wealthy family who was also interested in classical music," says Ray, adding that he learnt Rabindra Sangeet and Brahma Sangeet from his aunts on his mother's side.

The soundtrack is orchestrated from sound and music clips of Ray's films in keeping with the visuals and the comments by Ray. For example, when he talks about his grandfather, the sound track fills with the rhythmic beats of the pakhawaj. When the narrative mainly comprised of Ray talking about his music intercuts into clips from *Pather Panchali*, notes from a flute playing on the soundtrack enhances the tragedy of some of the scenes in the film. In this way, the narrative is a collage of Ray talking about how he evolved into composing for his own films since *Teen Kanya*, cutting into a voice-over as the visuals track back to clips of his films, sometimes closing on Bengali notations of his compositions intercut with the title card of each film, B&W photographs from his family album and from his films, and so on, evolving into a cohesive and aesthetically-structured documentary focussed only on the music of this great master.

The opening frames of Utpalendu's film capture the open window of Ray's apartment on 1/1A Bishop Lefroy Road as notes strung on a stringing instrument float into the visuals. The visuals are taken in long shots at night, so while the ambience around the house is dark, one discovers the lights in the windows up on the top floor of the building. This cuts to the rehearsal room where Ray is shown orchestrating with his musicians and singers to compose the theme music of *Ghare-Baire*.

According to Ray, every director should know what music to use in his film, where and how to place it within his film. Generally, for a director well versed in music "like I have been since I was a schoolboy, it would be best for the director himself to compose the music for his films. Since *Teen Kanya*, I decided to compose the music for my own films. The music maestros I worked with such as Pandit Ravi Shankar, Ustad Vilayat Khan and Ali Akbar Khan became very busy with their own concerts and recitals and I felt it would be ideal if I composed myself." Later on, he states that he rarely composed for other film-makers, such as for Merchant-Ivory's *Shakespeare-wallah* (1965), but had decided that he would not compose for other film-makers.

Ray perhaps is the first Indian film-maker to introduce the concept of theme music for every film that would fit into the environment, subject and plot of the respective film. The film closes with music rehearsals for *Ghare-Baire* and then finally rests in Ray's study capturing him sitting behind his organ, pipe in mouth, making notes and thinking, looking beyond, and trying to reach out.

The two omissions in the film make it less than a complete celluloid essay on Ray's music. One is the absence of any discussion whatsoever on the music in Ray's documentary films. The other is the absence of comments from some of the musicians and singers who worked under his music direction. In aesthetic terms, *The Music of Satyajit Ray* (1984) adapts itself to the style of Ray himself and yet Chakraborty manages to invest the film with his individual directorial stamp because he is a very good singer and knows music himself. Not at any point does the film deviate from its subject—Ray holding him in the centre whether he is talking, or reading out from his notations, or giving directions to his orchestra, or, through the films he made over time with the backing of clips from the films, the title cards and some flashbacks into the history of this musical genius.

It would be appropriate to sum up with Chakraborty who said, "Ray's music is imaginative, not melodramatic, balanced, not exuberant, functional, not decorative. It is music that grows from the film itself." *The Music of Satyajit Ray* produced by the National Film Development Corporation (NFDC) won the National Award for the Best Documentary in the non-feature section at the 32nd National Film Awards.

CONCLUSION

Ray had plans to make a documentary on Pandit Ravi Shankar called *A Sitar Recital by Ravi Shankar* and had also prepared part of the script. But the film was never made. The 32-page drawing book, with penciled in editing and camera movement instructions could be a godsend as a tutorial for students of cinema, for evolving film-makers and for film studies students and scholars. It was dug out of the archives of the Society for the Preservation of Satyajit Ray Archives that has collaborated with Harper Collins in the editing, compiling and publishing of the book.

Satyajit Ray's *Ravi Shankar* published by Harper Collins and edited by Sandip Ray explains what might have led to the rift between one great film-maker and one great music composer and artist that stopped the beautiful collaboration between the two. In his brilliant articles titled Unheard Melodies, The Sitar and the Camera in the book, Sankarlal Bhattacharjee recalls how in an interview with him, Panditji had said about the musical score of *Pather Panchali*, "Satyajit Babu was fairly liberal then with the editing of the score." Later in the same interview, Panditji adds, "Then awards and honours started coming his way. Thereafter, he started adjusting my scores, first in *Aparajito* (1957), then in *Apur Sansar* (1959). Even then the music of those films came out excellent." The message that comes across is that Panditji did not like the idea of Ray 'adjusting' his music for the film or making editorial modifications to the same.

From the title card with white font printed against a black background, the sketch book contains 106 sketches executed by Ray himself without any commentary to back it because the film itself was designed to capture Panditji actually in a recital, so it was to be an ideal blend of music, rhythm and visuals. Directions for the camera and for the musical phase penciled in by Ray mark the flow of the script from one sketch to the next. The first page has the word *alaap* (In Indian music, the improvised section of a raga, forming a prologue to formal expression) written in Bengali as the headline. The four sketches arranged angularly on the same page are marked with camera movement directions such as 'truck forward' moving on to the next page. Panditji captured in a long shot in silhouette with a semicircle of light used as backlight, according to Sankarlal Bhattacharjee, is Ray's homage to Panditji by creating a harmony between his name 'Ravi' with the sun which 'Ravi' stands for.

Making this script a unique example as a script per se, and Ray's script in particular are the director's sketches drawn from nature to give visual expression to the particular phase of the raga the maestro is playing on his sitar, such as the camera moving away from the maestro completely to display just the platform and then dissolve to a frame showing birds in flight, dissolve to dry leaves floating in space, dissolving to clouds, close-up of a pool of stagnant water and so on. A series of dissolving sketches of a beautiful woman in profile sometimes shifting her hands playing on the sitar shifts to a mid-close-up of the meditative Panditji as he works on the *meerd* (particular term within Hindustani classical music. The three main cadences in Hindustani classical music are meerd, *gamak* and *murchhana*) of the raga he is playing on.

To this writer's mind, the most outstanding feature of this visual script is the film-maker's playing around with the partnership between the music maestro and his percussionist held in different camera angles over several frames, sometimes moving from long shots of the pair of percussion instrument with the camera trucking forward to close on the hands of the percussionist playing on the tabla. Similarly, to strike a contrast and also to establish the varied manifestations the camera and the editing are capable of, in the next set of frames, the camera moves from long shot to medium close-up. The visual script invests the book with the unique quality of featuring an unfinished work by one great master with another great master as the subject of his film. Since neither of them is alive, this is a priceless gem.

Many small documentaries have been made on different aspects of Ray. Utpalendu Chakraborty made an interesting 77-minute documentary entitled *Child Artistes and Satyajit Ray*. Produced by Satarupa Sanyal, the film was censor-certified in 1997 but was never released. This writer watched its only screening at

Gorky Sadan, Calcutta, under the auspices of The Eisenstein Cine Club, Calcutta, a few years ago. This is the only film in India that explores the mastery of Satyajit Ray over children not only in terms of presenting them as characters within a film but also through stories written specifically with the child reader and child viewer in mind. He had the rare ability of handling them in a way that made them appear as if they had been picked out of real life. From *Pather Panchali* to *Agantuk* (1991), Ray tackled children as children. Chakraborty's 77-minute film is regarded as the only film in India that presents Ray's love for children and his ability to communicate with them at their own level—age-wise and mindset-wise. Yet, he took children out of their urban, educated, modern backdrop and placed them in a rural setting as and when the script demanded. And not once did they appear out of place. Nor did they once behave or speak like adults do. Unfortunately, these films are not available for viewing today and therefore could not be covered in this chapter.

NOTES
1. Chidananda Dasgupta. (1980). *The Cinema of Satyajit Ray*. Ghaziabad: Vikas Publishing House.
2. Ibid.
3. Marie Seton. (2003). *Portrait of a Director: Satyajit Ray*. Penguin Books: New Delhi.
4. Atanu Chakrabarty, *Cinemasangeet O Satyajit* (Bengali). Nandan Publication: Kolkata.
5. Found: Bala (1976, Satyajit Ray) and an Extant Recordings List http://cinemanrity-agharana.blogspot.in/2012/03/found-bala-1976-satyajit-ray-and-extant.html. Last accessed on 22 March, 2012.
6. Avanthi Meduri, Ann Cooper Albright, and David Gere, *Multiple Pleasures: Improvisation in Bharatanatyam* (Hanover: Wesleyan University Press, 2003).
7. Kushali Nag, "An Interview with Shyam Benegal,". *Telegraph*, 31 January 2012.

5
THE MILESTONE MAKERS

INTRODUCTION

The literal meaning of the word 'milestone' is 'a stone set up beside a road to mark the distance in miles to a particular place'. Expanding to its metaphorical meaning, it could suggest, 'a significant stage or event in the development of something'. If we put a human face to this metaphor, it can be elaborated to mean an individual who, with his work, defines a significant stage or event in the development, exploration, exposure or investigation into crucial questions affecting different pockets, groups, incidents and events and even takes his agenda forward through a consistency in his continuous effort to strive for the truth through his commitment to the documentary movement in India. His/her works carry the signature of their maker and therefore, can be recognized from the maker's choice of subject for his/her films, his/her approach to film-making and to his/her approach and style of film-making. These human 'milestones' are not only milestones by themselves but have also created 'milestones' through their films.

This means that the film-makers chosen for this chapter lend themselves to auteur critique of their works. By common perception, the making of a film calls for the contribution of many people for functions such as acting, screenplay, sound, cinematography, production design, music and editing. Yet, a dominant approach to films today believes that the 'director' is ultimately responsible for the finished film. The term 'auteur theory' describes a basic principle and method—no more, no less—of the idea of personal authorship in the cinema. The auteur critic takes on the concomitant responsibility of honouring all films of a single director through a systematic reading of each. This helps in bringing out characteristic themes, structures and formal qualities.[1] In this light, the idea of auteur does not solve all problems. Nor does this provide answers to questions raised about the director's claims to authorship. It offers a way of 'looking' at the films of a given director who has produced considerable work in which quality is more important than quantity. Not that any director actually comes forward to 'claim' authorship. The 'critic' decides whether a director lends his works to an auteur critique or not. Auteur criticism deals with the adequate though, relatively subjective distinction that makes the stylistic and thematic preoccupations of individual directors.[2]

Film-makers chosen for this chapter, despite their 'signature', connote diversity rather than unity, non-conformity rather than conformity and variation rather than repetition. Finding common elements of style, form, subject, etc. becomes a formidable challenge for the one attempting to study their films as an auteur critic to try and discover the auteur in the director. It has been a challenge to make this list too. It is by no means exhaustive but is based on the writer's personal experience of the works of these film-makers. There are no women directors in this chapter because a separate chapter has been earmarked for the discussion of their work.

ANAND PATWARDHAN

For around three decades, Anand Patwardhan has been making documentaries on many themes that earlier documentary film-makers would never have dreamt of. He has led the way for similar activists who followed suit. Says Patwardhan, "In every film I make, I strive to make the elements of film-making subservient to what is happening in the film. I measure the success of my films by their ability to make people think about the issues the film generates. Personally, I do not like to use the word 'art' because it is used badly and wrongly all the time. I do not think art can be divorced from society. Not that everything has to be political in the sense of everyday politics. But I think everything is political in a deep sense."[3]

Patwardhan's career in documentary films began with *Prisoners of Conscience* followed by *A Time to Rise* (1981). He hit the headlines with *Bombay:Our City* on the inhuman exploitation and victimization of slum dwellers in Bombay (now Mumbai) that won the National Award for the Best Documentary Film the following year. But the film was promptly banned from public screening by the same government that had bestowed the award on the film. It is a powerful essay on the politics of space and structure that dictate the blueprint of our country's irrational development.[4] The film marks a turning point towards a more specific definition of the political documentary that doubles as a social comment. The film led to the evolution of a movement towards the formation of counter-cinema.

His later films, *In Memory of My Friends* (1990); *Ram ke Naam* (In the Name of God, 1992); *Pitra, Putra Aur Dharamyuddha* (Father, Son and Holy War, 1994); *Jang Aur Aman* (War and Peace, 2002); deal with strong issues of the nation-state that involve us all. The first two films deal with communalism placed in different perspectives. The first is rooted in Punjab and the second is focussed on Ayodhya. In both films, Patwardhan takes the position of a left-wing rationalist interviewing scores of common people living in areas of conflict. He uses their pragmatic good sense to make his point. His point is that holocausts occur when passions are deliberately whipped up by political and communal manipulations that have a lot of axe grinding at stake. After making *Ram ke Naam*, Patwardhan said, "It is not so much that I have made the film from a Left perspective as that I made it as a contribution to the fight against communalism and the Left has been at the forefront of this struggle. During the Ayodhya Rath Yatra, no one else was opposed to the BJP. But Marxism is not the only way to fight communalism. We have a secular tradition in India, which Mahatma Gandhi emphasised, that is also opposed to fundamentalism. My support is for both."

Jang Aur Aman had to fight a prolonged, almost a losing battle with the Central Board of Film Certification for the public screening of the film. *Jang Aur Aman* explores the many impacts of the acquisition of nuclear weapons by India and Pakistan. Going from one topic to another in a somewhat non-linear fashion, Patwardhan manages to tie together the problems faced by people living near nuclear testing and mining sites, the horror of Hiroshima and Nagasaki, the psychological numbing in the United States with the consequent blind eye to the arguments against the bombing of the two Japanese cities and the global reach of the merchants of death, namely arms traders. But the film is not all gloom and doom—it also documents extensively the growing movement for peace in both India and Pakistan. In spite of the film having bagged prizes and praise from many who have seen it, the Indian Censor Board prevented its release for public screening in India for a long time and, like for his other films, Patwardhan was forced to fight several court cases to get the ban lifted. The attempt to censor Patwardhan's film was challenged by many.

Patwardhan's trademark style includes footage of actual events, sharp interviews with his opponents that often made them sound foolish and cutting between seemingly unrelated footage. "I like things to reveal themselves rather than tell people what is going on," he says. "Many of the things that appear shocking are not so shocking for the people who believe in them. It is only when you juxtapose their views with something else that the truth comes home." In the early 1990s, Patwardhan collected footage of the Bharatiya Janata Party's (BJP) *Rath Yatra* (ceremonial procession centred around a chariot carrying a holy image). In *Pitra, Putra Aur Dharamyuddha*, he makes the link between the feeling of threatened masculinity among the majority Hindu community and its increased communal feelings. Patwardhan aims to provoke audiences into rethinking their support for the BJP. "This kind of film-making is becoming rare," he said. "People react with surprise, not with horror."[5]

Jai Bhim Comrade (2011) is a brilliant portrayal of how music performed by the Dalits as a crusading, powerful weapon of resistance can raise consciousness and protest against the establishment, the ruling party and the police. Patwardhan worked on it for 14 long years and the trigger was pulled when a random firing by the police on 11 July, 1997 on a crowd of Dalits in Mumbai killed 10 young activists forever. The violence was spurred when a statue of Dr Ambedkar in a Dalit colony in Mumbai was desecrated with footwear. As the angry residents gathered, police opened fire killing 10 people. Vilas Ghogre, a leftist poet, hung himself in protest. Ghoghre was featured in Patwardhan's earlier film *Bombay: Our City* in which he sang his own songs of rebellion. Patwardhan was shattered by his death and *Jai Bhim Comrade* was born. "The film follows the poetry and music of people like Vilas and marks a subaltern tradition of reason that from the days of the Buddha has fought superstition and religious bigotry," says a promotional blurb.

AMAR KANWAR

Amar Kanwar is an independent documentary film maker who was awarded the Golden Conch-Best Film Award at the Mumbai International Documentary Film Festival in March 1998 for his film *A Season Outside* (1998). Subsequently, the film also received several awards at the CEC-UGC documentary film festival in India. His films have also received nominations for the Pinnacle Awards and have been screened in several international documentary film festivals. He is also a recipient of the MacArthur Fellowship for 1998 and is currently working on a film about masculinity and sexuality as part of the MacArthur Foundation Fellowship.

Narrated by Kanwar, *A Season Outside* uses India's northern borders as the inspiration for a personal and poignant meditation on the source of a violence acculturated through centuries of ethnic and religious conflict. Ritualistic military patrols and ubiquitous coils of barbed wire mark the point where the historic Grand Trunk Road traverses the international border, where only the butterflies and birds are free to cross or rest on the wire as they do not disturb the circuit. The white line running across the road has its origins in the communal conflict that led to the partition of India. It is also the symbol Kanwar has chosen to begin his search for new insights into the age-old yet omnipresent need for a politics of non-violence.

A post graduate in Mass Communication, Film and Television, from Jamia Millia Islamia, Amar Kanwar has been working as an independent film-maker for 10 years now. He has directed over 40 documentaries in this period (all of which have been broadcast) and has consistently worked on issues of health, ecology, philosophy, labour, law, politics, art and education.

One of the best examples of the new school of documentary film-making is Amar Kanwar's *A Night of Prophecy* (2003). The film collects protest poetry from across India, including Maharashtra, Andhra Pradesh and Nagaland. The poems give voice to feelings of anger, injustice and marginalisation. Kanwar made *A Night of Prophecy* after *A Season Outside* and a series of films about ecological destruction, for which he travelled to several conflict zones. "I felt that in spite of a very clear and strong articulation by people, nobody was listening to each other," says Kanwar. "I also got the sense that the understanding of issues was not enough. The form of poetry creates a certain kind of understanding that goes beyond information-based articulation."

The film's lyrical title stems from a hypothesis which Kanwar followed during the making of the film. "An economist understands agriculture by looking at information collected over a period of time," said Kanwar, whose *The Lightning Testimonies* (2007) was screened in Mumbai. "If you're able to understand the passage of time in society through poetry, can you predict the future? If I were to record poetry from a certain region over a period of time, would my understanding of conflict change?"

Kanwar's deeply felt explorations of conflict and violence question the government's claim which is endorsed by the private industry where India has made great strides over the last few decades. "Through the 1990s, and in the last nine years, the aspiration about a certain kind of India has been clearly and fully put to rest," Kanwar said. "People have seen through the project of India. My work tries to occupy a place between hope and despair. When you get to the pits of your despair, you begin to ask questions." *A Night of Prophecy* leans on the side of hope, he added. "*A Night of Prophecy* feels it comes out of despair. But after a while, you feel that you are now possessed with a need to figure out your future. If you're propelled, there is hope."

A Night of Prophecy was filmed in several diverse regions of India (Maharashtra, Andhra Pradesh, Nagaland and Kashmir) and featured music and poetry of tragedy and protest performed by regional artists. The sources of anger and sorrow vary from inescapable, caste-bound poverty to the loss of loved ones as a result of tribal and religious fighting. The footage is a stunning glimpse of India's diverse ethnic groups and topography from the rural mountains to its crowded urban centres. *To Remember* (2003) is a portrait of Birla House, the site of Gandhi's assassination which occurred on 30 January, 1948. Located in Delhi, Birla House has become a gallery and shrine attracting hundreds of visitors daily. This short, silent film is a homage to Gandhi as well as the visitors who embody the spirit of his pacifist teachings. Against the backdrop of a surge in militancy and Hindu nationalism, Kanwar's work is particularly telling. Clearly, the historical turn of events, from non-violence to nuclear armament, suggest a deep ambivalence about Gandhi's legacy. Then again, when Gandhi said turn the other cheek, he did not specify whether the left or the right.

The Lightning Testimonies is an eight-channel video installation that explores the sometimes repressed, always sensitive and newly urgent issue of sexual violence against Indian women. The visuals are disturbing in their shocking impact. They offer a complex montage of simultaneous accounts with stories on abduction and rape during India's partition in 1947 to the powerful anti-rape protest in Manipur in 2004, scanning a time span of nearly six decades of violence against women. The video installations are also a strategy to break through the conspiracy of silence—personal, emotional filial, social and political. He clearly states that this presentation is a two-pronged way of expression. One is to present the work as a multichannel installation in an art world setting and the other is to project it as a continuous film screening within the educational and activist contexts. Kanwar dots this with his own presence in the films through voice-over and first-person commentary, thus undercutting the objectivity of his political statements. In this way, he reinforces his own space within his larger framework, thereby investing this with the emotional empathy and subjective response he demands from his viewers.

Kanwar has mastered the art of gentle persuasion of making powerful political statements without the sound and fury that typically accompany critiques of this depth and magnitude. There is no commentary berating the government for its failures and the society for its wilful and arrogant maintenance of inequality. But lyrical as this film is, the viewer is never allowed to forget that *A Night of Prophecy* is not about poets and poetry but about the subjects of these poems; the people that speak the words and what they speak of. Kanwar's film takes the viewer from Kashmir to Andhra Pradesh, recording songs of oppression, pain, exclusion and marginalization.

RAKESH SHARMA

Rakesh Sharma needs no introduction to Indians who have been following the human rights movement in the media. However, *Final Solution* (2004) is not the beginning and most certainly not the end of his journey that established him as one of the most outspoken and independent film-makers who makes a strong statement against any violation of human rights. He fights with the powers-that-be and he fights with the censor board. The numerous awards which he won at international film festivals have not gone to his head. Rather, they have strengthened his determination to go ahead and make his statement at the best. *Aftershocks* marked his return to documentary after a gap of 10 years. Though today, Rakesh is better known for *Final Solution* that had to fight through a censor ban, he made an equally strong and powerful film, *Aftershocks*, before *Final Solution* (2004).

Aftershocks: The Rough Guide to Democracy (2002) sheds light on the politics of post-earthquake 'rehabilitation' in Julrai and Umarsar, two villages in Lakhpat. Though these villages were almost completely destroyed in the earthquake, no NGO, United Nations Organization (UNO) or earthquake relief agency bothered about them. Yet, the villages turned into instant 'gold' for the Gujarat Mineral Development Corporation (GMDC) for their lignite-rich soil! The GMDC was quick to pounce on them with false promises of 'relocation', 'jobs' and 'rehabilitation' to make financial capital out of a natural disaster. The film is a hitchhiker's journey through the labyrinthine universe of democracy, as it exists at its lowest-unit level—the Indian village. It is a brilliant expose not only on the exploitation of the poor by the powers, but also on the gross violation of human rights legitimized by the government to line its own corrupt accounts. It also sheds light on the casual indifference of NGOs and the international disaster relief organizations who allow such things to happen right under their snooty noses just because it suits them to look the other way at Bhuj and other such media-hyped places affected by the earthquake.

Final Solution is a study of the politics of hate. Set in Gujarat during the period Feb/March 2002–July 2003, the film graphically documents the changing face of right-wing politics in India through a study of the 2002 carnage in Gujarat in Western India. It specifically examines political tendencies reminiscent of the Nazi Germany of the early 1930s. About what motivated him to make *Final Solution*, Rakesh says, "Post-9/11, we live in a world where politics of hate and intolerance has gained mainstream acceptance, even grabbed centre stage. The 'War on Terror' dominated the electoral discourse in the US presidential elections, with both candidates promising to "hunt them and kill them" better than the other. The right wing seems to be tightening its stranglehold across Europe as well, a nationalism being fuelled by the anti-immigrant/anti-Muslim rhetoric. In a world where it has become legitimate to use fictitious intelligence to justify the bombing of innocents in Iraq, where it has become acceptable to launch precision bombs and rockets against non-'embedded' journalists, where shameless politicians divide up oil wells and farm out reconstruction contracts for their $36 million bonuses, where babies are killed and mutilated as acceptable 'collateral damage', we face a challenge greater than ever before. We have earlier lived through many dark periods in history, often justifying our barbarism by using similar rhetoric. Hate, despair, destruction and tragedy cannot possibly be the foundations of harmonious societies and a democratic world."

The censor banned it on the ground that it could incite communal flare-ups but finally cleared it for public screening. Sharma had appealed to the board to send the film for a review. The Censor Board had previously said, "the film promotes communal disharmony among Hindu and Muslim groups and presents the picture of Gujarat riots in a way that may arouse communal feelings and clashes. Certain dialogues involve defamation of individuals. The entire picturization is highly provocative". But when the film was shown on 7 October, 2004 to a high-profile revising committee comprising Censor Board Chairperson Anupam Kher, film-maker Shyam Benegal, activist Teesta Setalvad, theatre personality Dolly Thakore and film-maker Ashok Pandit, they said the film could be released without any change. The film has won the prestigious Wolfgang Staudte Award at the Berlin International Film Festival, where it also won the Special Jury Award.

Khedu Mora Re (Oh My Farmer, 2007), in a span of 62-minutes explores the myth of a 'vibrant' Gujarat by graphically documenting the tragic series of farmer suicides in the state. Moving away from the disastrous consequences of Godhra and the communal carnage that takes precedence in the media, Sharma goes behind these suicides to reveal the farmers' opposition to SEZs and the widespread anger fermenting within them against the Modi government's lopsided policies that claim the farmers in the film are tailored precisely into the scheme of corporates and industries. Ironically, the farmers point their accusing fingers directly at the much-hyped Sujalam Sufalam scheme for their misfortune especially during the recent floods in Saurashtra. "Till a couple of years ago,

Gokharwada in Surendranagar district did not experience a single flood. But ever since this Sujalam Sufalam project was activated, our village and our lands get submerged every year due to the faulty planning and construction of the new check dams. Modi keeps announcing packages running into hundreds of crores. But the people at ground level are yet to receive even five rupees out of the post-flood package announced for 2005. And the flood in 2007 has destroyed us totally," says one angry farmer.

Khedu Mora Re features shocking stories of suicides at a very personal and intimate level. Opposition to land acquisition for SEZs in Bhavnagar district and the havoc unleashed by private companies in Kathivadar are intercut with these stories. The film reports 10–12 suicides in Amreli, Surendranagar, Bhavnagar, Rajkot, Bharuch and Surat. The RTI data reveals shocking district-wise figures—Rajkot (63 suicides), Junagad (85), Amreali (34), Mehsana (48), Nadiad (44), Jamnagar (55), Narmada (30) and even in Gandhinagar (13), right under the CM's nose! At that time, Narendra Modi was the CM of Gujarat.

Chet'ta Rejo (Beware, 2007) shows another face of inhumanity in Gujarat. Over its 72-minutes running time, the film explores and exposes the saffronization of the Dalit–OBC population and its consequent plight. Its focus is on the patterns of arrests and litigations since 2002. It shows how most of those charged with rioting, arson, murder and similar crimes are either tribal or Dalits and other backward communities (OBCs). The analysis of those arrested from 32 police stations in Ahmadabad suggests that of the 1,577 detainees, only 30-odd belonged to upper castes. "Are these foot soldiers victims too? Cynically recruited, then discarded, left to rot in jails, what do the 'perpetrators' of the violence feel today about the VHP and the BJP?" These are some of the questions the film raises rhetorically as it also narrates first-person stories of some of the victims. The film shows six to eight families of S-6 (coach of Sabarmati Express) dead passengers speaking about how they were told (i) that people were going for a picnic tour, not *karseva* (refers to voluntary and free service rendered to religious institutions, organizations and structures within Hindu and Sikh religions); (ii) that the VHP–BJP exploited their tragedy for electoral gains in 2002, (iii) that ever since then no one has come to help, (iv) that how monies raised in their name never reached them, and (v) that how some of them who spoke in public about it have received threats from the Vishwa Hindu Parishad (VHP)!

The film points out that though VHP made tall promises to help the detained and the injured Hindutva cadre, the only 'help' were some rations and a little monetary help that came from them in the first two months. The VHP-BJP combine just vanished into thin air after that. A telling story is an account by Kanti and Deepak from Gomtipur—both caught by the police. They appealed to the BJP for help and even approached the CM but nothing was done. When they went to Togadia's own Dhanvantri hospital for operations/treatment, they were turned away unless they first deposited INR 50,000 for admission. An OBC Hindu and another Muslim boy, both friends, would often play cricket together in Behrampura. During the riots, both boys lost their right hands to bombs during the riots! The film ends with the two boys appealing to the youth not to join such parties or get involved in such violence as no one lifts a finger to help while it is they and their families who will suffer forever. The overall message that emerges through a range of voices is that violence and politics of hate destroys the Dalit-OBC-Muslim communities; it is best to stay away from parties that preach hate.

These two films are by nature a follow-up to the critically-acclaimed film *Final Solution* that dealt with the 2002 carnage and its aftermath, the *Gaurav Yatra* (procession of prestige), BJP's subsequent electoral victory in a sharply polarized state in 2002. In October 2007, *Final Solution* finally got recognition in its own country when the President of India gave it the National Film Award. Earlier, the film was screened at over 80 international film festivals and received over 20 awards (at Berlin, HongKong, Zanzibar, France, Argentina, USA, Bangkok, Spain, Kathmandu, etc). It also got the Best Film Award from the prestigious Index on Censorship Awards (UK); ironically the film was banned by the Indian Censor Board for a few months in 2004. However, following widespread protests by civil societies, the film was cleared without a single cut.

SANJAY KAK

Sanjay Kak is an independent documentary film-maker with interests in ecology, alternatives and resistance politics. His films include *Red Ant Dream* (2013) which is about the persistence of the revolutionary ideal in India; *Jashn-e-Azadi* (2007) is about the idea of freedom in Kashmir; *Words on Water* (2002) is about the struggle against the Narmada dams in central India; and *In the Forest Hangs a Bridge* (1999) is about the making of a thousand-foot bridge out of cane and bamboo in Northeast India.

His film work also includes *One Weapon* (1997), a video about democracy in the 50th year of Indian independence; twin films on the theme of migration, looking at people of Indian origin in the fringes of the city of London in *This Land, My Land, Eng-Land!* (1993); and *A House and a Home* (1993), a film on post-apartheid South Africa. Sanjay is the editor of *Until My Freedom Has Come—The New Intifada in Kashmir*.

Kak began making films in the late 1980s. At that time, the thin tissue of a post-Emergency social and political consensus, a patchwork of half-hearted gestures towards a more inclusive polity, was beginning to make its repercussions on world politics. Around the same time, documentary film-makers following the Emergency, to some extent led by Anand Patwardhan, came to take decisive shape.

Kak was joined by several other film-makers, including Pankaj Butalia and Ruchir Joshi, Reena Mohan, Vasudha Joshi and Ranjan Palit, Nilita Vachani and her brother Lalit Vachani, R.V. Ramani, Soudhamini, the Media Storm Collective—Rahul Roy, Saba Dewan and Amar Kanwar. Although this was a period of intense activity, Kak's films were yet to acquire the political edge they are known for today. He had already made a television film on everyday life in Punjab during the Khalistan movement (*Punjab:Doosra Adhyay*, 1986) and a television series on the Ganges (*Pradakshina*, 1987); documentaries on the post-Khmer-Rouge restoration of Angkor Wat in Cambodia (*Angkor Remembered*, 1990) and the Indian diasporas in Britain and South Africa in *This Land, My Land, Eng-land* and *A House and A Home*, respectively both in 1993.[6]

Kak's work has always been an attempt to engage with and understand the state's responses to peaceful as well as violent challenges to its power. To do this, Kak and his frugal crew have walked with thousands of people—to demonstrations, on patrols, to work, to count the living and the dead, to farms, to dam sites, to meetings and rallies, to gatherings, departures and fights. Over the years, these walks have taken Kak a long distance—from celluloid to analog and then to digital video, from being a consummately reasonable young man to becoming an agile and gracefully ageing rebel, from being a film-maker who would stand and watch people walk to a film-maker who began walking with them.[7]

In *Jashn-e-Azadi*, he recorded the struggle for freedom in the Kashmir valley. Much earlier, in *One Weapon* (1997), he looked at those who took up the vote, not the gun, as their weapon. *One Weapon* was part of a series called *India's Quest* produced by the Foundation of Universal Responsibility to commemorate 50 years of India's Independence. This marked Kak's stepping into the territory of mass expression of dissent and his strategy in the process of film-making which included walking along with the people he was filming.

Kak chose the electoral process and the way in which polls claim to represent the popular will. *One Weapon* was shot in two widely disparate locations—Tamil Nadu, simmering with the renewal of an assertive Dalit politics, and Punjab, still recovering from the violence of the Sikh extremism and state repression of the 1980s and the early 1990s.

In Tamil Nadu, Kak followed the reformulation of the demand for a separate electorate by Dalit activists, who were trying to renew Ambedkar's legacy in a political culture driven by the rhetoric of anti-caste movements and in the ground reality of continued caste-based oppression. In Punjab, Kak followed a range of candidates, from the Communist Party of India-Marxist (CPI(M)), the Communist Party of India, Marxist–Leninist [CPI(ML)], the Akali Dal and the Congress. His focus was on people in the margins, a Dalit Christian community campaigning for the Jat Sikh Congress satrap bitterly complained about how every promise was forgotten once elections were over; a CPI(M) candidate who stood up to Khalistanis and survived; a former Naxal-turned-Congress-worker who talked hesitantly, but clearly, about the meaning of state terror; and farmers and landless Dalit peasants who asked Kak whether he knew of any alternative to the vote as a weapon and whether such an option would work. Through these voices, Kak told the story of a society beginning to use the elections as a means to talk to itself, after years of grim silence. But after all these years, with stability in government bodies at the Central, state, local and panchayat levels spilling over with scams, corruption in politics and so on, using the vote as a weapon has exhausted itself and this makes *One Weapon* a wonderful historical treatise on the celluloid.

His next film—*Words on Water* (2002), defining a trek across all kinds of terrain—is a rich archive of the work of Narmada Bachao Andolan (NBA), one of the biggest and most organized resistance movements in the recent history of South Asia. Throughout *Words on Water*, one sees the NBA triumph. It mobilises thousands of people, shapes public opinion, isolates and shames a complicit bureaucracy and even persuades international agencies such as the World Bank and companies such as Siemens to drop their stakes in the project. The film shows us the movement acting like a model of how a democratic civic action ought to be.

The NBA, led by Medha Patkar (who is seen several times in the film walking, organizing, negotiating, getting arrested and staying her ground), began around 1985 as a small voluntary organization committed to saving the ecosystems and communities that thrived along the Narmada in central India from being wrecked by a series of big dams. As more and more people (totalling up to 250,000) began to be displaced by the development projects, opposition to the dams escalated, and the NBA emerged as the most significant and popular activist group within environmentalist politics in India. It attracted not just hardened grassroots organizers but also dissident engineers, lawyers and a wide spectrum of non-party Left activists who had reason to be wary of the local as well as global corporate interests that backed the big dams. The movement was confrontational but resolutely non-violent and was almost obsessively wedded to a legalist confidence in the judicial process.

Words on Water is a kind of mirror to the NBA; through the film, we see the organization thinking, changing tactics, retreating and advancing. Kak began filming the movement in 1999 and followed it until 2002. Every occupation of a dam site or a corridor of power is followed faithfully and every argument recorded. At every stage, the state's undemocratic willingness to impose its developmental aims on an unwilling population is scrutinised, sometimes with rage and sometimes with laughter and a song. The film showed the little disputes with lower-level administrators; the big tussles with global policy wonks; the protestors agitating in incessant rain; the counting of dead livestock; the vigil as water levels rose in a village; the debate over displacement figures; and the polemics over engineering, electricity and irrigation. In short, it countered a process that made people effectively invisible by reducing them to acronyms and numbers.

In October 2000, the Supreme Court, in a majority judgement authored by Justices B.N. Kirpal and A.S. Anand, gave the go-ahead to the Narmada dam projects. In their decision, the justices wrote, "the re-settlement and rehabilitation of people whose habitat and environment makes living difficult does not pose any problems." However, the film, which was released in 2002, would show what resettlement and rehabilitation mean. In a striking scene, a government contractor carpets the barren soil of a 'rehabilitation site' with a thin layer of fertile black soil.

Jashn-e-Azadi had almost no individual characters, no heroes and no bad guys—it just had the violence of a brutal military occupation, its routines of checkpoints, cordons and searches. It also showed the everyday life of resistance, slogans, singing, stone pelting and the hypnotic rhythmic incantation of the words that the film brought the south of Kashmir into the rest of India, "*Hum kya chahtey hain? Azadi!*" (What do we want? Freedom!)

One sees an unforgettable sequence from the film through Ranjan Palit's camera. Kak comes upon an old man walking through a labyrinth of headstones in the Martyrs' Graveyard in Srinagar in the midwinter, looking for his son's grave. When Kak asks him some questions, he responds in Kashmiri, as if he were not even registering the fact that someone was asking him what he was doing in a snow-covered graveyard. Finally, the father finds his son's grave. He clears the snow on the gravestone to read the date of his son's killing, stands silently for a while and then says, "That's it, that is enough. It was a feast day, and I thought I would come and spend some time here, that's all." Then he walks away. With every passing year, the number of graves in that graveyard only grows. But the act of looking for the headstone, of cleaning the grave—a small, private act—stands out as a mark of the things that need to be done so that the living may remain alive.[8]

Red Ant Dream (2013), his latest documentary, invites the audience into a journey within the world of India's Maoists, especially the members of the People's Liberation Guerrilla Army (PLGA), who are considered by the Indian State to be its 'most significant security challenge'. Right in the midst of the Dandakaranya forests in the Bastar district of Chhattisgarh, we get to see the real faces of the rebels who reveal their human face and not their insurgency-ridden angst. In some ways, this shakes us up into confronting the reasons and the social and economic circumstances that drive to create the guerilla who dances as merrily as he/she coldly trains an automatic rifle to shoot.

Red Ants Dream explores how in the Niyamgiri hills in Orissa, people have been constantly resisting the devastation of the forests and the displacement of tribal inhabitants for Vedanta's bauxite mine. They are quite easily bracketed as 'terrorists'. In Chhattisgarh, a recording of an intercepted police wireless message coldly instructs subordinates to make sure that no journalist returns alive from a foray into a combat zone, where torched villages, destroyed homesteads and the remains of 'neutralised' teenagers can be found. A lot of this material, which makes its way into the film through found footage, seems to point at the reality of India's massive counter-insurgency offensive aimed at destroying the Maoist presence in the central and Eastern India. This, Kak seems to say, is how the Indian State secures itself against its own population.[9]

AJAY RAINA

After a Diploma in Cinema (Film Direction) from the FTII, Ajay has been making documentary films about Kashmir, where he spent his formative years. His film with the PSBT, *Tell Them the Tree They Had Planted Has Now Grown* (2002), won the Golden Conch at MIFF, 2002, and *Wapsi* (2005) won the National Award the same year. Ajay taught screenplay writing at FTII and video production at ISB&M, Pune, and he was involved in training a group of semi-literate boys and girls from underprivileged slums/communities of Mumbai and Ladakh in video production.

Tell Them the Tree They Had Planted Has Now Grown is a powerful film made straight from the heart. It is a cinematic diary of a Kashmiri revisiting Kashmir after a 12-year exile to witness the scars of a paradise lost. Through the film, the film-maker, a Kashmiri who was there in November 1989 when militancy was just making its presence felt through random bombings and killings of the so-called 'Indian agents', mostly Kashmiri Hindus and leaders of the National Conference, returns to see if at all it was safe to return to Kashmir and to hear what people thought and felt about the long dark night that has reigned over Kashmir during this period. The film is replete with personal memories of the people he meets (some new and some again) and places he revisits as he searches for a time that is now lost.

The film follows the film-maker, a Kashmiri, through his travails and he is occasionally seen on camera as he meets various people and revisits places from his past. He has also provided the narration for the film and recorded it in his own voice thus making it as personal a film as possible which is precisely the strength of the film. The film-maker draws us into his journey as we meet his old acquaintances and visit his now empty house in Srinagar or his ancestral house in his village. Through this, we feel for him and wonder with him—will normalcy ever return to Kashmir? When will all these killings and violence ever end? Also to his credit, the film-maker takes no sides in the issue of Kashmir but meets as many people as he can from all sides and lets everyone have their say thus getting a multifaceted perspective on the issue and leaving the viewer with plenty of food for thought. One cannot but be shocked as one sees how resigned the people have become today to violence and killings as a normal part of their lives.

The camera, free flowing and often handheld, moves smoothly with the protagonist and draws the viewer compulsively into the world of the film-maker. The images of Kashmir are stunning because it shows us a land that looks ravaged and destroyed. This is no longer the Kashmir echoing with the cries of Shammi Kapoor's "yahoo" or Sadhana's bouffants. Today, it is a land of much destruction and mass killings.

In spite of its grim theme, the film has several moments of warmth and humour as well. The film-maker easily interacts with the various people he meets to get them to talk naturally to him. *Tell Them the Tree They Had Planted Has Now Grown* was funded by the PSBT. The film has been shot on digital video (DV), a format that is being increasingly used particularly for documentaries as it makes it extremely easy to go with a minimum unit and manageable light weight equipment to far-flung locations and shoot without difficulty. In fact, the unit of this film comprised just two people— the director himself and the cinematographer Tanmay Agarwal. The director and the cameraman also doubled as sound recordists taking turns to shoot the film. The film was shot over a period of two weeks and has come down to its present edited length from over 40 hours of raw shooting material![10]

Wapsi is an account of the film-maker's travels through the part of 'Al-Hind' that is now a foreign country and a most bitter foe. The journey to Pakistan is a journey of return to various kinds—to Nostalgia, hate, metaphor and reality. Starting from India's capital, Delhi, it takes a detour via Kashmir, Gujarat and Indian Punjab. It travels back and forth between memory and history to explore the 'idea' of Pakistan, the story of its making, what it has become and how it affects Indians and Pakistanis who, in spite of the divide, remain connected to each other through hate and through love.

In the times of a yet another thaw in the relationship between India and Pakistan, an Indian 'lover of cricket' finally manages to go to the other side of the Line of Control, to journey through the heartland of Pakistan. Much in the style of Al Biruni, a Persian scholar, who visited this part of India more than a 1,000 years ago to encounter an alien culture which he had called 'Al-Hind'. *Wapsi* captures the nostalgic moments of not just the film-maker but also of many who have travelled or yearned to go across the border into Pakistan.

The film travels through India and Pakistan during the India–Pakistan cricket series and returns not only to the idea of Pakistan or to the 58-year-old partition tales but also to much more. In the words of the director Ajay Raina, "*Wapsi* in Hindustani language does not only mean 'The returning' as its literal English translation would suggest, but it also means to go back, to start again, to give and to take. *Wapsi* means different things to different people. As for me personally, it was an unforgettable trip. I found out things that I did not know about, I had not been ever told about or had been lied to about."

Wapsi is an hour-long documentary that unfolds languorously but never indulgently as it searches through India and Pakistan in an effort to understand the genuine yearning for peace against the reality of continuing communal violence in the region. There is seldom denying the truths that come on the canvas of the screen. The slick editing as well as the fast transitions back and forth in time and location make this documentary a fast-paced revelation.[11]

Apour Ti Yapour (2011) explores the same themes as Raina's previous documentaries *Tell Them The Tree They Had Planted*

Has Now Grown and *Wapsi*. All the films explore geographical and psychological dislocation, the notion of exile and the yearning for a return to less fractious times. In *Tell Them*, Raina accompanies his father on a visit to their old home in Jammu and Kashmir. In *Wapsi*, Raina attends an India–Pakistan cricket series across Pakistan in 2004.

In *Apour Ti Yapour*, the attempt was to "go beyond the personal, to understand and address the question of Kashmir's struggle for azadi", said the film-maker, who studied direction at the FTII. "I have tried to look at Kashmir from the point of view of the people who have endured 20 years of violence and turmoil there. I can understand how the constant presence of security forces for the last 22 years can only mean occupation."

The film's elegant and elegiac tone comes largely from the silent passages between the interviews. The beautiful, crisp images of Kashmir in the summer were shot in a high-definition format by Raina and his regular collaborator Arun Varma in 2010. The film has a certain timeless quality to it even though it is taking place in the here and now. There's a serene sequence at Srinagar's Sri Pratap Museum, which houses artefacts from earlier, quieter times. *Apour Ti Yapour* is at its most poetic form in the images glimpsed through a near-invisible camera, an old man takes a walk through a tree-lined path; a young woman sits absent-mindedly in a grove; and an elderly woman tends to her field.[12]

"I wanted to make a film that was a departure in every sense from the kind of films I had previously made," Raina said. "I was also anxious not to return to the cinema verite style, which though it appears truthful only manages to scratch the surface of that which appears to be true."

The sense of exile felt by the residents is shared by the film-maker, a Kashmiri Pandit, who grew up in Kashmir and left in the late 1980s as militancy took root in the state. "I simply hated growing up there," Raina said. "I had expected to never want to look back but through the films I saw and read about, I understood why I had longed to get out of Kashmir. I found a motivation to return."

In June 2013, Ajay Raina and his peer in documentary films, Pankaj Rishi Kumar, put together an unique film festival under the umbrella title 'Kashmir Before Our Eyes', a festival of films that seeks to depict all aspects of Kashmir. This is not the first year for the festival. Over the years, there has been a sizable accumulation of films on Kashmir. Individually, they have been a part of different festivals, and it was only a matter of time before they commanded their own festival. Since June 2013, the festival has been travelling the country. From FD Zone in Mumbai, the film went to Asian College of Journalism in Chennai, Pondicherry University, venues in Thrissur and Hyderabad and reaching Delhi in September. Raina and Kumar were joined by writer and film-maker Siddhartha Gigoo.

On 7 September 2013, the same festival was violently disrupted in Hyderabad by a Hindu right-wing group for being 'anti-national'. On the same day, the Indian State was busy proving to the world that a fortified, very important person (VIP) concert in Srinagar was evidence of 'normalcy'. Whether by unsound violence or sonorously drowning out dissent, the intent is always to silence. Film festivals such as these are a much-needed shout in the dark.

RANJAN PALIT

Had Ranjan Palit and Vasudha Joshi not made *Voices from Baliapal*, few Indians would have ever known about the collective, peaceful yet active resistance of an ethnic mass against a wrong government policy. The government was trying to set up a nuclear base in Baliapal in Orissa that would uproot and displace the people from their natural habitat where they were economically self-sufficient through local crops and through fishing since the village is in coastal area.

Ranjan Palit has shot more than a hundred documentaries about subjects ranging from slum demolitions and protest poetry to the Bhopal gas tragedy and the Kashmiri struggle for autonomy. The 52-year-old cinematographer and film-maker has also made or codirected 11 films of which *Forever Young* (2008), a documentary on Lou Majaw, has the title borrowed from a Bob Dylan song. The 62-year-old rock musician Lou Majaw is the subject. Ranjan Palit is one of the most outstanding cameramen in the Indian documentary field. He has done feature films too, but the documentary has remained his lingua franca, mainly by choice. He has also directed many documentaries but is better known as a cinematographer than film-maker. His 79-minute documentary *In Camera—Diaries of a Documentary Cinematographer* (2006) is a nostalgic and introspective journey into his 25 years as a documentary film-maker and cinematographer. The film won the Best Editing Award at the

Image 5.1. *In Camera*

Courtesy: Ranjan Palit

57th National Film Awards 2010 in the non-feature section and Palit won the award for the Best Narration, a section he did not know existed!

For his celluloid diary *In Camera*, Palit turns the lens of the camera inwards, to take a nostalgic and introspective journey into his 25 years as a cameraman and film-maker "to take stock of my bearings," he explains. Made in 2006 with a film fellowship awarded by the PSBT, the film is motivated by the ethical questions of shooting investigative and activist documentaries focussing on human tragedy, varied manifestations of the violation of human rights, lives of the marginalised and the oppressed and then walk away with camera and film intact, leaving the subjects behind to carry on with the battles of survival in their daily lives.

"I have seen that one tends to get too involved with their lives. It is not only emotionally draining but also deeply disturbing. This is not just for *Follow the Rainbow*. It is also an outcome of the two films on Kashmir I shot—Sanjay Kak's *Jashn-e-Azadi* and Amar Kanwar's *Night of Prophecy*. In the former film, a father is looking for the tomb of his grownup son. In the latter film, a father believes that his son killed on suspicion of being a militant, was innocent. It is impossible to retain objectivity because the degree of involvement is tremendous," he sums up. It needs a lot of courage to face the camera for one who has always found himself behind it. Needless to say that Palit is not wanting in that department.

The film opens with a B&W frame, perhaps a clip from Palit's FTII diploma film *Bhiwandi* (1980), where one gets a fleeting glimpse of the cameraman, more black than white, investing the frame with an aura of intrigue about what one is about to see. When asked what made a young man in his early 20s choose to make his diploma film on Bhiwandi, he says that he had to accompany a journalist friend to Bhiwandi, a small town in Thane district close to Mumbai, who had to do a feature story for *Onlooker* to take photographs. He was shocked by the terrible working and living conditions of the power loom workers of the city and decided to come back and make his diploma film on the subject. Bhiwandi has the largest number of power loom factories in the country where workers, mainly Konkani Muslims, are exploited, underpaid, overworked and harassed by their employers, mostly Hindus. The film was made much before the communal riots in Bhiwandi that happened in 1984. It marked Palit's interest as a student in cinematography towards documentaries and not towards mainstream or off-mainstream feature films.

The narration in Palit's voice-over is not entirely free of emotional tone and pitch, but it is rich in content. The narrative moves back and forth in time, space and subject freely and smoothly. The viewer tries to explore the depth of the film clips—*Voices from Baliapal*, *Eleven Miles* (1992, Ruchir Joshi), *Tales from the Planet Kolkata* (1993, Ruchir Joshi), *For Maya* (1997, Vasudha Joshi), *Jashn-e-Azadi* (Sanjay Kak), *Night of Prophecy* (Amar Kanwar), *King of India* (2009, Arvind Sinha), *Bombay: My City* (Anand Patwardhan), *Kamlabai* (1992, Reena Mohan), *Sacrifice of Babulal Bhuiyan* (1988, Manjira Dutta), and *Forever Young, Bhiwandi* and *Abak Jaye Here* (both directed by Palit himself.) These are just a handful of films he chose to record because "not more than 30 to 40 films of the 100 documentaries I have shot are worth mentioning," he says.

The narrative is dotted with telling comments such as "the documentary is sometimes stranger than fiction"; "beauty is sometimes a hell of a burden" when visuals of a snow-covered Kashmir overlap the voice-over; "truth is sometimes unfocussed and blurred"; "when you are shooting the lives of displaced people, when do you shut off the camera?" while clips of *Jashn-e-Azadi* are framed, "is the cameraman a narrator, a storyteller, an observer, or a voyeur?" he asks, not expecting to answer his own questions. The last question—"should I continue to shoot, or should I look away?" perhaps places him on the edge of decision-making. "I do not even want to know what the answers to my questions are," he later explains.

The clips are voice-overed by his narration where, instead of dwelling on the aesthetics or form of cinematography or on the challenges he faced in the process of shooting or film-making, Palit explains the ethics of cinematographing these films. However, for the viewer, the clips offer an enchanting dossier of versatility in terms of the subjects he has shot, the insights into the issues the films deal with and the rise in the learning curve of the observer that results from a glimpse into the mindset of a creative documentary cinematographer. The 'journey', therefore, is marked more through his significant works than through the awards the films bagged or brought home to him or mundane facts of his childhood and growth which enter smoothly and incidentally over the 'pages' of this celluloid diary.

SUPRIYO SEN

Sen's first film, *Wait Until Death* (1995), was a 54-minute investigative documentary that explored the genocide caused by a stone-crushing factory in a tribal village. As he began his research, Supriyo found that he had become actively involved in the cause. He built up public opinion, mobilized villagers and finally followed the case up to the Supreme Court. In this way, the film reached a framework wider and deeper in scope and impact than it had initially set out to do. It established legal rights of the stone crushing factory workers whose safety had been compromised by the employers leading to tragic death and disease for most at a very young age.

Sen's next film, *The Dream of Hanif* (1997), was commissioned by the television channel Planet. It documented the story of one of the last traditional scroll painters of Medinipur in Bengal. *The Nest* (2000), bagged the National Award for the Best Film on Environment and Conservation and the BFJA (Bengal Film Journalists Association) Award for the Best Documentary in 2001. The 38-minute film is a documentation of the life of Jatin Mahato, whose love for the open-billed stork that fly in droves to nest, mate and breed in and around his home has cut him off from the rest of

Image 5.2. *Way Back Home*

Courtesy: Supriyo Sen

the village. His wife Sushila, three school-going daughters and his son are his sources of support in this lone crusade.

The Nest won the National Award for the Best Environmental Film in 2001. Says Supriyo, "I was fascinated by a feature on the strange life of Jatin Mahato in a Bengali daily. Since then I wished to document him on film. Money was difficult to come by. I put in my own funding and passed the hat around to my friends. Of course, it was not enough but we began the research" he informed. The Mahatos live in Kendua village. His house is located on the Jhargram–Jambani road in Midnapur district of West Bengal. His house looks like the rest in the village, with one difference, come June and thousands of open-billed storks arrive to breed in virtual colonies in the trees in and around Jatin's house. Jatin, now in his 70s, feeds them and his wife pitches in to help.

He made a two-part film on the partition of India entitled *Way Back Home* and produced by Jan Vrijman Fund for a worldwide competition of scripts from the International Documentary Film Festival of Amsterdam. "Since I was a child, my mother has been telling me stories of a village, a river and people she left behind as a girl of eleven. As I grew up, my father explained how the colonial rulers, religious fanatics and political power-mongers cheated the nation. All this made a deep impact on my development as a human being haunted by parents who were cut off from a cherished past for fifty years. For me it was a journey of history, a reconstruction of a lost land through slices of bitter-sweet nostalgia. It was a political journey too. Moving alongside burning houses, a smoke-covered sky and fragmented dead bodies, I wished to discover that country of déjà vu my parents were constantly living in, even while they coped with Calcutta (now Kolkata) for fifty long years. My journey was also to search for that courageous lady, my mother's cousin Kamli Didi, who dared to marry a Muslim at the cost of being cut off from her family, society and community forever," he says.

Hope Dies Last in War (2007), narrates the struggles of the families of some of the 54 Indian soldiers taken as prisoners of war (PoW) during the Indo–Pak war of 1971 who are yet to return home. Their lives are defined by a perennial struggle between hope and despair. But they refuse to give up the crusade for the restitution of basic human rights—the right to live and die in one's own country,

Image 5.3. Damayanti Tambay in a Still from *Hope Dies Last in War*

Courtesy: Supriyo Sen

the right to come back home and the right to a national identity. The fight has been on for nearly four decades. It is a saga of their individual and collective struggle, spanning three generations, to get their men back. It records a tragic stalemate, sufferings of love and shining moments of humanity, courage and hope.

Wagah (2009), a 12-minute documentary by Supriyo Sen bagged the Berlin Today 2009 Award. It was produced by DETAiLFILM. The Berlinale Talent Campus announced the competition inviting film-makers to make a 12-minute short film on the concept and the ideology of 'border'. *Wagah* was short listed among five finalists from 350 entries across 106 countries. *Wagah* is the story of an extraordinary event that takes place at the only border crossing between India and Pakistan. Every evening, thousands of cheering spectators gather to witness a patriotic parade for the ritual closing of the border. "I was fascinated by the way around 25,000 people from both sides of the Wagah border (that draws the metaphorical and political lines between India and Pakistan) in the north, gather in crowds just to watch the parade," says Sen about his inspiration for the film. He further goes on to say, "I discovered that kids, who live near the border, actually run an indigenous business in selling CDs and DVDs of films made on this parade and the watching crowds. My film is a point-of-view depiction by three children of this parade."

JOSHY JOSEPH

Joshy Joseph is low-profile but his portfolio of films is impressive. His films have won four national awards under four different categories on four completely different subjects. *Sarang—Symphony in Cacophony* (1997), won the National Award for the Best Motivational/Promotional Film in 1998. It is an inspiring documentary on a young couple's commitment to revive a valley through organic farming. Sarang or the Sustainable Agricultural Research and Natural Guidance is active in one of Kerala's small villages. In 1999, *Sentence of Silence* won the National Award for the Best Film on Family Welfare. It is a strong film that redefines the family ethos of changing social circumstances of the Indian Christian community the Catholic Church does not grant divorce to. The film resulted in the bringing of a new statute named Indian Marriage Act exclusively applicable to the marriages between Christian men and women.

Image 5.4. Mahasweta Devi Singing at Nandigram

Courtesy: Joshy Joseph

And the Bamboo Blooms (1999), won the National Award for the Best Film on Environmental Issues in 2000. The film is a study on the relationship between the tribals in the Northeast and the bamboo. The flowering of bamboo occurs once in 40–120 year life span depending on the species. This has a devastating effect on the lives of the local population. The rodent population multiplies uncontrollably (bamboo seeds are presumably aphrodisiacs), devouring crops and leaving the farmers bereft of a livelihood. *Wearing the Face* (2000), won the National Award for the Best Investigative Film in 2001. The film probes the 'face' behind the masked faces of Manipuri rickshaw pullers in a humane way. The social fabric, the collective psyche and the economic and political realities of Manipur emerge out as a resultant of this lens-eyewitness account of the illegal rickshaw-pullers who keep their faces veiled for fear of being caught.

Journeying with Mahasweta Devi (2008–09) was an ongoing 51-minute documentary produced by Drik-India and directed by

Joshy Joseph. Joshy's earlier film, *One Day from a Hangman's Life* 2005, was stopped from screening at Nandan II a few years ago, though it drew more crowds than Benegal's *Bose—The Forgotten Hero* (2004). The film captured a day in the life of Nata Mullick, the hangman who pulled the noose around the neck of a rape-and-murder convict Dhananjoy Chatterjee, shortly before he performed the act.

Journeying with Mahasweta Devi, thankfully, is not a biopic though Joshy imaginatively weaves in tiny nuggets the writer-activist-crusader's earlier life through B&W pictures picked out of the family album turning sepia with time. It offers a picture of this rebellious woman, who then 83 years old, could still belt out her favourite Tagore song spontaneously or recite Tagore's famous poem Proshno (The Question) extempore. The opening frames use a clipping from Ritwik Ghatak's last film *Jukti, Tokko O Golpo* (1974). It shows three silhouetted, shadowy dancing figures in black against a white background, symbolizing the three elements in human communication —logic, argument and story. Towards the end of the dance, two figures—'logic' and 'argument'—disappear and only 'story' remains.

When most of Kolkata's intellectuals remained silent, Mahasweta Devi's was the sole dissenting voice. In a letter to DRIK-India, she wrote, "I saw (the film) and was impressed. The treatment is entirely objective. No judgmental attitude towards other questions like whether death by hanging should or shouldn't be there. No moral attitude from the film-maker. No questions about the morality of a death sentence. It is a bare and savage documentation of a day in a hangman's life. It is just another day. Of course, the hangman is deeply concerned as one Dhananjoy every five years means bread and butter for him, but somewhere he also understands. This film actually points towards the reality, which is today in every viewers' life." This brought about the first meeting between the director and his subject.

"I use my cinema as a democratic space where my subject and I are placed on the same platform as equals. Otherwise, it would be difficult for me to make the kind of film I was seeking to make. Mahasweta-di is constantly on the move and that is precisely how I wished to capture her. I am against making a mobile person immobile just for the shooting. I prefer to position myself along and behind the camera instead of inhibiting my subject by bogging her down with my camera. Over two years, we evolved a mutual understanding and she developed respect for me and for my work. *Journeying with Mahasweta Devi* is just a tip of the iceberg of the massive project I have under way."[13]

KRISHNENDU BOSE

Krishnendu Bose, based in Delhi, is totally committed to the environment as a film-maker. He has been making conservation films under the banner Earthcare Films. Commissioned by PSBT-India, the 63-minute ***Tiger—the death chronicles*** (2007), in English with sub-titles takes a holistic look at the real tiger crisis. Travelling through tiger hotspots like Sariska, Panna and Buxa and shot over a period of nine months, the film also looks at states like Madhya Pradesh, Orissa and Goa to explore how they may be trading their tigers and their forests for greater economic revenue. What motivated Bose to make this film? What does he hope to achieve through its wide and repeated screening across the country? What hurdles did he have to cross while making this path breaking film?

Image 5.5. *Tiger—the Death Chronicles*

Courtesy: PSBT

"The tiger is the most magnificent animal that walks the face of the planet. Its largest population is in India. It is at the top of the food chain and a keystone species of the natural world. It has been made into a symbol of conservation efforts in India. Project Tiger was constituted around this animal more than 30 years ago. This was another way to protect the natural world in the name of the tiger. Unfortunately, I saw the decline of this charismatic animal purely for lack of engaged governance and lack of people's will and effort. I felt the need to document this disaster. Major lies had to be nailed. Lies that the state has been telling us for years. This includes its lack of transparency, initiative, policy, that points an accusing finger at the shape of the things to come for the tigers. The story was not of the tiger alone. It was more philosophical and existential. It was the way in which we live and grow. It was also about the world we are changing even as we live in it. All these inspired me to tell the truth, finally. No film has ever told the story of Indian conservation and of the tiger in particular, as this one has attempted to," says Bose.

His film, *Tiger—the death chronicles*, moves freely and tellingly across time and space to try and understand why tigers are rapidly vanishing from India. If things are allowed to go the way they are, resulting from ignorance, negligence, wilful and illegal poaching and hunting, it will culminate in one of the greatest violations of animal rights and a possible toppling of our ecological balance. The tiger population is in real danger of disappearing from the earth.

However, Bose began long back, setting up his independent production unit under the banner of Fluid Head Films, making his first 30-minute documentary called *The Godfathers of Dhanbad* (1988), a current affairs programme about the coal mafia for Doordarshan (DD) in 1988. He made it jointly with Sumit Choudhury, another film-maker. But the most interesting thing about the film is that DD has not aired it at all. "I am confident that had the film been aired in 1988, it would have set the trend of investigative audio-visual journalism through the electronic media which people like Nalini Singh later made famous," says Bose. Next, his company made a 33-minute documentary called *The Revolution and After* (1992). It proves his credo of "experimenting with form to make films away from the cut-and-dried documentary form patronized by established production channels and to grapple with bold and unchartered terrain that are creatively challenging."

Made for INTACH, *The Revolution and After* is a videofilm that traces the growth of the Green Revolution and explores its negative impact on the economic lives of the people. The film makes a convincing statement against the implementation of a modernised, updated methodology at random on a culture that is neither equipped nor prepared to implement it.

"We tried to show that the Green Revolution is a war against nature because it interferes, fights and even questions nature. Conventional technology that has been the common practice among grassroots people is in keeping with nature and also respectful to nature," he says. His next film was the 18-minute *My Camera and I* on Sikkim made by the Department of Tourism, Government of India. It is clearly a tourist-promotional film. But it spells out the maker's love for wild life photography on the one hand and for environment on the other. The film reveals the maker's fine feel for natural colours, natural light and natural sounds making the best use of these while making the film.

In his new 54-minute film—*The Forgotten Tigers* (2014) which Bose has written, edited and directed under his banner of Earthcare Productions produced by the PSBT—Bose, over one year, has captured the secret lives of the tigers living outside the borders of tiger reserves in the country. It has been shot extensively in Uttar Pradesh, Uttaranchal, Madhya Pradesh, Karnataka and Maharasthra.

Image 5.6. A Production Still from *The Forgotten Tigers*

Courtesy: Krishnendu Bose

"Very few know who they are. They are not filmed and put on the famous wildlife documentaries. Tourists and most tiger conservationists do not even know they exist. They are tigers who reside *outside* the famed tiger reserves. That is why I have called the film *The Forgotten Tigers*," explains Bose. The film explores an unknown, virtually 'invisible' world where tigers, with little legal protection and attention, have either gone completely or are going at a fast rate. Thirty per cent of tigers in the country live outside the preserves. Existence is their biggest challenge in these shrinking habitats and corridors. They have to confront the constant conflict with people on the one hand and development on the other.

"With a continued pocketed rise in the tiger population, this conflict will only increase," he adds explaining, "This film is an exploration into the lives of the forgotten tigers." Bose travels the length and breadth of wild life to find out how these tigers survive and what is their long-term future? Do these intrepid tigers teach us something new about conservation? The very fact that the film has captured tigers living out in the open forests and wild areas has been the greatest challenge for Bose who must have risked his life many times during the shooting of the film. It is the cause that is more important than the effect or the risks.

OTHER PILLARS

Many film-makers have been inspired to record on celluloid their perceptions of Indian socio-political reality, human rights violations, assertion of the rights of the marginal, the oppressed and the indigenous people. One among this counter-cinema is Utpalendu Chakraborty's *Mukti Chai* (1977, A Cry for Freedom) shot mainly with a hand-held camera. The film insists that from the time of the passing of the Rowlatt Act till the proclamation of Emergency, individual freedom remained in the grip of repressive forces. Goutam Ghose's *Hungry Autumn* (1974) took off from actual famine conditions in West Bengal in 1974 and analysed the basic situation of agriculture, widespread destitution and its impact on the Indian society. *An Indian Story* (1981) jointly directed by Tapan Bose and Suhasini Mulay probed into the forced blinding of 34 prisoners of Bhagalpur by the police. The film tried to examine the entire pattern of police brutality in India. They later made *Bhopal—Beyond Genocide* (1986) on the Bhopal gas tragedy. The film won the National Award but was kept away from public screening by the government. It was a straightforward, well-researched and painstakingly shot documentary about a great human tragedy that turned technology and industrial development with foreign funding into one of the sickest jokes of the modern world. Real footage of sick and pregnant women, blind men and dying babies helped the film evolve its own strong statement but was banned only to be later rescued by a court order.

CONCLUSION

To sum up, it would be right to recall that the auteur theory, according to Andrew Sarris, is not so much a theory as it is an *attitude*, a table of values that converts film history into directorial autobiography. A strong director imposes his own personality on a film. A weak director allows the personality of others to run rampant. This is precisely the criterion that picks out one director from a crowd of many others to place him under the auteur microscope. Edward Buscombe proposes other ways of looking at cinema.[14] These are (i) the examination of the effects of cinema on society, (ii) the effects of the society on the cinema (influence of ideology, economics, history, etc.) and (iii) a sub-division of (ii), the effects of films on other films.

NOTES

1. Alexander Astruc, "Fire and Ice," *Cahiers du Cinema*(English version), no.1, 70–71, 1966.
2. Andrew Sarris, "Towards a Theory of Film History," in *Movies and Methods*, ed. Bill Nichols, vol. I (Calcutta: Seagull Books, 1993), 237.
3. Meher Pestonji, "Getting Rid of Slumdwellers is Not the Solution," *Express Magazine*, 21 July 1985.
4. Vishwa Priya, "Patwardhan's Bombay, Our City: A Blueprint for Irrational Development," *Deep Focus*.
5. Nandini Ramnath, "Reel Change – Revolution Flows from the Reels of a Camera," *Time Out*, Mumbai, online magazine. Available online at https://mlfblog.wordpress.com/2010/01/. Last accessed on 18 May, 2015.
6. Shuddhabrata Sengupta, "A Long March – Sanjay Kak's Cinema of Rebellion," *The Caravan*, 1 July 2013. Available online at http://www.caravanmagazine.in/arts/long-march. Last accessed on 18 May, 2015.
7. Ibid.
8. Shuddhabrata Sengupta is an artist with the Raqs Media Collective and writes for kafila.org.
9. Ibid.
10. http://srinagar-memoirs.blogspot.in/2007/11/tell-them-tree-they-had-planted-has-now.html

11. http://li261-173.members.linode.com/films/2004/wapsi
12. Nandini Ramnath, "Kashmir Calling," *Time Out*, 9 December 2011. Available online at https://mlfblog.wordpress.com/2010/01/26/theme-parks-reel-change-an-article-in-time-out-mumbai/. Last accessed on 18 May, 2015.
13. Interview with the author.
14. Stephen Heath, "Comment on the 'Idea of Authorship,'" *Screen* 14, no. 3, Autumn (1973): 88 (a comment on Edward Buscombe's paper cited above [footnote 3]).

6
DIALOGUES IN DIVERSITY
Women Film-makers

INTRODUCTION

Documentary cinema was almost exclusively a man's world till around the 1970s. However, change in the direction of the wind brought in more and more women into the field. What does it mean to be a woman and a documentary film-maker? What perspectives and qualities do women alone bring to the screen? And when, if ever, should making films be about being female? The Indian documentary movement today has as many women film-makers as men, if not more since a demographic profile is not possible. The International Association of Women on Radio and Television (IAWRT) hosts an annual festival of films every year on a given theme. Despite its international character, the listing clearly points out the rich contribution of Indian women in terms of both quality and quantity. The title of this chapter—Dialogues in Diversity—is borrowed from the title of their annual festival. The term 'diversity' can be read in several ways—'diversity' stands for women film-makers in a world dominated by men for a long time. It also questions and comments on whether the female point of view is different from a male point of view or whether women tend to make films on certain subjects more than men film-makers do.

Does feminine sensibility differ from male sensibility? Is the feminine aesthetic sense in terms of cinematic image, while reconstructing reality, distanced from such counter-cinema made by men? Do they differ in their choice of subject, theme and issue? Not really, if one were to go by the telling works of women who have shattered the myth of cinema being a male creative field in their efforts at creating counter-cinema. Feminist film-makers such as Manjira Datta,

Reena Mohan, Nilita Vachani, Deepa Dhanraj, Madhusree Datta and the Jamia-based Mediastorm group made their first documentaries around the 1990s. Many of them came from a context of engagement with the women's movement and its politics. Remarkably, at a time when female film-makers were a rarity in mainstream cinema, a number of them began to use documentaries to consciously identify themselves as feminists. For many subsequent film-makers, this opened up several possibilities of how documentaries could become a political way of storytelling.

There are several angles to the woman question so far as the independent documentary movement goes. One angle is documentaries on and around women. The second angle is documentaries made by women. The third is documentaries produced by NGOs and educational institutes either through their own infrastructure and technicians or by commissioning other film-makers, men or women, to make films to further their agendas and/or cause. Directors who tackle women's stories, their problems, struggles and triumphs, are not always women. Men directors have made their arguments lucid, objective and sensitive without trying to draw on melodrama at any point.

Sometimes, packages screened at documentary film festivals spring pleasant surprises. The Roopkala Kendro (West Bengal)'s Social Communication Conference in 2003 brought forth an exciting package from the PSBT. The PSBT pack of films was professionally packaged and presented, each one strictly adhering to the 28-minute format. They offered insights into the known and little known areas concerning women. Among the known areas were—a follow-up on the Ameena child-marriage case in Hyderabad called *Brides of Hyderabad* (2001) directed by K.N.T. Shastry; *Parenting Alone* (2001)—a fresh insight into single parenting in Calcutta by the young Moumita Tarafdar; *Women in Conflict* (2002) by Radhika Kaul Batra; *Seismograph* by Gopi Desai that shed shocking light on how the earthquake has affected the children of Kutch; Meenakshi Rai's *Can't Take It Anymore* (2001) on sexual harassment at the workplace and Anupama Srinivasan's *On My Own* (2002)—a series of interviews with women in Delhi who have opted to live alone, even when they are not married, and after their relationships collapsed. In terms of artistic expression, the films tried to walk the delicate tightrope between aesthetics and social comment. In most cases, such as *Missing Young Women* (2001) or *The Women of Kisani Sabha* (2003), the directors chose to sacrifice aesthetics in favour of social comment when the ambience of the setting, weather conditions, technical infrastructure and most importantly budgetary and time constraints did not offer much scope for aesthetics. The rough edges—at times too rough to offer clarity of vision—notwithstanding, the dedication came across loud and clear.

CRITERIA OF CHOICE

The rough criteria for choosing the directors who qualify as women film-makers acting in the documentary film movement are based on (i) the author's familiarity with the works of these directors, (ii) the author having watched these films more than once, (iii) the authors' interaction with the film-makers and (iv) the consistency in their continuing to make documentary films. This choice in no way ignores or marginalizes the works of women film-makers not discussed in this chapter, but it is the consequence of the author's unfamiliarity with and ignorance of their works. Some of the film-makers discussed here are not making documentary films any more. However, their contribution to the independent documentary movement in India needs to be acknowledged and recognized. Some film-makers who have done excellent work have been kept out of this discussion because they have directed their films jointly with a man. The examples include Sumitra Bhave and Sunil Sukhtankar who have now shifted to feature films, and Kavita Bahl and Nandan Saxena whose brilliant films *Cotton for my Shroud* (2011) and *Candles in the Wind* (2013) have been kept out of this book because the author had no opportunity of watching these films or interacting with the makers. Other films by women documentary makers have found place in other chapters, so the author felt repeating them in this would be needless. Besides, they have not made too many films over time, and they are comparatively less experienced than the ones who find place here.

Ananya Chakraborty Chatterjee

However, some women have made women their beat in choice of subject, to shed light on issues not many bother about. Ananya Chakraborty Chatterjee is one of them. She has made many documentaries exclusively putting forth arguments and raising questions on gender issues. *Gandhari* (1992) described how women have naturalized the silent process of subjugation, suffering and oppression. *Half-Way Home* (1995) explored dimensions of the oppression of a certain group of women who were imprisoned in the Presidency Jail for many years by virtue of an outdated Draconian Act that did more wrong to them than any law would or could. *Uttaradhikar* (1997) dealt with the politics of marginalization of women who are used in the movement but are discarded during power sharing. *Najaayaz* (1998) was on children of sex workers that tried to explore the vulnerabilities of these children and their mothers. *The School That Karmi Soren Built* (1996) traces the development of a Junior High School in the backward pocket of Tulibarh, a village peopled by adivasi tribes where the children of the adivasi population could not go to school because there was not one. Then, one fine day, sunshine came in the form of Karmi Soren, a Santhal widow from Jhargram, who donated her entire land for the development and construction of a school because, through her life experience, she had acquired the awareness that education alone could lead to the uplift of the tribal community.

Understanding Trafficking (2010) won the National Award for the Best Film on Social Issues in 2011. The film tracks the trade across Nepal, Bangladesh and West Bengal in India, through interviews with NGO workers, victims of trafficking, victims who have been rescued and rehabilitated, some pimps and agents who pretend to be social activists, and some women who head organizations working to stop trafficking and rescue innocent victims from this illegal trade. Through captive audiovisual shots that go into forbidden ghettoes of the trade, it shows how trafficking is an integral part of an organized crime with a long human chain that begins with the girl's family, including her parents, and reaches her to the brothel she has been sold to, to live and die there as a sex worker. The film tries to explore the differences between sex work and trafficking, migration and trafficking, etc.

Are these girls 'bad'? Or are they 'good'? Chakraborti Chatterjee's film drives us to redefine the implications of what 'good' or 'bad' means for these tragic victims. The film tracks the trade across Nepal, Bangladesh and West Bengal in India, through interviews with NGO workers, victims of trafficking, victims who have been rescued and rehabilitated, some pimps and agents who pretend to be social activists and some women who head official organizations working to stop trafficking and rescue innocent victims from this illegal cattle trading.

Suhasini Mulay

"A film must portray reality. It may be a lyrical representation or a personal interpretation of an event or even a total figment of imagination but it should be rooted in reality," says Suhasini who has made over 60 documentaries, four of which have won national awards. An actress who made her debut in Mrinal Sen's classic *Bhuvan Shome* (1969) and returned many years later on screen to win the National Award for Best Supporting Actress for her role in Gulzar's *Hu Tu Tu* (1999), Suhasini Mulay has really come a long way. She is a human rights activist, and despite her busy schedule for television, she is already making two documentaries of significance. Suhasini is the daughter of Vijaya Mulay, known as Akka, a founder member of the Film Society of India and a strong activist within the movement in independent and documentary films. Suhasini was born in Patna. She lost her father when she was only three, and their mother brought up the three sisters single-handedly.

The first of the four award winning documentaries, *An Indian Story*, was based on the 1978 Bhagalpur blindings when a set of undertrials lost their vision when acid was forcibly poured into their eyes. The other three included *Bhopal—Beyond Genocide* on the Bhopal gas tragedy, *Citthi* and the fourth one was on the National Art Gallery of India.

"The films that shook me were Federico Fellini's *La Strada* (1954) and Louis Malle's *Les Quatre Cents Coup* (*Four Hundred Blows*, 1959). Film-makers and potential film-makers were frequent visitors. Then I saw S. Sukhdev's *And Miles to Go* (1965)... and I was hooked. I felt that if there was 'real cinema' it was in documentaries and that portraying reality was much more fascinating than a representation of it in fiction," says Suhasini.

"I held the naïve belief that documentaries reflected reality better and could make a significant change that India needed if we had break through this cycle of poverty-hunger-lack of education-lack of power, and its resultant—poverty. The films of Sergei Eisenstein, the cinéma-vérité movement, Vittorio De Sica, and Satyajit Ray in fiction and the works of Robert Flaherty, Joris Ivens,

Bert Haanstra and S. Sukhdev made lasting impressions. Their documentaries made you look at ordinary things in extraordinary ways, and because the faces and people were real they had a much greater impact. Through the documentary, you could analyze a situation, show reality as you saw it, and prove your case. The point had to made, like a lawyer presenting a case. It meant reading, investigating, visiting the actual place of the incident/ thought, come to a conclusion, and then set about trying to convince others through images. The whole gamut of the world—both subjective and objective reflection of reality—can be done with much greater impact through the documentary than through fiction. For a long time, what passed in India as documentaries was pathetic, and therefore the audience was instantly turned off. It was like feeding people a steady diet of badly written pulp fiction and then wondering why they don't understand the beauty of classic literature."[1]

She made a documentary for the Film Division on Motor Neuron Disease. Her *Bhopal—Beyond Genocide* was premiered at the gates of the Union Carbide factory in Bhopal with an audience of 10,000. It was subsequently screened by popular demand innumerable number of times in Bhopal with the gas-affected paying for the projector, etc. They watched it often and would raise issues on the nature of an MNC like Carbide. How did they function? How could they kill people in India and get away scot-free in the USA and India? Why were we suggesting that people do not sign over original death certificates to American lawyers? What alternate occupations could men undertake as now they were too weak to work as labourers, etc. Her first film shot in 1977 on Women's literacy, produced with her own money, was picked up by the United Nations International Children's Emergency Fund (UNICEF) with a print order of 10,000 and it was screened in Afghanistan successfully.

Deepa Dhanraj

Deepa Dhanraj is an award winning film-maker who has been actively involved in the women's movement since 1980. Over the years, she has participated in workshops, seminars and discussion groups on various issues related to women's status—political participation, health and education. Deepa has an extensive filmography spanning nearly three decades that include many series of films on education and health as well as award winning documentaries. *Enough of this Silence* (2008), *The Advocate* (2007), *Nari Adalat* (2000), *Itta Hejje Mundakka Thegiya Bediri Hindakka*, a series of 12 films for elected women in Gram Panchayats (1995), *The Legacy of Malthus* (1994), *Something like a War* (1991), *Kya Hua Is Shahar Ko* (1986) and *Sudesha* (1983) are a few of her films. Her films have travelled to numerous film festivals worldwide. The films have been screened on ARTE, CBC, and SBS. Her films have been invited to festivals such as International Documentary Film Festival Amsterdam (IDFA) at Berlinale, Leipzig, Oberhausen; and Films de Femmes at Creteil, Tampere, Vancouver and Chicago. She has a special interest in education, and she has created special video materials to address the challenges faced by the first-generation learners.

Her outstanding contribution to the independent documentary movement lies in the way in which she has commandeered herself to blend feminist concerns with other democratic movements as an inseparable part of her film-making.[2] *Mokarin* (1981) focussed on the oppressive working conditions of hundreds of maidservants in Pune, and it reported on how these women formed an organization of solidarity to fight for her rights. She also drew attention to two docu-fiction films. *Sudesha* focussed on a village activist involved in the Chipko Forest Conservation Movement in the foothills of the Himalayas. *This is Not a Mere Story* is a sensitive celluloid portrayal of the many faces of gender oppression. Madhumeeta Sinha calls them "early attempts at participatory filmmaking with social activists collaborating in the production and using the film as part of their subsequent change."[3]

Something Like a War (1991) is acknowledged as a film classic across the world. It not only documents but also brings across an incisive attack on the Indian government's anti-woman policies in the family planning programmes targeting rural women as part of a World Bank-funded initiative at the population control immediately following the Emergency. During the Emergency, thousands of rural men were forcibly subjected to vasectomies in makeshift camps. However, the congress in power was rebuffed at the next general elections for its anti-people stand. However, the focus changed and this time, women were targeted for sterilization. Deepa's film is a powerful feminist indictment and response to the new family planning strategies victimizing women in the name of their welfare, using them only as reproductive agents without human feelings and civil and political rights. The film points out that India's Family Planning Programme was first launched in 1952 in collaboration with the Western population control experts. Rural women, considered mainly responsible for the country's bulging population, were set as the targets of forced sterilization.

The narrative intercuts three strands linked to each other. One strand opens up a discussion among a group of women in a rural, feminist health workshop where they are taught about their bodies, discussing their problems of growing up, myths related to menstruation, sexuality and the experience of conditioned shame they suffer from. The second strand closes in on Dr Mehta waging "something like a war" at family planning camps performing 200 tubectomies in a single day in chilling and revolting conditions on women who are hardly aware of what is being done to them having arrived either through force or through cheap endorsements like a couple of buckets of water or money to the husband. The doctor proudly talks of his achievements to the film crew especially about the technique and the speed with which he manages to set his own records! The women already operated on lie on the floor of an adjacent room, in deep pain with a registration number pasted on their foreheads. This track takes the viewer into other city hospitals where patients are shown struggling to find out the reason for the many health problems a given patient has developed post tubectomy. It is discovered that the said women have been injected with Net-EN progesterone-based injectible contraceptive without the consent of the patients. The third track covers conversations with the rural government officials speaking of the pressure of filling the imposed target of women to be sterilized within a given time frame. They confess that if they do not get the targeted number of women sterilized, they might be penalized by delayed salaries, promotions and so on.

The film is an extremely effective critique and analysis offering not only stories of victimized women but also the inhuman and clinically insensitive manner in which the national and international agencies have handed poverty and population, spelling out that the answer to global issues like population growth and access to resources lies not in forcing the poorest of the poor to bear the heaviest burden of social change but in the national and international restructuring of priorities and a more planned and equitable redistribution of resources.

Kya hua is shahar ko (1986) is a pioneering political work of contemporary relevance: communal violence between Hindus and Muslims in 1984 forms the starting point for this film, whose complexity lends it immense political force. The film's historical perspective is provided by a thorough commentary, which gives the camera's particular presence the necessary depth and complexity. The mechanisms of political power struggles, the dynamics among those that hold power, the instrumentalization of economic relations and urban poverty make for a striking analysis, uniquely anticipating the subsequent development of communalist conflicts and the politics of marginalization. *Kya hua is shahar ko?* has been digitalized, restored and screened again for the first time in 27 years as part of the 'Living Archive' project. A DVD including additional historical and contemporary material was released in June 2013. It has some of the scariest footage of real life arson caught on camera during a turbulent period in Hyderabad.

"The film was shot in Hyderabad in 1984. As we were filming the Ganesh procession, a communal riot broke out and continued for 22 days. At the same time, the Governor who was a Congress appointee dismissed N.T. Rama Rao's government and appointed Nadendla Bhaskar Rao as CM. The BJP supported NTR and the Majlis Ittehadul Musalmeen supported the new CM who was being supported by the Congress. NTR asked for one day to prove his majority, the Governor gave the new CM a month for the same task. NTR removed his MLAs to a resort so as to keep them safe from temptation. The riots continued till the vote of confidence was placed in the Assembly to test the new CM's majority. As he could not summon up the numbers, NTR returned as CM. During that period, hundreds of shops and homes were destroyed and many people lost their lives," Deepa elaborates.

In her director's statement on this film, Dhanraj writes: "I am from Hyderabad and at the time I was close to members of a group called Hyderabad Ekta who were working on promoting communal harmony in the old city. The group comprised of activists, academics, intellectuals and residents of the old city. From 1980 the BJP had started holding massive Ganesh processions in the city. Hyderabad Ekta noticed that communal riots inevitably broke out either during or after the Ganesh processions. They felt that making a documentary film that could promote harmony and understanding between communities would be useful for their work and felt that it would be good to start with filming the Ganesh procession and trying to understand why thousands of Hindu youth were attracted to participate in it."

"We were filming for 22 days meeting victims of violence, politicians from the BJP and the Majlis and others. While editing the film, we decide to tell a complex story which would include a historical perspective, analyze political dynamics and show the suffering on daily wage workers who were pushed into destitution by long periods of curfew," she sums up.

Invoking Justice (2011) is another strikingly original political comment on the *Jamaats*. What are Jamaats? In Southern India, family disputes are settled by Jamaats—all male bodies that apply Islamic Sharia law to cases without allowing women to be present, even to defend themselves. Recognizing this fundamental inequity, a group of women in 2004 established a women's Jamaat, which soon became a network of 12,000 members spread over 12 districts. Despite enormous resistance, they have been able to settle more than 8,000 cases to date, ranging from divorce to wife beating to brutal murders and more.

In *Invoking Justice*, Deepa follows several cases, shining a light on how the women's Jamaat has acquired power through (i) communal education and (ii) the leaders' persistent, tenacious and compassionate investigation of the crimes.

There is some extraordinary footage of the Jamaat meetings, where women often shout over each other about the most difficult facets of their personal lives. The women's Jamaat exists to hold their male counterparts and local police to account, and to reform a profoundly corrupt system that allows men to take refuge in the most extreme interpretation of the Qur'an to justify violence towards women.

The 86-minute film shared the award in the Best Documentary (above 40 minutes) category at the MIFF, apart from snagging the Best Editor award for its talented editor, Jabeen Merchant. *Invoking Justice* brings together Dhanraj's decade old practice of drawing links between ideology and mobilization, political awareness and social change. It follows the decision-making process of the one of its kind—the Tamil Nadu Muslim Women Jamaat. Set up in 2004 by Daud Sharifa Khanum, the all-women organization emerged in response to allegations of chauvinism, corruption and abuse of power in the traditional, and all-male Muslim Jamaats. The female Jamaat tackles cases involving women and their families—a possible dowry death, domestic abuse—within the framework of the Sharia code, using their knowledge of the Quran, moral superiority when taking on resistant male gatekeepers of religious law, and wiliness during negotiations with potential allies.[4]

Dhanraj says she was fascinated by the 'organic manner' in which the Muslim women Jamaat had taken shape within the community rather than as a result of outside intervention. She was 'blown away' after attending a Jamaat meeting in 2010. "I fell in love with their energy, humour, and pragmatic understanding of what needed to be done, and their fluency in moving from the register of formal law to customary law, handling Jamaats and the criminal justice system of police stations and courts with equal facility and skill," she says. Dhanraj had previously made *Nari Adalat*, about an alternative legal dispute mechanism that resulted from the state-sponsored Mahila Samakhya programme in Gujarat. "I have anyway always had an interest in issues of justice and the law," she says. Nari Adalat got her thinking about how women deal with the law, create processes and institutions to tackle violence, and manufacture credibility out of nothing. These ideas find their way into *Invoking Justice*, in the meetings between the Jamaat members and their complainants and the often loaded conversations between the members and vacillating or obdurate male Jamaat representatives and police officials.[5]

Dhanraj has successfully turned the documentary format into not only a form of audiovisual expression but also very powerfully as a tool of political consciousness-raising, which began in the 1980s, and it continues even post 2000. *Kya hua is shahar ko?* highlights the economic and social costs of the insidious communalization of Hyderabad, *Something like a War* (1991) and *The Legacy of Malthus* (1994) lay bare the injustices resulting from a target-oriented family planning programme that denies women control over their bodies.

Madhusree Datta

A graduate of the National School of Drama, Delhi, Madhusree Datta came down from Calcutta to make theatre her lifestyle, and is a successful documentary film-maker, balancing her act with issues of topical relevance as well as abstract issues influencing the lives of girls and women. Her first film, *I Live in Behrampada*, was a well-made film that fetched her several awards. It was a sociopolitical feedback on the people of Behrampada, a slum-like neighbourhood near Mumbai's Bandra station where Hindus and Muslims lived peacefully for years together, a peace disturbed by the police atrocities on the minority community post the Hindu–Muslim riots in Mumbai. She then went on to make *Memories of Fear* (1995), concentrating on how girls from a very young age are socially conditioned into different kinds of fear, concrete, abstract and other kinds, which make them grow into suppressed individuals and complexed personalities.

Except *I Live in Behrampada*, Madhusree Datta's films are mainly docu-fiction. Then, why are they included in this study? Because the themes are real and have not documented or even appeared in a fictional form ever before. For example, *Scribbles on Akka* (2000) is a film that could not have been a documentary but it places Akka within a timeless perspective by drawing parallels with the situation of women in present times. The author has excluded the film-maker's *Sundari—An Actor Prepares* (1999) because though it deals with the life of Jayshankar Sundari, a popular male actor who was a female impersonator on the Gujarati stage in the early 20th century in Bombay, it was based on a play by Anuradha Kapoor, and therefore it should be read as a fictional biography of the actor.

Her second film, *Memories of Fear*, received the National Award for the Best Documentary Film in 1996. "The film is an attempt to capture the process of socialization of the girl-child to the very concept of impending violence she is vulnerable to at any given point of her life. I have used four parallel narratives to trace the growth of the girl-child through different age-groups," says Madhusree. "Through this film, I aspired to explore the interplay between sexuality, construction of fear, and the average woman's own contribution to the system which continues to slight all women." The film tries to capture the abstract emotion of internalized fear in the girl child through concrete visual images and sound, fictionalizing non-dramatic incidents intercut with the first person accounts bound to each other only by the universal experience of female fear.

Memories of Fear tries to contribute towards a better *reality* of the intended fear, rather than trying to make the film itself a better *vision* of that reality. It reinforces the inescapable, unpalatable truth that fear, when created through social and psychological means, and when directed only on a particular gender, defines itself as the first rung in the ladder of violence against women. But rightly, it does not offer either a solution or a remedy. These lie within women themselves.

Memories of Fear opens on a note of fun. A group of college girls are off on an excursion by train. They indulge in a bit of harmless adam teasing and singing but the lecturer stops them. A toughie walks up to a window and clutches the wrist of one of the girls. "Can't you behave decently?" asks the angry teacher instead of taking on cudgels against the guilty party.

From closing in on the drawing of a pierced heart on the outside wall of the railway bogie, the camera cuts to monkey tricks in a park. Further down, a couple sit talking, distinctly uncomfortable with each other. A couple of goons walk up, demanding money as a price for allowing them to 'make love' in a public place. They pay up and walk away, dejected. A collage of images like these is interspersed with real life interviews with women. "What is the use of being beautiful?" rues a once-beautiful, middle-aged woman wearing a deadpan expression, quite plainly. "I never face the mirror to look at myself any more" she adds, in response to a husband whose philandering ways her beauty could not put a halt to. Her husband walked out of the marriage after 21 years. Another younger woman says "I was so conditioned against talking to any male by my own mother that, as I grew up, I felt scared of my own cousins only because they happened to be male. Till this day, my parents are in panic about what will happen to me if I step out. Of course, I am too terrified to even try." She does not seem worried about her claustrophobic life.

Is fear a gender issue? Yes, says Madhusree Datta who has directed and scripted the 57-minute docu-fiction, *Memories of Fear*, which has received the National Award for the Best Documentary Film of the Year at the 43rd National Film Awards. "The film is an attempt to capture the process of socialization of the girl-child to the very concept of impending violence she is vulnerable to at any given point of her life. I have used four parallel narratives to trace the growth of the girl-child through different age-groups" says Madhusree. "Through this film, I aspired to explore the interplay between sexuality, construction of fear, and the average woman's own contribution to the system which continues to slight all women."

Memories of Fear tries to capture the abstract emotion of internalized fear in the girl child through concrete visual images and sound, fictionalizing non-dramatic incidents intercut with the first person accounts bound to each other only by the universal experience of female fear.

The society we live in creates a condition in which every element of a girl's life appears either potentially threatened or actually threatened. The most terrifyingly helpless feeling is that of recognizing that some danger is looming, but of not knowing exactly what that danger might be or what can be done to forestall it. Madhusree says, through her film, that there is no danger at all, adding, through a mixed collage of images and words, that the only danger is the danger that comes of being born a woman. *Memories of Fear* succeeds in getting its message across through subtle understatement and also through a designedly skewed narrative that is part fiction and part fact.

Fear itself is a form of violence perpetrated on the female of the species, states the film. This fear is egged on, fired with the imagination of a dominant patriarchal ideology that concretizes itself through domestic violence like wife and daughter abuse, through dowry and rape, humiliating the persona of the woman and marginalizing the humanity of her existence. Brick by cinematic brick, Madhusree builds a collage of ordinary, everyday happenings to share her personal conviction that fear in a woman is neither essential, nor fixed, nor genetic but it is created, sustained and manipulated by a patriarchal culture that is subconsciously threatened with the possibility of strong, brave and assertive women.

The film focusses attention on trying to construct collective identity through representations achieved by repeated screenings for a heterogeneous audience.

Is this fear the result of a patriarchy's naturally protective attitude towards the 'weaker' sex? Or, is the fear born out of the threat fearless women might pose to a patriarchy by proving that the so-called 'weakness' of the female is also conditioned by patriarchy and its dictates.

Scribbles on Akka, also a docu-fiction, has brought to light a precursor not only to the much-hyped women's liberation movement but also to Freud himself, is by itself an achievement of no mean merit. 'Mahadevi Akka' informs Datta "challenged social norms and discarded traditional notions of femininity in ways explosive enough to shock both men and women of her time. Why, she might have done the same had she lived today. Because, even now, we rarely find her kind of woman who is not afraid to live out, physically and spiritually, the courage of her convictions. She shocked the entire society of her time with her ideas and with her sensuous poems. Today, she is a presiding deity and an icon for many women, both among the educated and among the less fortunate. From painters to papad makers, Akka inspires women with her rousing *vachanas* (form of rhythmic writing in Kannada) or poems, throwing a long rope bridge across centuries so they can climb across. Her ideas, her questions and her actions may just as well have come from a modern-day feminist."

Datta created almost a new *genre* in cinema through her *Scribbles on Akka*—the *genre* of the abstract docu-fiction—broadening the historical parameters of the film to throw it open to the subjective interpretation by different sections of the audience—men and women. One might just accept it as a piece of pure fiction and find it exciting and interesting. Another may treat it as a biographical documentary that explores unknown areas of history within which lay the first seeds of a woman's inner consciousness which rouses her to shed her clothes in search of god. A third would perhaps look at the film as a multi-layered piece of abstract art which, on face value, may mean nothing, or everything, depending on how he/she interprets it. Journeying through the countryside of Udutadi in Karnataka with her camera (A. Mukul Kishore and R.V. Ramani), Datta tries to explore the meaning of Akka's denial and her asceticism through the works of contemporary painters who have identified the poet through their personal creative work. Nilima Sheikh, a Baroda-based painter, paints Akka as a solitary naked figure against a stark red background on a huge canvas. She says (in the film) that even if Akka had not lived, "we would have invented her because Akka is the icon we needed." Vaidehi, a contemporary poet concedes with admiration, "Everything I write seems to have already been written by Akkamahadevi."

7 Islands and a Metro (2006) is a hard-hitting and lyrical take on Mumbai's turbulent story, where the city's islands become metaphors for seven significant moments in its life to generate a provocative mix of images, anecdotes and information. The film is structured around imaginary conversations and debates between its narrators, Ismat Chugtai and Saadat Hasan Manto—the two legendary writers who lived and worked in the metropolis. This gives a unique historical and aesthetic dimension to the film because they often dot their narrative with references to their literary works. Sistema de Avalúo de Aspirantes al Magisterio (SIAAM) explores the various hues of the city's landscape and culture as reflected in the everyday life of the citizen and the historical acts over the 400 years of the city's existence that have shaped and informed this citizenry. In this sense, it could perhaps be called a docu-fiction or rather a documentary that uses famous literary figures who are no longer around as its framing device and a bridge to the city's past.

"The film is a celebration of formal cinematic experimentation as a tool of political film making, bringing together eminent writers, visual artists and mainstream political figures. Theatrically released in Mumbai in 2006, it has been widely screened at film festivals and on international television. The multi-lingual Bombay, the Bombay of closed mills, of popular culture, sprawling slums and real estate onslaughts, the metropolis of numerous ghettos, the El Dorado. It narrates the tale of the city through a tapestry of fiction, cinema vérité, art objects, found footage, sound installation and literary texts," says Datta.

Paromita Vohra

Paromita Vohra is a film-maker, writer and media activist whose work has focussed on issues of gender, politics, urban life and popular media. Her 15 years in film-making have included work in documentary, television drama and music shows, feature film and short fiction. Her first film *Annapurna: Goddess of Food* (1995) was about a woman's organization of food workers. *Cosmopolis: Two Tales of a City* is a diptych. One part was titled *Defeat of a Minor Goddess* (2004). In this film, Annapurna, the Goddess of Food, and Lakshmi, the Goddess of Wealth, battle one another for primacy in the city of

Mumbai. Other films she has made are *Q2P* (2006), *Where's Sandra* (2005), *Unlimited Girls* (2001) and *A Short Film About Time* (1999). She also coordinates a project called 'A Woman's Place', a collective of women from different countries using media to bring about a social change.

Her 25-minute short film in English, *Annapurna: Goddess of Food*, is in the lanes and bylanes of central Bombay's mill area, and the film is a portrait of a women's cooperative called Annapurna. Started in 1975 by 14 *khanawalwalis*—women who prepared meals for migrant workers, thus earning the name food lady—the organization has today swelled to a membership of 150,000, and it has its own credit cooperative bank, short-stay home and a catering centre. The film observes the everyday life of these women and intertwines it with the story of how the organization grew. An exploration of the politics and economics of women's work, the film is a tribute to the fearless women who started Annapurna, and the feisty women who carry it on. The film was part of an international series on women's initiatives entitled *Half the Sky: Women of the World*, made for the Beijing conference in 1995. It has been telecast in 11 countries.

Nearly 10 years later, she made another 12-minute film called *Defeat of A Minor Goddess*. This film was made for a Mumbai city festival called the Kala Ghoda Festival. Several film-makers were invited to make a film on food and the city, interpreting the theme, as they liked. "It was obvious that the idea was perceived as having warm and fuzzy meanings and I really did not feel inclined to pursue myths of the city's marvelous melting pot culture its diversity and so on, when what I see around me is a growing segregation and fragmentation, a marked mutual intolerance," elaborates Vohra.

She goes on to inform, "It was a chance remark by a friend that made me think of this theme of vegetarian buildings. While driving past a restaurant a friend of mine mentioned I wouldn't like it as it was vegetarian—at which point I remembered that the entire upscale neighbourhood of Walkeshwar was vegetarian—the restaurants and the residential buildings. So the film became an exploration of this phenomenon: food politics as an understanding of intolerance and the meanings of public and private space. Along the way I also remembered that someone had told me a story about a goddess who had blessed Bombay. On considerable enquiry I could not trace this story to any source or temple or known figure so I decided to make up my own story about the goddesses Annapurna and Lakshmi battling it out over the city. To my mind they represented the shift in the idea of wealth—from plenitude to money. But their personas too were important to me—the liberal Annapurna being a bit naïve and silly and the street-smart Lakshmi being a bit prim and sly under the guise of practicality. Sadly however, thanks to the total lack of distribution and exhibiting network for such short films that deal with little-known ethnic questions, including some on food, none of us get a chance to watch them."

Vohra goes on to say: "As an exercise in storytelling, the film also related to my basic love of fantasy, kitsch and popular culture, my enjoyment of mixing fiction with non-fiction to tell a story of ideas rather than events. The film did confront some challenges, not only the token budget; for one, how to anthropomorphize goddesses without mocking religion, with affection, not contempt; for another, how to talk to the vegetarian segregationists openly, without judging what they say; yet making my stand clear."

She has written, produced and directed *Q2P* (2006), a film about toilets, gender and urban development, *Where's Sandra* (2005), a film about sexual and community stereotyping of Christian women, often referred to as 'Sandra from Bandra' in Bombay (for the Bandra Citizens Trust), *Work In Progress* (2004) about the World Social Forum, which took place in Bombay in 2004 (for WSF India Trust), *Cosmopolis: Two Tales of a City* (2004), is a film that probes the myth of Bombay's cosmopolitanism through the politics of land and food. The film won an award at the Indo-British Digital Film Festival. *Unlimited Girls* (2002), is an exploration of what feminism means to different people in urban India. It won the Feminist News award at the Women's Film Festival in Seoul; *A Woman's Place* (1998), a film about women's legal strategies in India, South Africa and the USA (for PBS); *Annapurna: Goddess of Food* (1995) about an organization of women food workers in Bombay's textile mill area, which has been broadcast in 10 countries (made for the Beijing conference).

Morality TV aur Loving Jehad: A Thrilling Tale (2008) is a 26-minute documentary by Paromita Vohra, a film-maker, writer and media activist whose work is touched with humour and satire. She focuses mainly on gender, urban life and popular media. *Cosmopolis—Two Tales of a City* is a diptych. One part, *Defeat of a Minor Goddess* is about a fictitious fight between Annapurna, the Goddess of Food and Lakshmi, the Goddess of Wealth for primacy against the backdrop of Mumbai. Other films are *Q2P* (2006), *Where's Sandra* (2005), *Unlimited Girls* (2001) and *A Short Film about Time* (1999). She coordinates a project called A Woman's Place, a collective of women from different countries that uses media for social change.

She has worked extensively with young people. As a founding member of A Woman's Place Project, an international collection of women using media for a social change, she has co-coordinated a 2-year exchange project between teenage girls in Bombay and New York. The project focussed on media, identities and politics with an emphasis on creativity as a means of understanding and clarifying politics. As part of this sort of work, she has executively produced several audio documentaries, through workshops with young people, and some of these have been broadcast on community radio stations.[6]

Morality TV aur Loving Jehad: A Thrilling Tale realizes the impact of news programmes on television on some of the victims who unwittingly see themselves as the subject of these so-called headlines that capitalize on sensationalization. It is not a feminist film. It is an investigative film on how the media can be manipulated by some sections of the administration on the one hand and how the media itself can take advantage of the same administrators who promised it a break story as a sensational scoop. Anshu and Bittu, lovers, eloped after they were shown across television channels on Operation Majnu. However, when the noise died down, the young boy and girl came back and the respective families felt that getting them married would silence the gossip mills.

Morality TV aur Loving Jehad: A Thrilling Tale looks beyond the frames that weave the frenetic tapestry of Breaking News on India's news channels to uncover a town's complex dynamics—the fear of love, the constant scrutiny and control of women's mobility and sexuality, a history of communal violence, caste brutalization and feudal equations. Assuming the tone of pulp fiction and tabloid features, it examines the legacy of this kind of storytelling, from the relishing accounts of true crime magazines like *Manohar Kahaniyan* to the double morality of pulp detective fiction to the tabloid news on Indian TV, to unfold a thrilling but disturbing tale of its own.

Says Paromita Vohra, "I have had a troubled relationship with the idea of the expose, with an 'investigative' story that will finally reveal and fix the culprits from the time I began making documentary films. I felt that though self-aggrandizement and easy understanding are inherent in such stories, they are also wrought with problems. I felt it was a violent idea that needed to be executed seriously. The complexity of such situations needed to be understood properly. I felt this shows that we do not really live in a world of pure justice and democracy because when the media (television) and/or the police speak this language, they also speak a language heavy on morality, light on ethics."

The film justifies cinema as a rich visual medium with a virtual flood of images, repeated shots of multiple television screens, collages of cheap romance magazines that sell like hot cakes, heart-shaped pink balloons filling the skyscraper, to close in on the history of Meerut that has always been bedrock for sensational stories. There is a flashback to the 1987 Hashimpura killing of 42 Muslims who were shot dead with their bodies dumped into a canal but have not got justice till date. The film closes on notes of the famous song from Julie, which goes "My Heart is Beating" on the soundtrack. Anshu and Bittu came back and their families married them off.

Reena Mohan

Reena Mohan's *Kamalabai* (1992) (the first screen actress in India who was 88 years old during the making of the film) is still remembered vividly by those who saw it. It is a biographical documentary on Indian cinema's first female star *after* Dadasaheb Phalke's little daughter. It is filled with humour, satire and pathos as Ranjan Palit's camera follows the old woman in her daily chores. Kamalabai gets fed up with the paraphernalia of being in front of the camera. She wants some other excitement and asks cheekily, "What's the programme for this evening?" The amused director teases her saying, "The camera is on!" Kamalabai, the protagonist, the actress, thinks for a moment and replies, "Ooh... the camera is on!"

Reena Mohan is also one of the best documentary editors, and she has won many awards for editing. *Skin Deep* (2008) explores the patriarchal construction of body images and their impact on the consciousness and lives of women of diverse ages and social backgrounds. With nuance and empathy, it reveals the triumphs and traumas that women experience when almost every aspect of their lives is shaped through the power encoded in notions of beauty and body image.

Skin Deep takes us through a vast landscape—Tamil Nadu to West Bengal, Chennai to New Delhi, and beyond—looking for (and at) the various modes/models in which the female body finds acceptance in Indian society. There are these six extremely interesting women, whose experiences are presented to us in the form of revealing 'daily life' footage juxtaposed with direct-to-camera responses to questions that the film-maker poses to them. The young Sunila, who is a shy but quietly confident body builder; Neha, another college-going teenager who is relaxed about most things, except her appearance, and she wants to seriously pursue modelling as a career; Rachel, who is a well-known ex-model now running an ad agency breaks for us several beauty myths and reveals how she coped with the short modelling career and the traumas of ageing; Jyothi is a scholar in folk literature and a theatre activist who agonizes about having to remain backstage because of her dark skin and belonging to a 'low' caste; Asha is a beautiful, rich, happily married, middle-aged woman who confronts ageing with plastic surgery and getting shattered in the process; Paro is a successful Mumbai-based film-maker who reveals (and disdains) the frustrations that arise from the attitude that others, even friends, have towards her fat body. Four-year-old Maya is comfortably seated in front of a mirror in the act of a make-up/over. For her, lipstick and eye liners are already accepted tools of beautification though being clean and beautiful has little difference. This initial dramatization is a pointer that most of what is to come might be a drama! *Skin Deep* stands out in pointing out to all women everywhere how deeply we, as little girls, as teenagers and as grown-up women, have internalized the concepts of beauty and physical attractiveness constantly dictated and designed by patriarchal norms.

On an Express Highway (2003) is a short documentary, which traces the journey of a successful business woman renouncing the world for the austere life of a Jain ascetic. This film though biographical in nature is reconstructed through interviews with family members and friends and photos of the protagonist from the family album. However, when compared with films like *Kamalabai* and *Skin Deep*, this film looks very much like any commissioned film and slightly propagandist by nature, which could offer the wrong reading of trying to promote the whims and fancies of an extremely affluent young woman with a successful career who suddenly decides to become a Jain priestess.

Nishtha Jain

Nishtha Jain was born in New Delhi, India. She studied film direction at the FTII, Pune. Since 2002, she is working as an independent film-maker based in Mumbai. From her first film *City of Photos* (2005) to *Gulabi Gang*, she has been passionately engaged in the lives of ordinary people in lesser known areas and on lesser known issues. Her films have received several international awards, and they have been extensively shown in international film festivals, broadcast on international TV networks and regularly shown in schools and colleges in India and abroad. Her other films are *Family Album* (2011), *At My Doorstep* (2009), *Lakshmi and Me* (2008), *6 yards to Democracy* (2006) and *Call it Slut* (2005).

Lakshmi and Me is an eye-opening, 59-minute documentary. Jain tracks and explores the flux in the relationship between the director and her subject that is Nishtha and Lakshmi, breaking the hierarchy between the two. Lakshmi works as a domestic maid in Nishtha's home. Produced by Raintree Films and presented by Finland-based Steps India, *Lakshmi and Me* got a nomination for

Image 6.1. *Gulabi Gang*

Courtesy: Nishtha Jain

the Silver Wolf Award at the IDFA. It premiered in Mumbai on February 3, 2008. Jain has earlier made *City of Photos*, which looks at the change in the ubiquitous photo studios in small-town India, and *6 Yards to Democracy* on the fatal tragedy of a stampede in Lucknow during the distribution of sarees to women in an election campaign.

6 Yards to Democracy also won the best documentary award at the Birds Eye View Film Festival, London, 2007. Her sudden awareness of the maid who worked in their home motivated her to go behind the façade of this 20-year-old young woman. The camera closes in on Lakshmi in the opening sequence showing her performing a religious ceremony in Mumbai and then going off to work in different houses in the neighbourhood.

The turning point comes when Lakshmi elopes with her boyfriend that her father does not approve of. Soon after she delivers a girl child, her relationship with her husband turns sour. Her story is woven into against the backdrop of the backbreaking, thankless, poorly-paid chores she has to go through, forcing her, like millions of anonymous maids across the country, to age much before their time. The problem for Jain, she confesses, is that as film-maker, she remained dogged by the very uneasy question of whether Lakshmi allowing her to become the subject of Jain's film was forced or was a voluntary because Nishtha after all was Lakshmi's employer who it might be insecure for the maid to refuse.

At one point during the film, one does not see Lakshmi at all because in real life, she had gone missing. Jain also decided at the editing stage to clip out some lines of Lakshmi as an afterthought that perhaps Lakshmi might regret having been so open about her thoughts and feelings in the film that would be watched by an unsuspecting but perhaps judgemental audience.

"At one point of time, Lakshmi disappeared, so you can see she is missing from the film. We also left out a lot of footage, especially as we felt that Lakshmi may have said something she would regret later," says the film-maker. However, Lakshmi, as the film shows, is made of stern stuff and is incredibly candid on camera. "Before every shot, I would ask myself, is this valid? Can I shoot this? However, throughout, it was Lakshmi who would make the call. She would decide whether we could shoot this or not and we went along," says Jain.

In fact, it is the acceptance of Jain and her camera by all the people in Lakshmi's life that makes the film an absorbing tale, far more compelling than all the reality shows doctored for television these days. What was palpable was Lakshmi's desire to share her life with someone who cared enough to ask. "She had a strong, strong desire to tell her story—about her struggle from being a rag-picker and how she started working after her mother died. She also liked the formality of the shooting. She would say happily '*aaj* shooting *hai*' (we are shooting today), or tell her neighbours that we were coming to shoot in her neighbourhood," recalls Jain.

While initially the film was only about Lakshmi, Iikka Vehkalahti of Steps India suggested that Jain look at it from the perspective of an employer as well. That is when Jain realized she had been interacting with a virtual stranger for the last 5 years. "I saw a different Lakshmi during the religious ceremony. She was confident, even bossy, ordering people around—not the paragon of diplomacy I knew for the last five years. There was clearly a big disconnect between Lakshmi's working and non-working, everyday life."

At another level, the film also makes a gentle dig at the employer–employee equation, as it examines the behaviour of Lakshmi's employers. One employer spoke of the way she had rescued the girl from her rag-picking work, referring to her 'destiny' that places her where she is. Jain has not spared herself either: "In one scene, I seem like such a nag about the teacups and my editor took it out because 'I didn't sound nice', but we later decided to put it back into the film. Just because I control the camera, I can't paint myself white."

As Smriti Nevatia, producer at Raintree Films put it: "Having a maid has freed women, but the issue is how to treat them? How does one free the domestic maid and her kids in turn?" Even while the film was being made, its crew would discuss the issue. Housemaids are beginning to get organized and demanding an improvement in their working conditions, along with formal rights like leave, medical benefits, provident funds and pensions. *Lakshmi and Me* is a gentle reminder that this invisible worker must get her due—as a worker, as a woman and as a human. The process must begin at home.

Gulabi Gang follows the Gulabi Gang—an unusual group of rural women—the badlands of Bundelkhand in central India. It is a place of desolation, dust and despair. Led by the energetic and charismatic Sampat Pal, they travel long distances to fight for the rights of women and Dalits. They encounter resistance, apathy and corruption, even ridicule. Sometimes, whole villages connive against them to protect the perpetrators of violence. The film pulls us into the centre of these blazing conflicts, and it uncovers a complex story, disturbing yet heartening. It is a hope that this film discovers, as it follows the Gulabi Gang, an unusual group of rural women. The film was internationally premiered at IDFA, Amsterdam, in 2012. It won the award for the Best Film at Muhr Asia/Africa Documentary, Dubai International Film Festival, 2012, and also the winner of the Best Documentary, Kortfilmfestivalen, Grimstad, Norway, 2012.

"This spontaneous uprising of women in these villages is very different in tone and manner from the urban movements that we are familiar with. *The Gulabi Gang* has come to represent a kind of 'practical' rural feminism that's trying to grow within the mores of rural patriarchy. There's something taking place here that challenges many of our easy urban feminist assumptions; the ambiguities and dissonances, in fact, making it a phenomenon worthy of a film. I realized within days of meeting with the Gulabi Gang that my film will be a dialogue between these different feminisms which sometimes overlap and sometimes are at odds with each other," says Nishtha.

CONCLUSION

There are dozens of women, and men, who have ventured into documentary films but rarely have the chance to venture into their second film because of funding issues. *Aparajita* (2006) by Kanupriya Vijayvargiya is an interesting 4-minute animation film on how a bride-to-be puts her foot down about dowry demands. Another Indian film *Kaveri* (2011) by Shilpa Munikempanna unspooled the sad tale of 13-year-old Kaverii whose carefree world turns upside down when she attains puberty that marks the end of her formal education and the beginning of an early marriage that will trap her forever. Shabnam Virani's 4-minute film *BOL* screened earlier across the world is part of a larger celluloid essay on domestic violence in India. It was a public service television campaign on the issue of domestic violence; these spots instigate a range of people to 'speak out'. India's Sonia Jabbar in her 65-minute film *Autumn's Final Country* (2003) unspools the story of four women who have suffered displacement, reveals an intimate dimension of the Kashmir conflict and raises questions about patriarchal values, communal identities, patriotism and war.

Shoojit Sircar and Gary's 5-minute music video *Mann ke Manjeere* (2000) remains as topical as it was around a decade ago when it was first screened. It sings out a special anthem about a woman who reconstructs her life after a long period of having suffered domestic violence. The script is based on a true story of a woman who now drives a truck to make a living for herself and her daughter. It remains an all-time favourite with Prasoon Joshi's lyrics sung by Shubha Mudgal and visuals provided by the powerful performance of Mita Vashisht.

In 2005, children of sex workers in Kolkata's Sonagachi red light district came together to form their own collective, ('We Are Foot Soldiers'), drawing inspiration from the work that their mothers have been doing to demand their right to sex work as work. The film journeys through the lives of five *Amra Padatik* (2005) members whose entangled realities do not paint a picture of helplessness but of political assertiveness and social consciousness. This film, jointly directed by Oishik Sircar and Debolina Dutta, won the third Prize at the Jeevika Film Festival last year. The idea for this film came out of a year-long research project funded by Child Rights and You (CRY). Interestingly, the directors are practicing human rights lawyers.

Dr Lokendra Arambam, chairperson of the United Nations Association of Manipur, is a renowned theatre person. Through *Soldiers in Sarong* (2005), he lifts one layer after another of the slow but steady torture of the women of Manipur leading up to an analysis of protests led by a coalition of local women's organizations. These have since been escalating, primarily demanding the repeal of the Armed Forces (Assam and Manipur) Specials Powers Act, 1958. This legislation gives sweeping powers to the army of detaining any person for months without legal redressal on the suspicion of being a militant or a supporter to the militant cause. Why did some elderly women strip as a way of protest? What is the present situation for women in Manipur? Why has the Manorama Devi rape and murder been swept under the bloodied soil of the land? These are questions raised within the film and some of the answers come up seamlessly.

Paradise on a River of Hell (2002) jointly directed by Abir Bazaz and Meena Gaur won a Special Recognition Award at the Karachi Film Festival in 2003. Produced by PSBT, it opens with memories of one of the directors, Abir Bazaz, who looks back on the ruins and debris of a land where he spent his childhood and adolescence, with memories washed with the tears of loss. It is no longer livable because the women do not know whether the men will come home or not, and the men are uncertain not about their future, but about their present time. It is a beautiful film that constantly confirms that aesthetics and social comment can create a happy marriage within the documentary.

More than a decade has passed in which the work of women directors, both fiction and documentary, art-house or commercial cinema across the world sharply suggests a subtle but strong shift from films consciously or unconsciously imitating films directed by men or picking up a woman's cause or a woman's agenda as the message of their films. Most women directors do not quite care for the word 'women' used as a prefix to the word 'director' because they feel this might ghettoize them further into a gender trap. However, the present focus highlights an important feature of cinema—compared to men directors, women directors can almost be counted on one's fingers, so unless they are given special focus at least for another couple of decades, they will not find space for showing their work to a discerning audience.

NOTES
1. Interviewed by the author for the cover story in *Dignity Dialogue* in 2006.
2. Madhumeeta Sinha, "Witness to Violence: Documentary Cinema and the Women's Movement in India." *Indian Journal of Gender Studies* 17 (2010): 365.
3. Ibid.
4. Nandini Ramnath, "Deepa Dhanraj – Justice League," *LiveMint and The Wall Street Journal*, 15 February 2014. Available online at http://www.livemint.com/Leisure/1R2rO5eWbRzZdDbqUsxWXI/Deepa-Dhanraj--Justice-league.html
5. Ibid.
6. C.V. provided by Paromita Vohra to the author.

7
POSITIVE DOCUMENTARIES ON SUSTAINABLE DEVELOPMENT

INTRODUCTION

Sustainable development is the development that meets the needs of the present without compromising the needs of future generations to meet their own needs. It contains two key concepts: (i) the essential needs of the world's poor which should be given overriding priority and (ii) the idea of limitations posed by the state of technology and social organization on the environment's ability to meet present and future needs (Brundtland, 1987). Sustainable agriculture is a system that can evolve indefinitely towards greater human utility, greater efficiency in resource use and balance with the environment favourable to humans and most other species (Harwood, 1990). Sustainable development involves devising a social and economic system that ensures that the goals of (i) rise in real income, (ii) rise in the standards of education, (iii) improvement in national health and (iv) advancement in the quality of life are achieved (Pearce, Makandia and Barbier, 1989).[1]

Documentary film-makers have long realized the power of cinema to spread awareness, concern, information and education about sustainable development through well-researched documentary films. There are several ways documentary film-makers go about making films that contain positive stories on sustainable development. The first is to make a self-funded film that is free from pressures placed by external funding sources. The second way is to seek organizational sponsorship and/or support to make the film. The third way is when organizations committed to a given cause that falls within the scope of sustainable development create a separate cell to make films. Organizations might also commission independent film-makers to make films on a given project.

The difference between the cinema of sustainable development and other kinds of documentary films lies in that this needs total commitment of the film-maker and his team so either activists jump onto the film-making bandwagon or film-makers who make such films become activists along the way.

SOME EXAMPLES

An example of an organization making films on sustainable development is the Centre for Science and Environment's series of films on water under the common title *Changing Currents* that forms a compilation of 28 films drawn from across the world. "Visual images often have greater impact than written words. These video resources create awareness and understanding on issues of water—its 'scarcity', pollution, politics and management. They provide 'real life' examples, which learners can relate to," says the brochure. One might cite the example of *Plumbing the Rights—Part 1* of this series. This 26-minute film in Hindi focuses on the issue of water as a common property and a right that is indistinguishable from the right to life. The film documents local communities from India and South Africa striving to maintain this right in the face of official opposition.

Another film *Tell-Tale Signs* explores the significant subject of climate change and its impact on the availability of water in Odisha in India and Mozambique in South Africa. The film puts forth a strong case for communities and official agencies to work together to adapt to changing climate. *Pumping Pressure* documents the plight of people affected by mining in South Africa and a case study in Gujarat where communities have found new ways of catching rainfall showing how water scarcity has made farmers innovate.

On the other hand is the individual effort of Susanta Biswas, a documentary film-maker, who exclusively concentrates on making films on sustainable development. Though his films are mostly produced by the Government of West Bengal to publicize their programmes on sustainable development, his films have featured in several documentary festivals and been positively panned by critics. His film *Jal Dharo Jal Bharo* (Preserve Water, Reserve Water) produced by the state government of Trinamool Congress, within its 11-minute footage, deals with water resource management in water-scarce regions of West Bengal where the population depends primarily on agriculture. The lack of adequate water resources has invested the local's lives with uncertainty and increased their insecurity. *Jal Dharo Jal Bharo* is an initiative undertaken by the state government to provide a replicable framework to solve this ecological inequality in the face of the impact of climate change.

However, all government-produced/sponsored documentaries are grossly propagandist as one discovers in *Jal Dharo Jal Bharo*. It is an unabashed promotional film that describes the government project asking locals not to waste water but to preserve it. No feedback from local inhabitants to find out about the functioning of the project has been documented. In fact, the only voice-over narration is by the director who expounds the different bodies under the government involved in the project. The credit titles at the end of the film list names of high-ranking officers under different administrative offices of the project. There is even a 'manufactured' folk song-and-dance number to add to the aesthetic value of the film. There is no countering comment, or questions or opinions, on the viability of the project from experts on the subject. In other words, the total absence of objectivity tinges the film as being made with propagandist intentions.

The same argument applies to the previous Communist Party of India-Marxist [CPI (M)]-ruled government that made similar films under the auspices of the Roopkala Kendro; the West Bengal government under the CPI [M] rule had set-up as an educational institute for film-making. This ran counter to its aim as defined by Anita Agnihotri, IAS, who headed the Roopkala Kendro till some years ago and was instrumental in organizing the Social Communication Conference held annually in Kolkata in February. "The main objective of the festival is to interact with the common and marginal people about the reality of their existence, their struggles and their triumphs and develop our own social communication video films from these inputs. These inputs would then be taken to people through the broadcast network of television and the narrowcast network through small groups working at grassroots levels like NGOs, Panchayats, and women's organizations and so on. Our focus is not on information, but on the multi-layered reality of people's lives," she said but this has no evidence in practice and has failed to stand the test of time.

In this chapter, the author cites illustrations of some brilliant films on sustainable development with respect to indigenous practices in agriculture, how local people struggle to find their own solutions to problems of preservation, conservation, food and medicine when political, administrative and legal reforms do not offer the solutions they can and need to.

Ek Ropa Dhan

Ek Ropa Dhan (one seedling per hill) is a 26-minute film that traverses the farming fields of Bihar to explain, educate and promote a new technology in paddy cultivation that the locals have given the name *Ek Ropa Dhan* from which the film borrows its title. Basically, the film takes a look at the basic problem of food—the first of our survival needs and points out one way of solving the problem, known as the system of rice intensification, or the SRI method. The advantages of this relatively simple technique is that it needs less fertilizers, seeds, insecticides, labour and, most importantly, much less water than is needed in normal modes of cultivation. Water needed is only about one-third of what is needed in the traditional system.

The opening frame of the film shows a green farming field with a voice-over explaining the acute scarcity of food, mainly among the farming population. One of the farmers interviewed in the film says that most farmers produce less than subsistence levels and can barely live for three months out of what they normally produce. But the SRI method or the *Ek Ropa Dhan* technique has bettered their lives in a significant way. This farming method was introduced by a Catholic priest, Father Henri de Laulanie, in Madagascar, around 25 years ago.

The exorbitant prices of fertilizers, seeds, irrigation, electricity and labour have adversely affected any possible profits from farming. However, an increase in productivity does not always require higher investment. Farm yields can be enhanced by improving the methods of cultivation and this is precisely what the film points out. One striking feature is the proliferation of the woman's voice throughout the film. Kunti Devi who has adopted this method for her farms smiles into the camera and proudly claims how numerous farmers took her example to adopt the SRI method and got very good results. There are dozens of rural women who not only look after their own farms, but also spread the message and help.

Image 7.1. A Poster of *Ek Ropa Dhan*

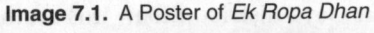

Courtesy: Meghnath Bhattacharya (Akhra)

In India alone, farmers in more than 100 districts are using the SRI method. In Gaya district, Bihar, this method of cultivation has taken the form of a mass movement. The whole district is reverberating with different sections of the people discussing SRI and the success stories of many women who have adopted this method. More than 35 countries have adopted this revolutionary method of paddy cultivation. Some important features of the SRI method are:

- The paddy seeds have to be treated before sowing.
- For each acre of cultivable land, four nursery beds of 20 × 4 ft each have to be prepared.
- 18–15-day-old seedlings are transplanted using this new technique.
- The principle of *one seedling per hill* is used in the transplantation lending it the local name of *Ek Ropa Dhan*.
- 10–12-inch distance is maintained from plant to plant and row to row.
- A specially designed weeder is used for the weeding.

These methods are explained in detail graphically as well as through voice-overs and interviews with an agricultural scientist, a district magistrate, an agricultural activist and other pioneers who are working towards the aim of helping small farmers make a living with dignity. Instead of first educating and persuading the big farmers to use this technology, this movement begins from the small and marginal farmer and moves upwards where big landowners and farmers take the example of practicing the method of cultivation. The SRI technique of paddy cultivation can go a long way in providing an effective answer to the challenges of sustainable agriculture and addressing food security concerns.

Food is the most essential requirement, after air and water, for the survival of living organisms. Our ancestors worshipped food, and they did not see it merely as a commodity to be sold in the market. Today, agriculture in India is passing through a crisis. Farming has become a loss-making proposition. *Ek Ropa Dhan* shows one way of resolving this crisis. Man has been evolving and developing technologies and processes for making food available to communities. Modern farming is the result of at least 10,000 years of evolution. This is one more example of human imagination and innovation in modern times. Scientists and others associated with agriculture are convinced of the effectiveness of the SRI method.

This method of root intensification has been successfully introduced in other crops such as wheat, sugar cane and vegetables.

The film is also aesthetically expressive without being too pedantic filled with advisory oratory. The visuals capture the beautiful mosaic of nature—blue skies, green fields, local women in colourful cotton saris, their hair sprinkled with vermillion dotting the picturesque canvas beautifully. The music track runs like a living constant throughout the film. The commentator often retreats to allow local voices to express themselves freely in their local dialect. Towards the end, the music of a popular Bengali folk song, famously sung by the Indian People's Theatre Association long back, fills the soundtrack meaningful because it is a farmer's song. The film drives home the point that an increase in productivity does not always require higher investment. Farm yields can be enhanced by improving the methods of cultivation. That changing the method of cultivation from broadcasting to transplanting will dramatically change the yield of paddy is a common knowledge today.

The film won the National Award in 2011 which went to Meghnath Bhattacharya and Biju Toppo for the Best Agriculture Film. The citation from the jury said "A succinct and well-researched film that looks closely at an innovation in the farming of rice." What do the directors have to say? "It is nice to get national recognition," beamed Biju Toppo, also a cinematographer. Meghnath adds, "It is more important to spread the message. Our films have been screened by universities in Germany and Denmark, but Ranchi University didn't bother. This could be a very good film for use in agricultural colleges and institutes of agricultural technology."

Niyamgiri You Are Still Alive

In 2006 Sterlite, a subsidiary of the UK mining company Vedanta built a refinery in Niyamgiri Hills, Odisha. The intention was to mine bauxite from the Niyamgiri Hills, which is in reserved forest. It is also home to indigenous communities who are dependent on it for their livelihood. Niyamgiri is the source of two rivers, Bansadhara and Nagaballi. The refinery consumes 30,000m^3 of water per day severely affecting the ecological systems and the communities. The toxic waste material from the refinery pollutes air, ground and water. Since 2003 different groups have mobilized to fight Vedanta. Has the mining project thrown hundreds of tribals living off and within Niyamgiri Hills into an uncertain future that spells their death?

Poet-turned-journalist-turned-documentary film-maker Suma Josson's film *Niyamgiri You Are Still Alive* won the Vasudha Environment Award at the International Film Festival of India, held in Goa, in 2010. The film sets up an inquiry into the illegal mining of bauxite by Vedanta in and around the Niyamgiri Hills in Kalahandi District, Odisha, which will severely threaten the lives, habitat and lifestyles of the Dongria Kondh tribes who have lived and worked there for thousands of years, in harmony with the environment and dependent on it. After scanning the lush green mantle of green that fills the landscape, the camera cuts to a brown and arid area with some kind of mining machine positioned in the frame. The voice-over visualizes that this is what Niyamgiri will turn to if the mining lease is granted to Vedanta.

The voice-over points out how this ₹10,000 crore project was cleared with the full backing of the Government of Odisha flouting environmental laws of the land. But local, national and international groups garnered strength and decided to fight to stall the project. When asked what motivated her to make the film, Josson says, "Raising awareness is one of the main intentions of making such films. Mainstream media will not talk about Kumti Majhi, Sukli Majhi or Mukta who live in Niyamgiri Hills and whose ancestors have taken care and protected this ecosystem for millions of years. These films are windows through which the outside world can listen to the sound of their voices. Can see their faces and feel the pain that they go through. Such films reach out to governments and various other decision-making forums."

If the lease was to get going, it would result in the cutting down of 1.2 lakh trees and 3.3 lakh shrubs, herbs and ground-level flora and fauna. The camera focussed on the rich wildlife of the region. This comprised of the four-horned antelope, the barking deer and the near-extinct species of the gecko lizard. These fall within Schedule I of the Wildlife Protection Act, 1972. These animals will disappear from the landscape of Niyamgiri with the mining project. The 36 streams that flow directly out of the two rivers will dry up. The Vedanta Project has already appropriated 26 hectares of village land of its proposed land area of 660 hectares that is in gross violation of the Community Claims Provision of the Forest Rights Act, 2006.

The bright colours in the lives of the indigenous groups whose entire life, culture and religion depend on and are determined by Niyamgiri Hills come across when the camera moves to Kamli, a local in a purple sari going to the market to sell some of the forest produce of vegetables and farm produce in the market after home needs are taken care of. The sound of local drums, the process of worship of nature as a regular ritual with local music, songs and chants, comes across, underscoring the lives of these tribals in a world of their own. Though poor, some of promise to give up their lives, but not give up Niyamgiri to corporate killers.

Kumti Majhi of Sindhbal says "*Niyam* means principle of law which is never partial. So, we look upon Niyamgiri as our God. How can we live without our God?" he asks angrily. Kumthadi Vedaka of Kajuri says, "We do not have any land and depend on the mountain. If these people begin to mine in the mountain we will have nothing to eat or drink." Adds Bhima of Belamba, "We will not get a single drop of water even if we dig deep."

Around 8,000 Dongria Kondh adivasis, a Primitive Tribal Group (PTG) notified by the Union Government, will be affected by Vedanta's mining project. They revere Niyamgiri Hills as their God. We get aluminium out of bauxite. It takes millions of years to form bauxite. There are rich ecosystems wherever bauxite is found. It means the destruction of the entire ecosystem that keeps alive Niyamgiri and its surrounding parts in Odisha. A high percentage of the aluminium output, an estimated 30 per cent, has always gone into the arms industry to make bombs, tanks, fighter planes and so on. So we have to ask the question whether we need to leave behind black deserts both in Niyamgiri and wherever wars are being fought. When Jheelu Majhi says, "If Niyamgiri is taken our gods and goddesses will eat us up, the earth will eat us up," he symbolically refers to the end of civilization. "The company has forcibly taken away our lands, run bulldozers into our homes, built roads without our permission or consent and laid pipelines against our wishes," says Dakka Majhi of Bandhaguda.

Over its brief run of 16 minutes, *Niyamgiri You Are Still Alive* lucidly spells out how Niyamgiri is an ecologically sensitive area. It is one of the richest areas of biodiversity in South East Asia. All this will be destroyed with bauxite mining. The work that already began on the project has had serious effects on the health of the locals. Wastes dumped on the ponds and lands include effluents that are toxic, filled with heavy chemicals and are also radioactive.

There is hope at the end of the dark tunnel. As the momentum against Sterlite and Vedanta began to escalate and gather strength from local, national and international corners, on 24 August 2010, based on the findings of the Forest Advisory Committee (FAC), highlighting improper practices, including manipulation and use of coercion, the government rejected the company's bauxite mining proposal for Niyamgiri in Odisha, and initiated further investigations into project discrepancies.

The film closes on lines from the report: "It is the responsibility of the ministry to enforce the laws passed by the Parliament. It is in this sprit that the decision has been taken." But as this goes into press, the cabinet reshuffle has a new minister in replacing Jairam Ganesh. No one can tell what will happen now.

In a pithy, summing up, Josson says, "It is the story between the ant and the elephant. On the one side there is the insatiable greed of the Multi National Corporations who have the money and muscle power and on the other id this desire of ordinary people to be left alone. As a filmmaker I place myself with the victims—the forests, rivers and streams—an ecosystem which basically wants to breathe undisturbed. For me it is a question of survival. Everything is so connected. If they go they, we will also be pulled along with them."

These films have been picked at random, among hundreds of others, not in the order of merit or popularity or festival prizes and screenings, not weighted by values like 'good' or 'bad', 'for' or 'against', but to point out that over the past three decades, this documentary film movement has visibly shifted from the making of any specific *genre* of film to the making of films that defy genre trapped within its rigid definition. The independent documentary movement applies, therefore, to a wide range of film genres, where the making of the film itself is political.[2]

Johar—Welcome to Our World

Nilanjan Bhattacharya's *Johar—Welcome to Our World* explores the intricate relationship the tribals of Jharkhand have with their forests. The film explores traditional recipes, medicinal qualities of

Image 7.2. *Johar—Welcome to Our World*

Courtesy: Nilanjan Bhattacharya

various herbs, weeds and fruits and the traditional knowledge of their sustainable management by the adivasis. The film also talks about how mindless, aggressive development and the government's wrong-headed conservation policies have damaged the tribals' relationship with their land and pushed them deeper into food insecurity. In other words, the film changes our entire perspective on India's food culture based on taste, delicacy, nutrition and health needs. We are introduced to a world where food has to be collected directly from the forests and processed indigenously and painstakingly over days and nights to make them edible enough for the people to survive on a day-to-day basis. A local leader points out that the depletion in forest produce that gave them medical herbs and eliminated the needs of a qualified doctor, have now become scarce which forces them to go to the nearest doctor they cannot afford.

Nearly 70 per cent of Jharkhand's rural population faces the prospect of going hungry at some stage during the year. The food supply is assured for only about three to four months, following the harvest in late October–early November. Food supplies tend to run short by the end of winter. The 'starvation period' begins by mid-summer and, in many cases, continues till the end of October. Though depleted, the forest remains the only source for a large number of tribals in Jharkhand in those adverse 'no-food' periods of the year.

The narrator stresses on the important role women play in the procuring, processing and preparing of food. The role of women is critical for the survival of tribal households, in terms of provisioning food and income, as well as in resource management. Women are major earners from the sale of 'non-wood forest products' in the forest-based livelihood systems in Jharkhand. The women in tribal societies of Jharkhand are the de facto managers of the households.

Though the adivasis own the right to the forests they live in, these rights have been taken away from them by vested interests including political parties and parties in power. That they are aware of their rights has been proved again and again. One visual focusses on an agitation demanding the regularity in distribution of food grains through ration shops. The locals complain how the ration shops are not delivering essential food grains at a price they are entitled to. Some frankly state how their below poverty line (BPL) cards are being kept on hold while there are others who complain that their appeals fall on deaf ears every time they approach the authorities.

The film points out that (i) every biosphere reserve in the country is on adivasi land; (ii) every major dam since the 1970s has been submerging adivasi land; (iii) every wildlife sanctuary in India is on adivasi homelands; (iv) 90 per cent of the mines in India are on adivasi land; (v) nearly 50 per cent of the mineral wealth of the entire country comes from adivasi areas, yet 80 per cent of the entire adivasi population in India lives below the poverty line; and (vi) lack of food, minimum work opportunities, systematic opening up of tribal territories for the so-called 'development' projects forced the adivasis to migrate. In the rich mineral belt of Jharkhand, the adivasi population has dropped from around 60 per cent in 1911 to 27.67 per cent in 1991.

Arzoo

Documentary film-maker and researcher Shashi Gupta did a 26-minute short film called *Arzoo*, focusing on a fearless woman named Sulekha Ali and on her brainchild Arzoo. Sulekha Ali is a woman of courage. She is totally committed to salvaging the lives and childhood of children from the margins affected by the communal riots in Gujarat in 2002. "After the riots, relief camps were set up in many parts of Ahmedabad to take care of the victims who had lost everything in the carnage. I entered one of these camps, Alam camp, as a volunteer. The camp had around 15,000 affected people with children moving around aimlessly. It was as if my family had expanded from four or five to 15,000. I was first posted in medical examination and then shifted first to injections and then to the dressings section. The experience was shocking. If one person came with a finger dangling from a hand, another came with a lost arm with blood flowing from the limb. One came holding his entrails slipping out of his slashed stomach. But I learnt to take it all. My interests increased when I got involved with the children. When I came home, I felt emptiness around me. Life was no longer what it used to be before the camp. I wanted to do something concrete," says Sulekha.

Before her Alam Camp experience, Sulekha was a simple girl of a Gujarati Muslim family who was good at drawing and embroidery and loved to rear goats. She was very religious and was the first in performing all rituals perfectly. "But the riots changed all that. I am still a believer but my perspective on God and religion has changed dramatically. Religion is something that lies deep within the psyche of a person. No religion can be the reason for people to kill one another in anger or in cold blood. Minorities are victimized across the world in different ways and India is just one country. But that does not mean that it should be a cause for violence," she says. In course of time, Sulekha founded Arzoo, an organization that began a school for the rehabilitation and mainstreaming of marginalized children, children who have been orphaned or affected by the communal riots in Gujarat in 2002, children who are very poor and hardly go to school, children of all communities living in shanties and *bustees* of Ahmedabad.

The white-washed walls of the small premises Arzoo works from headed by Sulekha Ali are splashed with colour crayon sketches of flowers, houses, musical notes drawn by the children of Arzoo. Some have even written their names, 'Sharif', 'Ashraf', 'Raj' while some little kid has scribbled "Sulekha didi is my friend" complete with 'friend' spelt wrong. "I had gone to Bangalore to learn paper craft and had thought that when I come back, the money I would make with my paper craft would go into funding Arzoo. But I soon learnt that this would not work. So, I began to teach the kids simple crafts like making greeting cards, paper work, picture framing so that we could sell these through suppliers and earn money," elaborates Sulekha.

The journey was extremely tough and an uphill climb all the way. Sulekha is still climbing and will not stop because she considers her work with Arzoo an ongoing project. As a volunteer working with riot victims, Sulekha had worked mainly in Muslim-dominated areas. When she came to work in a ruined neighbourhood dominated by Hindus, she was sceptical about whether the Hindu community would accept her. "So I brought in a carrom board, some puzzle games and waited for the kids to come in. They came first out of curiosity and then got involved. I thought of making them perform short, simple skits with subtle messages of communal harmony, the value of education, woven into them. It worked. Then I began to teach them paper craft." The name Arzoo was born out of Sulekha's dream and aspirations for the children she feels responsible for. There are Hindu and Muslim kids and they sing and dance in front of Shashi's camera with natural spontaneity. In the process of her involvement with children, Sulekha has rehabilitated herself too, from being an ordinary woman to a woman committed to the upliftment of children who live below the poverty line.

From the time of its inception, Arzoo has diversified from being a small play group to an activity centre and more. The Gujarat riots of 2002 had affected the young minds beyond repair. The need of the hour was to infuse fresh hope in the minds of riot-affected children of both Hindu and Muslim communities and to channelize their energies positively in the right direction.

Asked how she broke the barrier between film-maker and subject, Shashi said, "Sulekha is an extremely warm and honest person and breaking the barrier was not an issue at all. Somehow we drew a comfort level between us, much before I shot her, which is why she is completely at ease in front of the camera. I believe it is important for the subject to speak rather than for me as a film-maker to speak on his/her behalf. I showed the edited film to Sulekha. She had a couple of suggestions which I implemented. On the whole, she seemed happy about the film. I had met Sulekha a few months after the 2002 communal riots in Ahmedabad, through a friend of mine who had been working as a volunteer. Around two years back I met her again, as I was planning to write an article related to the Gujarat riots. That is when I decided to make the film," Shashi sums up, adding, "Making the film has strengthened my belief in basic human values and integrity. Each of us has something unique, something we truly believe in. But few are brave enough to cross the bridge. Sulekha Ali has reaffirmed to me that it is possible to do so. All that is required is courage and faith."

Earth Witness: Reflections on the Times and the Timeless

Earth Witness: Reflections on the Times and the Timeless is a documentary film made by Akanksha Joshi. It won the Best Film (Climate Change and Sustainable Technologies) Award and the Best Cinematography Award at the Sixth CMS Vatavaran and was screened at the MIFF in 2012. Four people—a father, a teacher, a farmer, a shepherd—find themselves on the frontline of the Earth's biggest, most complex crisis—climate change. Shikari Biaga is a Biaga adivasi who lives and works in Chhattisgarh. Doongra Rabaari is a semi-nomad who comes to herd his sheep in Gujarat. Seno Tsushah who speaks English is a Chakhesang Naga from Nagaland. Sukdev-da is a farmer in the Sunderbans.

Joshi is no stranger to documentaries. Her first effort, *Passengers: A Video Journey in Gujarat* (2003), was a 52-minute-long film that explored communal violence in India chronicling the journey of a Hindu and a Muslim family during and after the

Image 7.3. *Earth Witness*: The Director on Location with Locals

Courtesy: Akanksha Joshi

carnage. After five years, Joshi visited the carnage area to document the stories of people who had saved others during the violence. This came out as 'Profiles of Courage and Compassion' in a book she co-authored with Harsh Mandar titled *Towards Healing*. She received the Karmaveer Puraskaar, or the National People's Award for Citizen Social Justice and Action, for *Chilika Bank* (2008), which highlighted the ecological issues around Asia's largest brackish water lake. The film received the Livelihood Award in the Fifth CMS Vatavaran Environment and Wildlife Film Festival.

Earth Witness travels across Chhattisgarh to explore the local people's indigenous Forest Ecosystem, the Dryland Ecosystem of Gujarat, Nagaland's Mountain Ecosystem and, finally, the Coastal Ecosystem of the Sunderbans. Each system reflects adaptation to the immediate environment by the locals who are familiar with the ecology, the geographical mapping and the benefits of the environment in which they live. The film zeroes in on an expert who talks about his/her system of taking advantage of the ecological circumstances of their lives and gaining from it without causing any harm to the environment in any way.

Yi As Akh Padshah Bai (There was a Queen)

Kavita Pai worked as Programme Executive at Jnanapravaha, a centre for arts education in Mumbai. She has worked on numerous television programmes on women, health and environmental issues. This is her first independent documentary. Hansa Thapliyal graduated from the FTII, Pune in 1997 in direction. She collaborated on an audio novel project with Vipin Bhati on a grant from SARAI, Delhi. She has assisted in works of fiction, written for papers and the occasional journal. The two ladies co-directed the documentary *Yi As Akh Padshah Bai*.

"Difficult ethical questions are a part and parcel of documentary film-making," says Kavita Pai who, along with her friend and peer Hansa Thapliyal, was commissioned by Other Media, an NGO that functions in Delhi and Bangalore, to make a film on women, war and peace in general, and in particular on peace initiatives by women in conflict-ridden states. The outcome is a 105-minute incisive documentary called *Yi As Akh Padshah Bai* on peace initiatives by the women in Kashmir. Their work is concentrated on conflict-ridden areas the media generally keeps away from.

The beginning was uncertain. "We were uncomfortable with the entire premise of the film. We were not sure whether their gender predisposes women to non violence," explains Pai. "At that point, we were not even sure what the word 'peace' meant vis-a-vis our film, the women we were going to research and the life-threatening situations they live and work in. When we first went for the field survey, above everything else, they wished to talk about injustice, the brazen violation of human rights, and their total lack of geographical, social and economic freedoms."

After the first field survey, Pai and Thapliyal went to shoot with a technical crew composed entirely of women. For all that, the film does not reveal any gender bias. So, alongside the women who come across with very powerful voices, we find the camera closing in on some men. One of them is a former militant. The second man had sent his son for training across the border with his blessings. The third man is a school master who lost his son in gun battle only to realize that he was a militant. The fourth is a schoolboy whose brother was killed in crossfire. And as they spoke to the men, they realized there is a difference in the narratives of men and women.

"While every story in Kashmir has the power to shock and move, and the stories of both men and women were compelling in their honesty—in their rage, in their grief, in their helplessness, in their contempt, in their fierce refusal to forget,—the women's stories are markedly different in their determination to survive, to nurture," Pai elaborates. It is through these women—proud, strong, with an undying zest for life—that they have tried to explore what peace means and how it can come about in Kashmir. *There Was a Queen* is a film of conflict and peace in Kashmir. It is about Kashmiri women who talk openly about terrorism, militarism, peace and their daily life. It is a record of political voices of women representing many sides in Kashmir.

While documenting the plight and pluck of women, the film demonstrates the uncertainty the everyday lives of young girls and women whose lives could be trapped in a no-exit situation at any moment, without dramatizing this constant risk. A young girl learning tailoring in the Zainab Skill Centre in Maisuma in the heart of Srinagar is being teased by her friends for wearing lipstick. She says, "Who knows whether I will remain alive tomorrow? So, why not fulfil my desire and have some fun while I am alive today?"

The Zainab Skill Centre was established around 1991–92 to provide support to girls affected by conflict. The Centre was founded by Agha Ashraf, father of the late Kashmiri poet Agha Shahid Ali. It is run with donations from non-resident Kashmiris. Kavita says that every girl here has lost a brother, father, husband, son or some male member. "Their smiling faces say that this is nothing extraordinary for them. They dot their stories belting out lines from popular Hindi film songs, sometimes lamenting when this onslaught would finally end," Pai adds.

The crew reached Sopore two days after two young girls Shahnaza and Ulfat, both 17, studying in pre-university were killed. Kavita Pai says that they did not wish to shoot the funeral of the two girls because it would be intruding into very private moments of grief. "But the family insisted that we do, because they wanted the rest of India to know what was happening in Kashmir. As one of the dead girls was being bathed by her wailing mother, I could not bear it anymore and Hansa took over. 'Did you see the mehendi in her hands,' Hansa asked me afterwards. I hadn't because I felt guilty in some way," says Kavita.

Hansa was stronger. "My predominant emotion was rage, which made me place the horror, the shame and the sorrow of it on record, for all to see," says Hansa. "So I shot the mothers bathing their little girls, stroking their seemingly unscarred bodies, gently combing their hair and kissing their fingers," she adds.

A year later on the editing table, they debated whether they should use the funeral footage at all because it was too sensational and too intrusive. "We finally decided to keep three shots to drive home the gravity of the crime—the murder of two innocent girls," Pai points out. Some said they were killed in crossfire while others said it was the Indian army who were responsible. In the end they decided it did not matter who had ended the lives of these children; what mattered was that two innocent girls had been killed, just when their whole life was about to unfold ahead of them.

The documentary not only traces the plight of the women, but also shows the video footage of the movement of the convoys of security forces personnel in busy areas of Srinagar city. Parveena Ahamgar, whose son is missing, and Parvez Imroze, a lawyer who works in the area of human rights, founded the Association of the Parents of Disappeared Persons (APDP) in 1994. The APDP is an important initiative by women towards bringing peace in Kashmir. Tasleema Bano, a resident of Malangam-Bandipora and a member of APDP, says how her husband was picked up some years ago, and has never been seen or heard of again.

Women who have lost their near and dear ones are united in carrying forward a joint struggle, demanding the return of their missing husbands, sons, brothers and fathers. "If they are dead, give us their dead bodies so that we can give them a decent burial," says one woman. These women are neither involved in the political issues that plague the state nor are they part of militant groups. Their tragedy is that the male members of their families have been picked up either by militants to join the movement for Azaad Kashmir or by the security personnel or by the Indian Army.

Hajra had lost four sons. Yet, a ray of hope keeps this old, frail, but brave woman get on with the business of living. She says that conceiving a situation of peace is impossible in an environment where guns keep roaring and where women lose their dearest ones, taken away by the security forces, never to be seen again. The camera closes on the wrinkled face of Ghulam Rasool Paddar, father of

Abdul Rehman Paddar, killed in an encounter (a 'fake' encounter, says the father) at Ganderbal.

While many voices are anguished, some are vengeful and harsh too, and the film does not overlook these. At one point in the film, we see a young girl who is ready to take up arms to avenge the killing of her sister by the security forces at Sopore. Her mother echoes this, proclaiming she would take up arms so as to 'eliminate' the security forces personnel.

The film pans through extensive interviews, the nature of crackdowns carried out by the security forces and how the women cope with the situation once the security forces cordon a given area. Naseem Shifai, a famous Kashmiri poet, says that it is necessary to remove the stigma of every Kashmiri being labelled a militant by the rest of India. Hameeda Nayeem, reader in the English Department of the University of Kashmir, claims that every Kashmiri should be given the right to self-determination, and asks why the militants would kill their own people.

Misra, one of the men interviewed, who lives in Malangam, said that more appalling than the indifference of the state was the tragedy of the Kashmir leadership abandoning the families of those they call martyrs. "Some of them seem to have seen the light after the Amarnath protests last year when there was a consolidated attempt by some parties to give compensation to the families of those who had died in the firing, to pay for medical aid and for the education of the children. But given the scale of devastation as a result of the 20-year-old conflict, much more needs to be done," he said.

There 'Was a Queen leaves us with strange feelings of shock and guilt—shock because of the meaningless death and disappearance of hundreds of people, and guilt because so many of us have done nothing to help these women who are trying to carve out pockets of peace in their disturbed lives. The conflict has created a large number of widows, 'half-widows' (those whose husbands have disappeared), mothers who have lost their sons, daughters who have been subjected to rape, women pushed out of employment and people suffering from acute stress and trauma. The sheer banality of such acute suffering is striking, throughout the film.

The film ends with the recent protest demonstration by the parents of disappeared persons at Jantar Mantar in New Delhi. The scene is ordinary, by the standards of high emotion elsewhere in the documentary. But its ordinariness also captures the everyday nature of the pain that people live with, and the alternating realities of intense conflict and peaceful democratic protest.

Have You Seen the Arana

Sunanda Bhatt's *Have You Seen the Arana* had been on the forefront of many awards and outstanding citations. She not only believed in direct feedback from her subjects, but also admitted how community screenings of the film gave her a different way of looking at the film. Among a string of highly prestigious awards, *Have You Seen the Arana* won the Golden Conch for the Best Documentary in the National Competition at MIFF 2014. The citation states, "This film is elegant, patient, meditative and subtle. The director gently moves her audience towards a deep appreciation of the tribal, mythical connections between humanity and ecosystems that sustain us all." The award was shared with *Invoking Justice* by Deepa Dhanraj. The film also won the Best Cinematography for Saumyananda Sathi and Best Sound to Christopher Burchell.

Wayanad district that lies on the northeast of Kerala was formed on 1 November 1980 as the 12th district, carved out of Kozhikode and Kannur districts. The etymology of the word Wayanad is *vayal* meaning 'paddy' and *naad* meaning 'land'. This translates into 'land of the paddy fields'. The district is flush with indigenous tribes who

Image 7.4. *Have You Seen the Arana*

Courtesy: Sunanda Bhat

form rich repositories of knowledge in conventional forms of rice cultivation, how to extract medicine from the forests in the area, the use of these medicinal herbs, roots, branches and plants and so on.

Wayanad is positioned against the backdrop of the picturesque hills of the Western Ghats with altitudes ranging between 700 and 2,100 metres above sea level. The district is unique culturally, ethnographically and lifestyle wise, because it comprises a large population of aboriginal tribes consisting of Paniyas, Kurumas, Adiyars, Kurchiyas, Ooralis, Kadans and Kattunaikkans who own land while the other tribes are labourers. Wayanad makes for 36 per cent of the total adivasi population in the other districts of Kerala. Wayanad forms the setting of Sunanda Bhatt's *Have You Seen the Arana*.

Have You Seen the Arana is about Wayanad in Kerala inhabited by original adivasi tribes who carry their own heritage of medical, agricultural and other practices inherited from their ancestors. "I have tried to explore the effects of a rapidly changing landscape on people's lives and livelihoods. Set in Wayanad, the film takes you on a journey through a region that is both witness to and victim of the drastic transformation in the name of 'development,'" Sunanda elaborates.

Sunanda worked on this film for over six years, looking for ways to represent the complexities of the people and the places. Much of the film rests on the relationships she was able to build with the characters. "I was deeply inspired by what David McDougall, an ethnographic film-maker, said. He [had] said, 'Before films are a form of representing, they are a form of looking ... with a certain interest, certain will. To look carefully requires strength, calmness and affection. The affection cannot be in the abstract; it must be an affection of the senses,'" she quotes.

As the film journeys through the earthen roads into the lush green villages of Wayanad, Sunanda zeroes in on the subjects of her film. Raman Cheruvayil belongs to the Kurichya tribe known for their knowledge of traditional rice cultivation. Along with his wife Geetha, he collaborates with NGOs to grow and preserve over 30 varieties of indigenous species of rice. He holds workshops for children which include his little grandson who often bunks school to be with his grandad. He lives with his family in Kammana and Mananthavady, Wayanad. Raman recently won the P.V. Thampy Endowment Award for his work in traditional farming. The narrative of the film moves in a zigzag manner and returns to Raman often, the camera capturing him with his little grandson who is taught to catch insects from the slush.

N.P. Joschi is a traditional healer who belongs to the Adiya tribe. Jochi is an integral part of the tribal initiative that protects and regenerates disappearing medicinal plants from the evergreen forests of North Wayanad. She imbibed her knowledge and training in medicinal herbs and plants from her father who was also a traditional healer. The forest has been her home since she was a little girl. She has been witness to the rapid spread of tourist influx into the region that constantly eats into the growth and evolution of medicinal herbs because tourists have neither knowledge nor concern about the value of these traditional medicinal plants and herbs. Along with a local school teacher, a forever smiling Jochi has gathered support from the tribal communities of Thirunelli to protest the mushrooming of tourist resorts in the area. A mother of two, Jochi lives in Thirunelli in North Wayanad.

George Joseph is a Syrian Christian whose family migrated from South Kerala to Wayanad. He worked in Saudi Arabia but came back with a lot of money to settle down again with his wife and two daughters in Pulpally, Wayanad. Foreseeing prospects of cultivating ginger in the neighbouring state of Karnataka, he invested all his earnings and savings into ginger cultivation and trade. But there was a sharp fall in the price of ginger and this liquidated his entire investment leaving the family on the edge of survival. The family is now considering going back to Saudi Arabia to get back its bearings. But his wife narrates the sad tale of their financial downfall with cheer in her voice and a smile on her face.

Holding these three stories together is P.K. Kariyan, former President of the Thirunelli Panchayat who is a *moopan* (Vanniyar subsect in Malabar) or elder of the Adiya tribe. He sings the *pulapattu* or 'song for the dead' that traces the travels of a mythical couple across Wayanad. The myth is chanted in the hope that souls of the dead will find their way back to the ancestors. This lyrical myth is the thread that weaves a garland of stories of people. This song is a narrative and musical thread drawing parallels with the lives of the people where Arana is itself a myth that people are scared of because there are different stories doing the rounds of the 'Arana' but no one knows what it is. Kariyan learnt the song from his uncle,

P.K. Kalari, a renowned *Gadiga*—an invocation to the Goddess Malli—performer. As the film crew journey through public busses and on foot across Wayanad and try to discover worlds they did not know existed, they try to link the *pulapattu* with the content of the film and use it both as form and part of content. Along with his troupe of young adivasis, Kariyan is invited across Kerala to perform the *Gadiga*.

"It has been a year since I finished making the film. Since then, I have repeatedly gone back to Wayanad to show the film to different audiences of the district—college students, film clubs, camps for tribal kids and adivasi communities. Once I was asked to show the film at one of the oldest libraries in Wayanad. Initially, they had planned to screen it in their reading room. But over 200 people came for the screening; so we had to move outdoors where the film was projected on the wall of the library building. The occasional passing traffic did not take their attention away from the film. A road cut through the audience and men and women sat on either side of the road. Some men sat on the wall of a neighbouring tea shop," Sunanda reminisces.

"During the many screenings, I found the kids very excited during the post-screening interactions," says Sunanda, adding, "one said—we never realised that so much was disappearing so fast." Another said, "I liked it when the farmer says—we have to know the soil and the soul has to know us. A third kid said—"Joschi puts it across so well when she says that she took such good care of her daughter that she kept her on her lap and did not place her on the ground." Ironically, the film shows how Joschi is completely estranged from a grown up daughter.

For Sunanda, the journey is an ongoing one and the film is just a part of that journey. "As my involvement with the people and place grew, I looked for means to bring this positive energy into a film that was initially more about 'victims of an exploitative culture' rather than equal stakeholders. I began exploring ways that would make the landscape and the people speak. I looked for ways to interweave bus journeys with the wetness and the dryness of the seasons, the changing contours of the land and the textures of the faces as they are all closely linked. I decided to tell the story of Wayanad through the lives of three ordinary people who engage in different ways with the land," she elucidates.

The Tribal Cultural Heritage in India, a Dutch organization that works with tribal groups in India, is supporting Sunanda and her team for community screenings in Wayanad through a local environmental group called FERNS. These screenings happen in adivasi settlements and are sometimes followed by discussions. "Reactions vary from some asking why we did not cover all the tribes of Wayanad to some talking about how they are aware of the disappearance of important elements in the landscape but realized the extent on watching the film. In one community screening a woman healer appreciated that we had shown the disappearance of medicinal plant adding that she does not get support from the government and has to constantly battle the growing popularity of allopathy."

Some screenings in Bangalore were attended by the characters in the film. The audience loved interacting with them, asking questions and often offering solutions! "I often find that young audiences treat them with great respect and awe as if they are rock stars!" says Sunanda.

CONCLUSION

It would be in the fitness of the subject to sum up by what an 'outsider' has to say about the independent documentary movement in India. John Fishcher of Yale University, in his article,[3] roundly criticizes the hurdles of financing faced by independent documentary film-makers, though he labels them under 'Independent Political Documentaries'. But he ends his thesis with more than a few notes of optimism. He talks about the enlarging canvas of funding sources that would allow for more film-makers to enter the documentary world and established documentary film-makers to make more documentaries or complete their unfinished ones. As examples, he mentions the founding of media collectives such as Media Storm in Delhi and the Janamadhyam Cieds Collective in Mumbai who have been funding and producing documentaries independently of the Films Division.[4] According to Iikka Vehkalahti, an executive producer for Steps India, a Delhi-based non-profit organization supporting documentary films, "In Europe today, most documentaries are boring because film-makers are living in a very 'safe and stable environment'. In India and China, where tremendous changes are happening, many interesting stories are emerging. Because people have to work in tight budgets, they are passionate about their work."[5]

NOTES
1. http://www.ecifm.rdg.ac.uk/sustainable_development.htm
2. Trinh T. Minha, "Rethinking the Subject of Ethno-documentary," in *Visual Anthropology and India*, ed. K.S. Singh (1992). Brundtland Commission, "*Our Common Future*", (1987), Oxford: Oxford University Press.
3. John Fischer, "Oppression: The Indian Independent Political Documentaries and the Ongoing Struggle for Viewership," *The Columbia Undergraduate Journal of South Asian Studies*, 1(1): 41–53.
4. Manjunath Pendakur, "Cinema of Resistance: Recent Trends in Indian Documentary Film," *Documentary Box* 7 (1995).
5. Mini Pant Zachariah, "Making Business Sense of Documentary Filmmaking," The Hindustan Times (9 February 2007), http://www.hindustantimes.com/newsmartimportedstories/making-business-sense-of-documentary-filmmaking/article1-204738.aspx

8
OUT OF THE BOX

INTRODUCTION

'Out of the box' is a broad term that expresses things that are out of the ordinary that may or may not fit into our perception of what is generally termed 'mainstream'. In this chapter, the writer tries to create an artificial classification of genres where one includes ethnographic and anthropological documentaries apart from films that might fit into either category or not quite fit into either. Films that the author considers ethnographic or anthropological or out of the box are included within a broad spectrum touching on some films watched and written about long ago and therefore faded a little from memory tracked back a time when there were no computers and no memory discs to save one's writing. Most of the films discussed here are quite extensively analyzed with quotes from the makers of these films. The choice is based on the author's repeated viewings, interviews with some of the makers of the films and the perceptions they project over the film.

In global terms, anthropologists, such as Gayatri Chakravorty Spivak, choose the word 'subaltern' to define the 'marginal'. The word 'subaltern' has a more precise meaning because it covers the marginalized as well as the oppressed. Is there a difference between the two? Not really, because marginalization and oppression are too closely intertwined to be separated through discussion and debate. Groups of people are marginalized because they are oppressed. In the same way, persistent oppression of a weaker group by the more powerful in terms of caste, class, age or sex automatically marks them as 'marginalized'. The Concise English Dictionary defines the word 'subaltern' as 'one of inferior rank'. It is used as a name for the general attribute of the subordination in the South Asian society whether this is expressed in terms of class, caste, age, gender and office or in any other way.

This chapter deals in one way or another, with the 'subaltern' or, rather, the marginalized, the oppressed and the ignored. This also proves that classifications may be considered necessary for a certain understanding of the terms of negotiation involved in them, but they are not really possible and might become subjects of debate among scholars, academics and film critics.

OUT OF THE BOX

Within this created classification that does not exist in factual history of documentary cinema, the writer has tried to focus on films that tackle little-known areas of human endeavour and struggles that might have remained invisible and unknown to everyone had these films not been made. If they ask to be categorized, the genres would overlap and perhaps create a new genre independent unto itself. The common ground they hold is that the films have been made very recently and, therefore, might not have been written about or seen widely. The author has chosen five films made over the past two years that shed light on little-known areas of human rights violations of different kinds, at different pockets of the country carrying different repercussions. The films define an assorted, versatile group in terms of issues tackled, and the statements they make that take priority over the aesthetics of the films though this by no means implies any lack of aesthetic expression or compromise on issues and arts. The films are—*Exploring Madness* (2006), *Nirastra Padatik* (2001), *Nakusha—The Unwanted* (2012), *Angels of a Troubled Paradise* (2010), *Ocean of Tears, Char—The No Man's Island* (2011) and *Flickering Angels* (2012). All these films except the last are made by very young film-makers who are still groping their way to find their footing in the independent documentary film movement in the country.

Parvez Imam, a psychiatrist-turned-film-maker, who decided at a point of time that there are many extramural issues within the social environment beyond the mere clinical diagnosis and treatment of mental patients, tried to work out a functional balance in his 19-minute long documentary on the mentally ill called *Exploring Madness*. In actuality, the film encapsulates within its 19-minute footage, six three-minute films trying to portray shades of the differently abled in terms of their reason. He does this through different subjects ranging from those who seem to have been cured but may relapse at any point of time, to a completely cured mentally sick patient who has found his place in the mainstream and now works for other mentally ill people. The film was screened at the Max Mueller Bhavan under the auspices of Anjali, a city-based NGO that works for human rights of mentally ill persons and also works towards raising awareness about the mentally ill.

The aesthetics of presentation versus the ethics of representation are the two polarities that place the film-maker concentrating on the mentally ill neatly between the horns of a dilemma. Should he concentrate on aesthetics? Or, as a former practicing psychiatrist, should he focus on the ethics of presentation—such as protecting the privacy of his subjects, perhaps at some cost to the aesthetics of the language of cinema?

"I was disillusioned with the clinical aspects of psychiatry when I realized that there are more social issues involved in the entire spectrum of a patient being diagnosed mentally ill till the point when he is completely cured and is poised to step into the mainstream. To reach out to the common masses and make them aware of the problem through communication was what triggered me on to this different language of cinema," says Imam, whose films have been screened nationally and internationally over the years."

Different Strokes (2006) throws up perceptions of mental illness among the mainstream ranging from the man on the street to an expert on the subject. *Sentenced for a Lifetime* (2006) explores how the world has its own definite notions about abnormality and tends to label anyone behaving beyond these norms or contrary to them, as 'abnormal'. This is especially true of women within the family whose mental state, if and when considered not normal, is swept under the carpet. *Mental Illnesses—People and Policies* sheds light on the dismal situation of institutionalized, professional and administrative situation for mentally ill patients in the country. "Can you imagine that India has only 3,000 professionally trained and academically qualified psychiatrists juxtaposed against the millions in want of expert treatment, counselling and advice?" he asks.

Three Women and the City (2006) traces the lives of two daughters and their mother, all mental patients, who live a shadowy life forever vacillating between illness and relapse. Imam takes care not to focus on their faces and the film narrates the story without revealing their identities. It is the most moving of all the six films mainly because of the low-key treatment Imam gives it. *Once upon a Madman* (2006) is, perhaps, the sole note of hope that would strike the viewer as he sees how a raving mad person can be completely cured and then brought back into the mainstream. *Mind Games* goes back to popular perceptions on madness, albeit in a different light where many a time, most of us do not even recognize a mental sickness even when we see one in front of our eyes. Is this a sign of our insensitivity? Or does it point to our ignorance? Rather, could this perhaps be the consequence of social conditioning resulting from both insensitivity and ignorance?

Exploring Madness is a social statement made through the language of film in the best possible way this subject can be articulated. Therefore, in a manner of speaking, it rightly precludes any questions about its aesthetics. However, Imam tries to make the best of the situation by structuring the film like a physical journey through arid roads in a car and comes back from that journey. This could perhaps be interpreted metaphorically as a larger journey into unknown territory. The films could have been of five minutes duration so that we could have begun to internalize some of the ideas rather than the blink-and-you-miss-it impression they carry.

King of India

King of India (2008) is a moving documentary by Arvind Sinha. He picked up a few children from the same family when he was making his earlier documentary *Journeyings and Conversations* on migrant people from Bihar, UP, and other states who have made Howrah and its periphery their homes. He began following the children as they wandered from one street to another, went back home, shared a cheap thali of food and sang, danced, performed acrobatics with cheap and crude make-up on their faces, over a period of six years, from 2002 to 2008. *King of India* was screened at the IDFA in Amsterdam, one of the two Indian films ever to have been selected for its main competition.

The children are named after names of popular Hindi films such as Raja Hindustani, Toofan, Jyotsna, Reshma and Chandni. They are wandering performers on the streets, pavements, funfairs,

Image 8.1. *King of India*

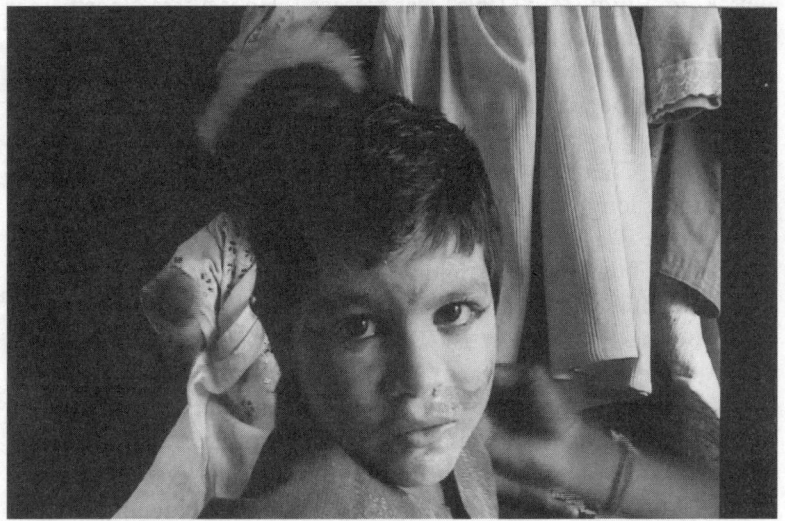

Courtesy: PSBT

carnivals, markets, grounds, bridges and railway platforms of Calcutta. Ratan Singh, their father, a migrant from Chhattisgarh, claims to be a descendant of the 'Nats' of Rajasthan but lives in a tent-like temporary shanty in the suburbs of Kolkata with wife Radha and the children, two sons and four daughters.

"For several months each year, hundreds of wayside performers called 'Nats' make the chaotic and colourful metropolis of Calcutta their temporary home. They live in tents pitched a few hundred meters away from the railway tracks. 'Nats' are traditional performers—singers, actors, dancers, acrobats, all rolled into one. They spend their nights in the tents and their days in the big city where there is a ready audience for their entertaining skills. This film is about one of the 'Nat' families living in these tents in conditions that even the most primitive municipality should not approve of," explains Sinha.

Today, the 'Nats' are outside the caste system and are considered untouchables. The medieval Rajputs were fearless warriors while Ratan Singh and others of his 'Nat' fraternity earn their living as wayside performers. The camera opens on the crudely painted face of a little boy of six or seven. His name is Raja Hindustani, after the popular Aamir Khan hit because his parents say he was born the day *Raja Hindustani* (1996) was released. He is a street performer who performs on the streets of Kolkata, on railway platforms of Sealdah and Howrah, with his elder brother Toofan and sister Jyotsna, to the accompaniment of a cheap *dholak* (a percussion instrument played in Indian musical performances) that has seen better days. This little boy Raja and his kin are the heroes of Sinha's 107-minute long *King of India*.

Sinha is a leading Indian documentary film-maker. He has won some of the most prestigious awards in the world for his films—in Leipzig, Bilbao, New York and Japan. He also won the prestigious Hoso-Bunka Foundation TV Documentary Competition in 2001. He won the National Award (President's Award) eight times, five times as director and three times as producer. "'Nats' are mentioned in texts like *Manu Smriti* and Kautilya's *Arthashastra*, each at least 2,000 years old. 'Nats' are to be found in practically every part of the Indian subcontinent; they hold their separate social identity close to their heart. They are often gifted both in looks and artistic qualities, being robust, sensuous, nomadic, and carefree. They are also known to encourage their women to practice prostitution on the side to augment their earnings," he elaborates.

Raja, Toofan, Jyotsna, Reshma and Chandni are neither good-looking nor healthy. Janaki, the eldest, would have been good-looking but she does not perform. They commute every day to Kolkata by local trains without tickets, carrying their equipment and dholak along to perform for money. The earnings are taken away by their parents to keep the family fires burning. The parents are not bothered about their education, health and nutritional needs. *King of India*, picking the story of these children, exploited by their own parents, grows up with them as, one by one, they go their separate ways, with the younger, very small siblings filling in the vacuum they leave behind.

Ratan Singh's time is spent on putting make-up on their faces with indigenously prepared black kohl for eyes, moustache, etc., some garish red paint for lipstick and rouge and talcum powder for the face. The rest of his time is spent drinking and dancing away in merriment, singing old Hindi film songs and taking pride in his ancestry. The deep influence of Hindi mainstream cinema on the lives of the family and on the performances of the children comes across strongly. When the family walks out of a temporary theatre after watching a Bengali film, Singh spells out the names of three popular Hindi films from which ideas and plots have been lifted in this film.

The wife pitches in cooking and cleaning as the debts begin to mount. When asked why they do not send their kids to school, Ratan Singh says they cannot afford to, adding, "What will they gain from schooling?" A while later, Radha smiles and says, "We are smart people you see? Our children earn a lot; so instead of our spending money on education that will hardly bring in ₹6,000 per month, without education, they can bring in much more every day." However, her daughter-in-law Julie repeats that she wants to send her son Kishore Kumar (named after the playback singer) to school because "he will be able to read and write and keep *hisaab-kitaab* (keep track of one's money) and maintain accounts and will not be cheated".

Over the six-year span the film covers, Sinha shows how the eldest girl, Janaki, is married off to a boy from another family of 'Nats' in their Chhattisgarh village. Toofan grows up to marry Julie, a love marriage. Along with his wife and infant Kishore Kumar, he heads the siblings in their daily routine. Ranjan Palit's camera returns again and again to the performing kids, closing up on the smiling painted face of Raja Hindustani, or on Julie's collection plate as she goes around the crowd to collect the money. There is one touching shot showing Toofan and Julie's toddler carted around for the shows, turning on his stomach to puke on the street. Another shocking sequence shows Chandni fall off the makeshift trapeze during a performance that hurts her but no one talks about taking her to a doctor, including Chandni herself. Another scene shows little Kishore Kumar trying to learn the tricks of the trade when he has not even begun to talk!

The film is a wide canvas of life lived off the dredges of poverty that Ratan Singh lives in with his family. The camera travels into streets and bylanes of a Kolkata we do not generally get to see, thus throwing up a collage of the city from a perspective we are not familiar with. "I have tried to take both a macro and a micro view of the 'Nat' community of performers in the backdrop of a totally insensitive 'mainstream' India which is unwilling to provide physical space to these people living in the margins. No one either cares or notices their presence among pigs and dogs and rodents and I found them co-existing without any qualms in blissful harmony along the railway tracks," informs Sinha who grew close to the Singh family over the six years he took to shoot the film.

Through the story of these children, their parents and their pathetic state of existence, Sinha makes a scathing indictment on the skewed development that globalization has brought forth. "The story of children like Raja Hindustani is just a tip of the massive iceberg of a growing population that remains completely forgotten when the benefits of globalization are shared by the fortunate few. Ratan Singh, his wife Radha who he throws out when Julie enters to take charge, their children and grandchildren are merely a metaphor for the massive poor whose lives have not been touched by the booming economy," sums up Sinha. The names of these children stand out in stark irony against the films they are named after. In this sense, *King of India* is a powerful sociopolitical statement. At the same time, it also raises questions and points an accusing finger at a Shining India of which we are a part, where even the radiance of the glitter does not reach the lives of these children who light up their street audience with joy and fun, but they remain in the dark themselves.

Between the Devil and the Deep River

This documentary directed by Arvind Sinha, tries to discover the authenticity of a downtrodden people, where the setting is north Bihar, from deep feelings of nostalgia. Sinha is from north Bihar himself. He has tried to fix his emotional perspective within a social process, which naturally evolves into a strong political statement.

Arvind Sinha is not an astrologer or a soothsayer. He is a documentary film-maker. Precisely four years ago, in 2004, Max Mueller Bhavan of the Goethe Institute, Kolkata, screened his documentary *Between the Devil and the Deep River* (1999). The film is born out of the personal pain of belonging to north Bihar, of helplessly watching his homeland being washed away just because of the failed planning of the powers that be. He has witnessed, at first hand, the devastation that has ravaged his region year after year. The film was so moving that most of us, including film-maker Mrinal Sen, wished to see it again. Therefore, thanks to Mrinal Sen, the film was screened a second time some time later, drawing a full house for both screenings. The film takes the viewers back to show readers how clearly the present ravaging floods in Bihar—resulting from the Kosi shifting its flow that took a toll of several lakh villagers who are now forced to live in tents and eat handouts for survival—was foretold in this film.

Bihar is easily identified in the national psyche with a mafia Raj, with a politics that presents the best model lesson in corruption, exploitation and dehumanization of its people, with Lalu Prasad Yadav, his cronies, their circus antics and their magical tricks forming the centre of its sociopolitical map. Lurking behind this mafia landscape, in north Bihar, a living history of tragedy is being written since 1947. It is a history that defines a strange conflict between man and nature, where nature is constantly defying man's persistent attempts to control and conquer it. It is a history where the once-affluent peasant populace, sandwiched between these two strong powers, has been reduced to impoverished destitution, having lost their land, their close ones, their homes, their lives. A history where a once-lush green mantle of enchantment has been converted to sheets of water, till as far as your eyes can reach, angry waters, wavy waters, dirty waters. For the first time in the history of cinema, Arvind Sinha, a dedicated young film-maker, decided to archive this incredible real-life story of human tragedy on celluloid, for posterity. The apt name of the film is *Between the Devil and the Deep River*.

The crux lies in the forced embankment of the Kosi River passed in the parliament and the Bihar Legislative Assembly in 1953 as a 'solution' to this most flood-prone state in India. Soon after, other rivers of north Bihar were also embanked without debate, just by citing the example of the Kosi. The results have been disastrous. Before the embankment in 1954, when the length of the embankment was 160 kms, the flood-prone area covered 2.5 million hectares of land, mostly fertile and cultivable land. In 1999, with the length of the embankment spanning 3,465 kms along the Kosi and other rivers in north Bihar, the flood-prone area has extended to 6.9 million hectares, almost three times more than what it was in 1954! This, after having spent ₹8,000 million of the taxpayers' money. Today, 900,000 hectares of land is permanently waterlogged because of this state 'intervention', and 6.5 million human beings in these waterlogged areas are now human 'amphibians' and continue to be so. This incredibly true story of man's inhuman apathy to fellow humans comes across in this aesthetically beautiful statement on celluloid.

"Embankments instil a false sense of security and people continue to occupy the flood plains till a breach occurs, when a tidal wave hits them with tremendous force because the river beds of the embanked rivers have risen by 15 to 16 feet and thus the countryside is much lower now. The Kosi embankments have been raised by two metres in the lower reaches, keeping pace with the rising level of the river bed," says a graphic in the film. The locals have discovered their own solution—breaking the embankments on both sides! Their act, at the first instance, has been taken to be illegal. But they go on nevertheless "because this is the only way to reclaim our lands for us, to live a life of dignity and not depend on so-called relief," they say.

Sinha has worked out a beautiful blend of aesthetics and documentation, interviews, live footage, graphics and music, as his camera pans across a village fair, a skeletal marriage 'procession', a group of young men ruing the day the government decided to twist their fates for all time in the name of 'development'. He uses music, mainly in the shape of Kabir's *dohas* (a form of self-contained rhyming couplet in poetry) on the soundtrack, alternating this with a Hindi film song from *Teesri Kasam* (1967) ("paan khaaye sainya hamaaro") blaring forth on the loudspeaker at the fair. The camera often closes in on the face of a woman, a face that bears wrinkles belying her age, who speaks of mass male migration to Punjab and Delhi and Calcutta, effectively reducing landed peasants to daily wage workers. "What's the use of your taking photos?" she asks, her question making its own statement. The faces are more puzzled than sad. Their voices are a deadpan monotone, because that cruel 'instrument' called 'induced reality' has blunted their emotions. Sinha has stuck almost rigidly to the straightforward development of a linear narrative. The organizing sensibility of the film gives respective representation to the victims of this designed 'carnage', to experts, to social activists, to young, old, men and women victims.

Shot extensively in north Bihar, the film articulates, in various dimensions, the lives of people whose fate is inextricably linked to the forces of nature. Even before flood control measures were started, north Bihar had been witnessing floods every four to five years—so this was not an unknown feature for the local inhabitants. Over the years, with each consequent flood, they developed their own coping mechanisms, which soon became integral to their culture. The technocentric flood control measures that were started in the 1950s primarily included embanking of rivers. The embankments have not been of much use—on the contrary, they themselves resulted in large-scale flooding and waterlogging that have, over the years, submerged vast tracts of land and in the process, left millions destitute.

Stripped even of the basic amenities of sustainable livelihood, the people of north Bihar are compelled to leave their families in search of employment. Thus begins a new and continuous diaspora—a whole mass of people constantly in the elusive search of employment, security and some stability. They are viewed as nothing more than cheap labour. This enhances their vulnerability. The tragedy is paradoxed by the fact that north Bihar is a fertile land with an abundance of water. Yet, the primary reason for the wretched condition of its people boils down to these 'man-made floods' resulting from the disastrous and unplanned embankments.

"For the people of Bihar to get out of this morass, they must find hope and ideals once again. They must benefit from the bounties with which Nature has endowed their land. They must discover themselves with the pride of ancestry and hope for their progeny. They must once and for all, shed the shackles of inequity, which have been imposed on most of them. And they must discover a new politics," says the optimistic graphic towards the end of the film.

Sinha has convincingly established all possible subtexts that the issue of floods, waterlogging, massive displacement and ruthless trampling of human rights have thrown up. He has not permitted the film the oft-repeated cliché of a blurred focus. He has emphasized issues such as migration, the vulnerability of women and child labour and so on. The film probes deeply into the reality that lies behind stark facts. "The idea that nature can be conquered, carries within it, the seed of human destruction. The onus of adaptation lies on human beings, not on Nature." This is the central theme around which Arvind Sinha's *Dui Paatan Ke Beech Mein* (Between the Devil and the Deep River) works.

Kalo Shekh

Alok Das' has a deceptively simple appearance. However, behind the simplicity lies a heart that beats for unusual subjects of human empathy he transforms into a documentary film. Alok Das' creative juices seem to get triggered by nature. His first film, *Lyrics of No Life* (1995), explored the subhuman living conditions along the slum dwellers on either side of the squalor and mush-filled Rajabazar Canal in Calcutta. It was a no-holds-barred expose of official apathy to the plight of people already living amidst the debris of a city, a microcosmic view of the face of nature distorted beyond recognition. It was screened at the MIFF some years ago. His second film, *The Last Lady*, was a personal tribute to Lady Ranu Mukherjee, the woman who enhanced and enriched Calcutta's world of art and culture with her personal contribution to it.

His third film is *Kalo Shekh* (2010), a documentary he produced with his own money. It is about the single-minded determination of an unlettered man named Kalo Shekh who is tall, very dark, muscled and strong, who wears a loose band around his head, looks as ferocious as a dacoit. However, his life is dedicated to the preservation of trees in the Kashiara village near Labhpur in West Bengal where he lives. Within its brief, 13-minute span, the film shows how Kalo wanders around the tree-lined, earthy roads and stops a police officer who tries to touch a tree. When Kalo protests loudly, the officer tells him that he is a high-ranking officer. However, Kalo is not to be deterred by the man's designation. It is only when the man walks away from the scene that Kalo calls him and asks to be forgiven for his rudeness. "It's okay. I have done something wrong. Sorry," says and police officer, walking away.

A villager tells the film-maker, "The collective effort of villagers of Kurumba, Malari, Thesera, Budhura, Aamnagar and Sheikhpara saw the planting of many trees in this forest. The Panchayat has cooperated with us. Kalo Shekh was given the responsibility of looking after these trees under the new project. Earlier, under the Kelar Company's project, people would cut down the trees. But now, Kalo bhai has given up all other work to guard these trees." However, Kalo bhai's wife is far from happy. "He gets no money at all. He has stopped working as daily labour and guards the trees in the forest," she comments with a sad face, adding "The two of us, mother and daughter, work with clothes and we have some goats and somehow manage to eke out a living. Kalo does not even look our way. The trees are his family and his home. He spends his days and nights with those trees."

"I I discovered him in one of my journeys and through a small bit of news in a Bengali daily. I went to find out what he is all about. The result is this film," the film-maker sums up. The cinematography and the sound design of the film leave room for improvement. The film closes with a Baul performer walking down the roads where Kalo is doing his rounds. The Baul keeps singing a famous folk song that goes, "I will live under the tree, I will not leave it," which is also the theme song of the film.

Nakusha—The Unwanted

This is a documentary film jointly directed by Rima Amrapurkar and Sanjay Shukla. The film narrates the shocking story of 292 *nakushas* today in Maharashtra's Satara district. What does the word 'nakusha' mean? Roughly translated from Marathi, it simply means 'unwanted'. And this is the name these girls have been christened with at the time of their birth because their parents, families and relatives did not want a daughter!

Image 8.2. *Nakusha—The Unwanted*

Courtesy: Rema Amrapurkar and Sanjay Shukla

Satara is among Maharashtra's comparatively financially better off districts. This does not change the fact that families still have a strong preference for the male heir. The film shows how in an effort to change attitudes towards daughters, its district collector (DC) initiated renaming ceremonies and rewards for families who agreed to give their girls a 'new beginning'. "We do many film projects for various NGOs. While shooting for one such project last year, we came across this school girl named Nakusha. This did not ring a bell till someone told us that her name had been recently changed because her original name meant 'unwanted.' Then, a few more conversations with people in the area revealed that it was quite a common phenomenon," said Amrapurkar, a noted documentary and feature film-maker who has worked in different capacities for films both features and documentaries.

The directors approach girls of different ages but mostly from impoverished backgrounds in different pockets of the Satara district. One says that she was named by her grandmother while another says she does not know who named her but it has been a cause for embarrassment for her in school till she got used to it and so did her friends. With the thought of carrying around the fact of being unwanted from the time one remembered and that too simply by name, one is not only constantly reminded about being unwanted but also unwittingly spreading the news across one's world that one is really unwanted. "We realised the impact of the psychological torture these girls must be going through. We felt this urgent need to tell the world about this cruel social truth because few know about this. This motivated us to make the film," informs Rima.

Nakusha—The Unwanted is produced by the non-resident Indian (NRI) Madhav Namjoshi who lives in New Jersey and was impressed with another documentary made by the director duo on female foeticide and wanted to fund films on critical issues to create social awareness. Madhav Namjoshi Productions produced it and Amrapurkar and Shukla's Samvedana Film Foundation handled the production of the film.

Haima Deshpande informs us that Satara's villagers do not hold naming ceremonies for baby girls. Nor do they spend on their nutrition, welfare and education. Many lactating mothers are not allowed to breastfeed their little daughters. Girls who are privileged enough to have been breastfed are not entitled to milk once they are weaned off their mothers' milk. Typically, even otherwise, male kids get to eat first and their sisters make do with leftovers. Likewise, new clothes or toys are a boy's prerogative. Incidentally, Satara, home to a majority of Maharashtra's politicians, has a sex ratio of 881 girls for every 1,000 boys.

Sometime in August–September 2011, the DC, Dr Ramaswamy N., hoped to change things for the better and, towards this end, he launched a house-to-house campaign to identify all girls named Nakusha, and accord them dignity. The DC's office identified 900 such girls since the campaign but the older girls confessed that they were already so used to Nakusha as their name and known by that name within the family, school and neighbourhood that the change in name did not quite matter anymore but did make them feel a bit better than they did before.

The collectorate held a lavish naming ceremony for all Nakushas, and gave them all a new name. This name defined a new identity for them and was registered with the civic body or municipality. It does not stop there. Their parents are given free rations, and the renamed girl child gets access to the state government's free education and transportation schemes. Social workers have promised to monitor such families and ensure that the child is treated well at home.

However, the film does not get into the minute details of this official renaming and chooses to focus on the girls instead. Says Rima, "Personally, we believe that official renaming has not changed the status quo of their lives because as long as everyone around them does not call them by their changed name, they will never be able to forget that their names were such." The film includes interviews with a psychiatrist, a social worker and a religion expert, which, feels Rima, were necessary to bring out the finer points of the issue. "This was a private project, so we did not face any pressure for interviews of leaders or government officials," she says.

Having lived for several years with the socially ostracizing name, the feeling of betrayal by their loved ones is still deeply rooted in their hearts. So, even if their parents and others in the family do call them by the new names, they are confused about whether they are being called by their new names because the government wants this or whether the family really wants to call them by their new names.

"Basically, the girl identifying herself with her childhood name says that she is still not sure if her status as 'unwanted' has changed. To put it straight, these girls were betrayed by their family by being labelled 'unwanted'. Then, the government made an event of renaming them, but did not bother to change the names in places where it mattered...on birth certificates, on school/college registers, gazettes.... So the confusion of their status wanted/unwanted still continues," sums up Rima.

Angels of a Troubled Paradise

This is a 26-minute long documentary directed by Raja Shabir Khan. The film tracks three years in the life of 11-year-old Adil who grows to be 14 when the film ends. The film is dedicated to the memory of film-maker Raja Shabir Khan's cousin who was shot dead in 1992 by Indian forces when he was just 11. Adil, the protagonist, is also 11 when the film opens. There is a beautiful prologue that shows visuals of a shikara being rowed by a boatman on Dal Lake shot in silhouette against a setting sun. This is followed by the beautiful landscape of Kashmir filled with snow-capped mountains and tall trees with the soundtrack playing traditional Kashmiri music. The scene cuts to a boy and a girl walking through tall blades of grass to school. This rhythm of peace and harmony is suddenly shaken by the sound of gunshots as the camera cuts to scenes of armed forces walking through smoke-filled gullies and pictures of wailing mothers grieving the dead.

The film tracks the everyday life of Adil who lives in Srinagar, based on an occupation no civilian in the rest of India can even dream of. Adil is the sole earning member of a very poor family. He is a school dropout who collects used tear smoke shells from different places in the city and sells them as scrap to the scrap dealers to eke out a living. The scrap dealers do not accept shells with the remnant of the gas inside. So Adil and other boys like him must empty the shells. Some of these are 'live' which carry the risk of the boys losing their lives in case of an explosion. "Are you not afraid of the police and the military?" asks the voice-over. "I used to be, but I am not afraid anymore. I pose to be a gentle boy and they don't say anything," he says. He puts a pinch of salt under his tongue in case he begins to experience tears from a live shell because, "salt dilutes the effect of smoke".

Adil has become an expert in removing the detonator and take out the explosive material from inside. He says, "It is better to die bravely collecting shells than out of hunger." His dream is to buy a study desk for his little sister. When he saved enough from his meagre earnings to buy one, the money had to be used in a nasal surgery for the sister! So he is saving again. He is able to sell around 2–3 kgs of shells per day and gives the money to his parents for the family's expenses.

"I spent almost three years on making *Angels of Troubled Paradise*," says director Shabir Khan about this film which was one among three prizewinners at the *Asian Pitch* in 2010. "Because of the nature and theme of the film, I faced a tough time while shooting it. The security scenario demanded extreme care and caution and it was not advisable to move with a full-fledged crew," he adds. The film also received the second prize in the documentary section at the Third Siliguri International Film Festival. It received high commendation for its in-depth and time-based exploration of the conflict in Kashmir seen from a completely different perspective. "Having got close to Adil, his family and his friends, I practically experienced at first hand the truth behind the adage 'survival of the fittest' as children like Adil know it best," Khan sums up.

Ocean of Tears

Ocean of Tears is a 27-minute documentary film directed by Bilal A. Jan that portrays the oppression, humiliation and torture of Kashmiri women because of the ethnic conflict that is raging across the state. The film has been produced by the PSBT, New Delhi. Nusrat Andrabi, social worker and civil rights activist, says that no action has been taken on 2,500 rape cases by the security forces, which is the highest in the country.

Ocean of Tears scans incidents of concrete rapes, beatings and murder of women across time. This is the very first documentary that focusses on the physical, social, psychological and emotional violence inflicted on the girls and women in the valley. The violence has been inflicted both by Indian security forces and by Kashmiri militants. It covers rape, beatings and murder, and victimization of women whose husbands have gone missing. *Ocean of Tears* narrates the untold stories of victims who endured social, economic, physical, mental and emotional abuse and reveals their struggle for justice.

Image 8.3. *Ocean of Tears*: Bilal A. Jan on Location

Courtesy: Bilal A. Jan

Bilal and his crew came across a high percentage of violence against women due to the ongoing conflict of the past 23 years, in terms of sexual violence—rape, abduction, eve-teasing of women and girls. Insecurity is the biggest issue in Kashmir, particularly in rural areas where military bunkers or police and Central Reserve Police Force (CRPF) checking spots are a common sight.

The film goes back to the Kunan Poshpora mass rape incident in 1991 in the frontier district of Kupwara, the most high-profile gang rape during the two decades of conflict. On the night of 23–24 February 1991, according to the villagers' statement and newspaper reports, over 32 women and children were gang-raped in Kunan Poshpora.

Neelofar, 24, and Asia, 18, of Shopian were molested, raped and killed and their bodies dumped in a stream nearby by two members of the Rashtriya Rifles. There were three investigations into these deaths—the Jan Commissions' investigation, the Special Investigation Team's (SIT's) investigation and the Central Bureau of Investigation (CBI) that was brought in before the SIT could even submit its report. However, the CBI distorted the report and tweaked the medical reports so that the culprits could be protected and go unpunished.

The gruesome and cold-blooded killing of two sisters, Akhtara and Asifa, by militant gunmen is another case. One of the attackers, Wasam Ganai, was killed in an encounter while Muzaffar Naik has not yet been captured. Ashmal, a young woman, was raped when she had gone to collect grass by some men of the Rashtriya Rifles on 20 April 2012. Her 13-year-old daughter Kulsum saw this from behind a tree. Ashmal died of cardiac arrest on the way to hospital and her daughter's eyewitness account did not stand in court because she was a child at the time.

The Association of Parents of Disappeared Persons (APDP) was formed in 1994 by families of victims of enforced and involuntary disappearances of family members. The Association records that between 8,000 and 10,000 people have been missing during different regimes since 1989 and APDP is carrying an ongoing campaign against their disappearing family members. Mymoona Banu's husband Akhtar Hussan has been missing for 14 years and she is left alone to take care of the family. He disappeared after he left to attend a friend's funeral. She is a microcosm of all the half-widows who are members of APDP. *Ocean of Tears* is a shocking film. It is also a learning experience and a political statement that militates against government inaction.

110002

It is the story of Kunwarpal, father of an 11-year-old who went missing in November 2010. Since then, Kunwarpal has been running from pillar to post only to be left disappointed and empty handed. Through Kunwarpal's search for his missing child, *110002* (2013) documents the pain and misery of millions of such parents. It speaks about the trauma that they have to undergo each day of their lives in the hope that their loved ones would return some day. They do not.

The mother of a missing child beats herself every day with her slippers in the hope that this self-punishment will reward her with the return of her missing child. Another mother says that she keeps visiting *dargah*s (a Sufi Islamic shrine built over the grave of a revered religious figure) and masjids across the city but does not have any idea about whether her missing girl will be found or not.

Image 8.4. 110002

Courtesy: Vivek Asri

"The police do not help us and tell us to fend for ourselves," says one father who sticks posters of his missing boy on tree trunks and outside shops. "There is a certainty when a child dies. But when a child goes missing, the uncertainty is killing," he adds.

110002 is a documentary by activist-journalist Vivek Asri. 110002 is the office where every parent of a missing child runs around. This is the office where their hopes lie only to be shattered because of the insensitive and unresponsive system. The address is—Missing Person's Squad, New Police Station, Daryaganj, New Delhi-110002.

"The film was triggered by a sense of guilt and shame within me. A few years ago, I had found a crying child at a Delhi bus stop. She was too small and too terrified to answer my simple questions about her parents, her address, etc. Not knowing what to do, I handed her over to a policeman. But till date, I have no idea about whether the police traced her roots and took her back to her parents or sent her back to the streets. I should have followed the case myself knowing that the police functions irresponsibly in these cases. But should I not have shown more responsibility?" the film-maker asks rhetorically.

"Daryaganj is filled with people essentially from the lower middle and working classes where most residents, Hindus and

Muslims, lead almost a hand-to-mouth existence. So, their children are not kidnapped for ransom. Nor do they just walk away on their own. They do not simply vanish in thin air. They are kidnapped as the major source for trafficking which spans a large chain of operators in connivance with the police. I have tried to bring this across in the film because the poor are victimised not only by their ignorance and their poverty but most importantly, by police apathy and by an establishment that does not have a monitoring system in place," says Vivek.

Yeh Hai Malegaon Ka Superman (The Superman of Malegaon)

Faiza Khan in her first film negotiates a relationship between the documentary and the making of a feature film called *Yeh Hai Malegaon Ka Superman* (2009) by a group of cinema lovers rooted in Malegaon, within the Nashik district in the State of Maharashtra. This film within the film is being directed by a local named Shaikh Nasir who has a family business in readymade garments but has preferred to surrender to his obsession—films and film-making. The film opens on this passion the entire community of Malegaon lives with. A small boy plays a street game to attract crowds.

Image 8.5. Superman of Malegaon

Courtesy: Faiza Ahmed

The pebbles or boxes he plays with are named after three top female stars of Bollywood. Hair-cutting saloons proudly display posters of male Bollywood stars promising to copy starry hairstyles according to their clients' choice. Her film is also called *Supermen of Malegaon*.

Supermen of Malegaon unravels a fascinating story of a ragtag crew of people from Malegaon who have set out to make a 'Superman meets Bollywood' take on established box office hits such as *Sholay* or *Don* (1978) or *Superman* (1978) on a shoestring budget with local actors who usually work in the power looms that form the major source of employment for the men. Malegaon's population is 70 per cent Muslim and 30 per cent Hindu who live on either side of the local river. Though there is little love lost between them, the one great factor that bonds the two is their love for films. In its form and content, the film touches upon a wide landscape of issues ranging from the documentary form and its changing aesthetics, mission and content, particularly within the Asian subcontinent, to the question of how this regional, low budget cinema in the country can strike so endearing a chord among the local audience. "We give a comic twist to the original source to make it credible and appealing," says Shaikh, simply. How is that done? "Well, we show that a given character, say Superman, is affected by environmental pollution and is suffering from asthma and, therefore, cannot fight his enemies all the time," he explains, raising laughter among the audience. It also deals with issues of adaptation, parody and the relationship between mainstream Bombay cinema and regional cinemas, among other things.

The film provokes laughter, offers entertainment and also educates and informs without either reducing itself to becoming pedantic or turning into a sombre critique of contemporary reality. It does not take potshots at the establishment. Nor does it become a diatribe against any given communal or linguistic group. It sets out to entertain and entertain it most certainly does.

Char—The No Man's Island
The movie, directed by Saurav Sarangi, won accolades and awards right across the world. *Char—The No Man's Island* points out how even nature has neither sympathy nor understanding for this vulnerable group of people who live a precarious existence on a tract of land that has risen up on the Ganges near Farakka Barrage in

Image 8.6. *Char—The No Man's Island*

Courtesy: Sourav Sarangi

West Bengal in the fear of losing everything to the eroding shores of the river and the rising tides which can happen any minute, washing them away. The island is named 'No Man's Island' because it is as fragile as the people who live on it.

The film follows the journey and lifestyle of 14-year-old Rubel who lives in the Char and has dreams of making it big in some other city because he knows about the fate of Char. Rubel is the single earning member of a family living on the dredges of poverty not knowing where the next meal will come from and if it does, whether they will still be around to eat it. Rubel crosses the Ganges which divides this section of India from Bangladesh. He smuggles rice from India to Bangladesh where the point of crossing acts as the international border. They are basically from India but the river eroded the residents of these people from mainland India when Rubel was only four years old. He wanted to study but there is no school and his parents are not interested in his education because that will place their lives at stake.

The camera that is also an invisible 'character' in the film and a 'voice' speaking silently about Rubel and his fellow beings follows the lives of these people, sometimes with candid forthrightness and often, quite clandestinely in the middle of the night through a monochrome green light that invests the scenario with a strange, mysterious aura, throwing up the people in the tragic reality of having their lives dictated by the border patrol, merciless in their dealings with them. Sarangi has painstakingly followed the cycle of seasons across the panoramic landscape whose picturesque beauty stands in sharp contrast to the tragic reality of their lives teetering between life and death. There is no school, no medical facilities, no NGO to take recourse to when a young married girl is not accepted by her husband and in-laws because her parents cannot shell out ₹50,000 dowry!

Rubel's first visit to Kerala ends in failure, and he loses the money he had earned and saved to seek greener pastures there. In the end of the film, he deserts his home and family again and Sarangi comes to find him missing. We, the city dwellers who live in the comfort of shopping malls and multiplex theatres and luxury cars, cannot imagine that not very far away, some of our own people are living every day with the fear of death either out of poverty or due to the erosion of the island they live in, or both. The editing is sequential because Rubel's story has a linear narrative moving away for moments to detract and focus on other lands and other people. Sarangi talks to the residents, asking them normal questions about their lives yet keeps an objective distance that helps the viewers to draw their own conclusions. "The Char may disappear but I will not" is Rubel's message to us through Sarangi.

Flickering Angels

Directed by Subhrajit Mitra and produced by Gaurang Films, *Flickering Angels* is a documentary that takes us on a learning journey into the lives of some of the girl children of prisoners—undertrials and more, who, with the help of concerned citizens of society, are trying to triumph over the social and financial hurdles life has carved out for them. Separation from their parents has not been much of a hurdle for these girl children of West Bengal in the sense that they are being taken care of by a home run by a group of kind-hearted nuns. The home is called Daya Bari, situated in a remote area in Ranaghat, along the India–Bangladesh border. This heart-warming tale of the children of convicts had been selected at the Utopia Film Festival, Greenbelt Maryland, Washington, D.C., the 30th Teheran International Short Film Festival (TISFF), Teheran, and the Kolkata International Film Festival (KIFF).

Image 8.7. A Poster of *Flickering Angels*

Courtesy: Gaurang Jalan

The film is an exception to society's ignorant state of indifference towards these young children marginalized for no fault of their own. *Flickering Angels* is the most ideal title one could have created for a group of girls ranging between the ages of 6 and 16. They are lights that are not fully switched on by life nor are they immersed in complete darkness. Their parents are either undertrials or inmates in prisons across West Bengal. They look with vacant expressions without a smile until they warm up to some people from the mainstream trying to bring new meaning into their lives.

The film focusses on a few of the 40 girls living in Daya Bari. The most tragic story is that of Afroza. Her mother was arrested while crossing the Bangladesh–India border illegally. Afroza was just five years old in 2009. Her mother, Manowara Begum, died during her prison term. No one knew where her father was. Afroza's brother Munna had already been sent back to Bangladesh. However, it was difficult to repatriate Afroza. Hope is not bright but flickers all the time as they prepare themselves in the home to face the future when they are 18 and have to fend for themselves in the world out there. The girls in Daya Bari are children of parents who are in prison often caught while crossing the India-Bangladesh border illegally, or captured for being Maoist extremists, or for some other reason.

"We arranged the admission of Afroza under 'Cottage Scheme' through the Directorate of Social Welfare, Government of West Bengal, for her education, lodging and rehabilitation at Daya Bari run by 'Sisters of Charity of Saint B. Capitation V. Gerosa' based in Kolkata. It was not easy because Afroza was a foreigner and red tape came in the way of her admission to any Indian mainstream school. Munna, her brother was repatriated to Bangladesh in 2011 but Afroza remained behind," says B.D. Sharma, Indian Police Service (IPS), Additional Director General (ADG) (East), Border Security Force (BSF), in West Bengal who has been a key figure in organizing the rehabilitation and training of these girls who are sheltered in Daya Bari. He takes personal care of each of these children and monitors their progress every now and then through personal visits.

When Sharma informed the West Bengal Human Rights Commission about the death of Manowara Begum, the Commission awarded a compensation of ₹150,000 each to Afroza and her brother Munna Pervez for their mother's custodial death at Berhampore. The money has been handed over to her at the time of her repatriation.

Others who have enriched the narrative of *Flickering Angels* with their expert comments and concern are Justice Shri Ashok Kr. Ganguly, Chairperson, West Bengal Human Rights Commission, Ranvir Kumar, IPS, Inspector General (IG), Correctional Services, Government of West Bengal, and Dr Sabyasachi Mitra, consultant neuropsychiatrist.

The film follows the past journeys of some of these girls who go through the rudiments of elementary education in Daya Bari alongside training in some technical skills to equip them for financial independence later on in life. This process protects them from the evils that dog girl children of prison inmates and undertrials from being trafficked as the state of West Bengal is bordered on three sides that often become easy ways of trafficking these unprotected girls. Shri Ganguly stressed on the legal details of these children who are practically persona non grata and have no locus standi in society.

"Worse is that they carry the social stigma of their parents' imprisonment even when the parent has been wrongfully imprisoned for a simple crime like trying to cross the border without legal papers," informs Sharma. "These girls are doubly handicapped by poverty and by the fact that they are identified with parents who are prison inmates who, it is assumed, are criminals. Even worse is the position of girls who belong to Bangladesh and must be extradited on legal grounds even when they have no home to go back to. They long to belong to the mainstream and it is our duty, as open-minded citizens, to accept them into the mainstream. This will go a long way in establishing a secure future for them and by them," sums up Dr Mitra.

"The story of Afroza will go a long way in promoting mutual friendship and understanding between India and Bangladesh. It will also hopefully reinforce the basic child rights of all children of the entire world regardless of their nationality, religion, caste and creed," sums up Sharma. *Flickering Angels* is an optimistic film filled with hope because the brief narratives of the little girls are often intercut with people who really care for them. Afroza's story is a sterling example of the power of cinema in changing lives and mindsets.

During director general-level talks between BSF, India, and Border Guard Bangladesh, Dhaka, Sharma handed over the first copy of *Flickering Angels* to Major General Anwar Hussain, DG, Border Guard, Bangladesh, requesting him for the safe repatriation of the child to her native place. Hussain was touched. He was so emotionally moved by the film that he assured Sharma he would take charge of Afroza's education till graduation, including her marriage. Afroza was officially repatriated on 14 September 2013 accompanied by B.D. Sharma to Dhaka. Afroza, who hardly smiles or talks, was sent back, smiling at last. She would have been lost completely if she did not get shelter in Daya Bari under the tender care of Sister Marietta, Superintendent, Daya Bari.

Our Family
Our Family (2007) is a 56-minute Tamil (with English subtitles) documentary, written and directed by K.P. Jayasankar and Anjali Monteiro, a husband–wife team who combine academia with activism and film-making. Jointly, they have won more than a dozen national and international awards for their films. This film elucidates what it means to free oneself of the social construct of being male and explores life beyond a hetero-normative family. It was produced by the Centre for Media and Cultural Studies, Tata Institute of Social Sciences, Mumbai. What does it mean to cross that line

Image 8.8. *Our Family*

Courtesy: K.P. Jayshankar and Anjalie Monteiro

which sharply divides us on the basis of gender? To free oneself of the socially constructed onus of being male? Is there life beyond a hetero-normative family? These are some questions this film tries to address and deal with, some answers provided by the subjects within the film.

Set in Tamil Nadu, *Our Family* is a different kind of documentary film that for the first time perhaps puts across a powerful statement on alternative sexuality and on new forms of family that one would not generally conceive of. With a running time of 56 minutes, the film makes a statement and also raises questions. "We decided to make the film when we met Aasha through Pritham, who is our friend. We wanted to do it as a collaborative project, not one that dictated terms to them," says Anjali Monteiro who has jointly directed the film with her husband Jayasankar. Who is Pritham? Pritham K. Chakravarthy is a transgendered subject who does a one-person performance called *Nirvanam* which means 'liberation'. The name of the performance is taken from the traditional name given to the ritualistic surgical removal of the male genital that finally converts a male to a female. The film, through the point of view and first-person narrations of three generations of transgendered female subjects, unravels the strange story of how these people have knit themselves together into one family.

Aasha, Seetha and Dhana are bound together by ties of adoption. They belong to the Aravani community called '*hijras*' in some parts of the country. However, these three women are not biologically born as eunuchs. They opt to get out of their male bodies because "we are females trapped within male bodies," says Pritham who enacts the experiences of having been gang-raped, having turned into a prostitute to make both ends meet, and, finally, to come and settle down in Chennai with a one-woman performance called *Nirvanam*. Though she is one of the 'family' for some intriguing reason, they consider her the only 'outsider' and one is not clear why they qualify her like this. Her facial expressions bear the pain of her life, but one can see through the surface pain, the pride that comes across for having been able to make one of the most difficult choices an Indian can make—the right to choose her sex and leave the biological fact of her sex behind her forever.

Asha Bharathi is the 'grandmother' of the family. She is also the president of the Tamil Nadu Aravanigal Association of Chennai. Seetha, the 'daughter', lived with her male partner Selvam in Coimbatore. But sadly, Selvam passed away before the film was publicly screened. He was a young man who understood the needs of his partner completely and did not come in the way of her choices. "The issue of getting married simply did not arise and we are pulling on like a normal couple," says Seetha during the course of an interview. Dhana is the youngest. She is the adopted daughter of Seetha but her own family has also accepted her choice. So she keeps shuttling between her natural parents and her adoptive one. The film documents their journey as they discover their sexual identities and progressively blur the lines between themselves and what is seen and interpreted as normal social behaviour. "They become a regular family. So the woman Seetha does the cooking. She does assert herself but in trying to do so she asserts her womanly identity even more, one of the things that struck us was that they were normal but in trying to be normal they had to play out the politics of being normal in some sense," said K.P. Jayasankar.

"The local residents have accepted Seetha as one of them. We had a good rapport with them, so when we shot in public spaces there were no issues," says Jayasankar, who along with Montero has made 30 odd documentaries that tackle very unusual social issues. The undercurrent that runs through all their films done to date has been a detailed and insightful exploration of notions of the 'Self' and the 'Other', of 'normality' and 'deviance' of the local. "This film has been very special because it deals with a marginalized, socially oppressed and humiliated community ridiculed by most of us and avoided like the plague. We wanted to discover for ourselves and consequently for the audience, what it means to cross the gender divide, to be free of being 'male' just because the biologically determined birth has decided that one is 'male'."

"We wanted to make a film which would question the way people look at the *hijras*. We wanted to look at the human rights violation, the stigmas and also look at the warmth and celebratory aspect of it," says Monteiro. *Our Family* has been made as a collaborative project with the subjects, giving them the space to voice their concerns and reflect on the process of becoming an *Aravani*. It has been made on a shoestring budget. The directors have researched, scripted, shot and edited the film, completed production management, graphics and special effects as well as the sound design and subtitles. It has been a mutually enriching experience, for the protagonists and the directors.

"We regard the film as a useful device in their struggle to question social stigma and advocate for the rights of Aravanis in Tamil Nadu," say the directors who have kept away from peeping into the private spaces of their real-life characters with voyeuristic delight, refraining from any kind of titillation. The film attempts to bring this off-beat family into the mainstream and make it socially acceptable, throwing up how despite the apparent lack of a power base, the same hierarchy of power that ails patriarchy sustains. The film also explores how all identities are fraught with equations of power. As Dhana points out, becoming a 'woman' has its own attendant problems of lack of freedom and access to public space. The family of Seetha and Selvam reproduces, in many ways, the patriarchal mores of the larger society.

The film has been edited slickly and with imagination, clipping out much of technical detailing. It takes the viewer to the noted

Pal Utru Vizha or the 40th day celebration of Nirvanam, with graphics detailing the meanings of the alternate terms. The film closes on the discussion that boils down to a fervent appeal from this family and the community they belong to, to look upon them as normal human beings with normal desires and not as genetic freaks.

The camera designedly avoids a voyeuristic gaze and uses 'their' stories to raise questions about 'us' and our sexualities. The directors have attempted to problematize the terrain of sexuality by mainstreaming the off-mainstream. The four women question the straitjacketed sexual identities and preferences society has thrust on its unquestioning masses. At one point in the film, Dhana points out that becoming a 'woman' is not easy at all. It brings along with it associated problems of lack of freedom and access to public space. Anjalie and Jayasankar have tried to familiarize the unfamiliar, familiarizing the unfamiliar: the 'normality' of the lives of Aasha, Seetha, Selvam and Dhana question the futility of trying to straitjacket sexual identities and preferences. *Our Family* subverts all ideas of the family, whether they are patriarchal, biological or heterosexual, to give it new dimensions and dynamics.

A Poet, A City and A Footballer

Joshy Joseph's long documentary, *A Poet, A City and A Footballer* (2014), shows how the dynamics of death unfolds in varied manifestations. People filled with the vibrancy of life even after they have survived death-like situations, larger-than-life personalities such as P.K. Banerjee, one of the greatest footballer the world has ever produced, continue to infect everyone with his throbbing energy escorted by his nurse right into the football field, directing youngsters to develop the right focus in lobbing the ball, in kicking it back to fall on the front foot and so on. On the other hand, one encounters a very low-profile, occasional film-maker and gifted poet Gautam Sen who begins to shoot a documentary on the great footballer and a feature film with a superstar at the same time just after he has been diagnosed with fourth-degree terminal cancer of the lungs. This is another manifestation of death. Gautam knows his days are numbered. However, he was determined to complete both films before the final summons arrive. Sadly, he has left both films incomplete.

Image 8.9. Gautam Sen in *A Poet, A City and A Footballer*

Courtesy: Joshy Joseph

Gautam and P.K. are bound by a throbbing city that seems sometimes to be in the throes of death and sometimes wakes up to processions, crazy fights, Chinese breakfast places, colourful banners floating in the breeze, the dark night around the Kidderpore Docks and so on. It is the city of Kolkata. While Banerjee has been cited by FIFA as the Indian footballer of the 20th century, Sen is known among his close friends more as a Bohemian poet who lived life on his own terms than as a committed film-maker, though he did win the National Award for a documentary on witch-hunting.

"The trigger happened when the jury asked Gautam whether he would be able to take up the shooting or not due to his ill-health. The question invigorated his spirit. But the idea of making a film struck V.S. Kundu, Direct General of Films Division, who was in the jury and is now the creative producer of this film," says Joshy who has won five National Awards for his films among which one is for the 'best writing on cinema'.

The film meanders across the night sky against the backdrop of the Kidderpore Docks, panning across a reclining pensively Gautam passing a hand over his shaven pate post one of his many chemos, with actress Laboni Sarkar's voice-over reciting one of Gautam's poems. The voice precedes the visuals that show Laboni, once married to Gautam, talk about how a Bohemian-like

Gautam does not understand the pain that affects his close ones who are not Bohemian and cannot understand how the Bohemian mindset works.

The film is broken up into four parts and P.K. comes almost in the last segment. The mood of the film changes completely once P.K. enters as he infects the viewer with his magic charm, chatting with his star friends from football, narrating funny anecdotes and one realizes that he is perhaps the best anecdotal man in Kolkata! Once P.K. enters to present himself for Sen's documentary, Gautam sits wearily on a chair wondering what went wrong as P.K.'s larger-than-life image unwittingly takes over the entire scenario and Gautam, the director, resigns himself to this! Earlier, we also see Gautam shooting the feature film with a visibly off-mood Rituparna Sengupta waiting inside her car for the director's say-so. "Are you off-mood today?" asks Gautam but she just nods her head to say 'no'.

"The narrative technique adopted to hook the viewer is a constant shift of perspectives, from my film to the film Gautam was dreaming, then the shooting of the film on P.K. Banerjee and the fiction film. At times all these multiple perspectives converged, blurred, mingled or separated. But I also wished to signal my viewer to a somewhat linear comprehension because I am a Malayali making this rooted and organic Bengali film," explains Joshy. He has shown Gautam's dead body wreathed in flowers but has kept away from exploiting the tragedy with his camera.

In one scene within the larger film, Joshy asks Sen whether his choice of making a documentary on P.K. was motivated by the contradiction between himself—the indisciplined, crazy Bohemian who lives life by his own rules—and his subject P.K., who lives within the rigid, discipline of sports. Was this in keeping with Joshy's personal take on this contradiction or, was it something else? Joshy explains that this question came from the director Mr Kundu. "I have no clue of why Goutam was attracted to his subject P.K., I was more charged by 'how' this will bring its own tensions. I could sense rich raw-material for my film. It was a contradiction difficult to handle for Gautam.... You can see the drama in the fourth chapter," he says.

"I liked the title because it pronounces the three characters lucidly. Also, in a manner of speaking, it will prompt the discerning viewer to imagine the probable contradictions and allow him/her to make his/her own connections to it. I personally feel that Gautam was definitely a better poet, compared to Gautam, the film-maker. So, I call him a poet, in the sense that it leaves a sense of the incomplete journey of an artist. He did not consider himself a poet, even in the film. But what one thinks of oneself as a public person is not important. What is more important is what the world around is thinking about me. For me, as a film-maker and as an individual with two levels of functioning—as I also write—both dimensions are important," Joshy elaborates. The way Gautam accepts the certainty of the final exit with stoic and calm acceptance is as amazing as P.K. recounting anecdotes in his bright red tee shirt, just after a close brush with death.

A Poet, A City and A Footballer is the most difficult film Joshy says he has ever made. "Meditation on Death and Celebration of Life" may be a great tagline for the final film. "But believe me, I had to constantly turn down Gautam's invitations when he kept calling me whenever he wrote a new poem or shifted to a new room with a different view. The first day's shoot was a disaster. A film-maker himself, Gautam was conscious of the movie camera which impacted on his behaviour. The second time, I hid myself while my crew pretended that they were waiting for me to begin the shoot. My DOP [director of photography] shot him without his knowledge when Gautam was speaking naturally to his assistant Subhashish, spelling out his conception of the documentary on P.K. These are the richest moments in my film but the process was not only very difficult but also very painful," sums up Joshy.

A Poet, A City, A Footballer is a documentary created, orchestrated and synchronized by Joshy Joseph, an immigrant to Kolkata by virtue of his government job with the Films Division, who was inspired to place these two distinct individuals in the same film. While Gautam, the film-maker within the film becomes the 'subject' of Joshy's film, P.K. is the subject of Gautam's film within the film. The two individuals are also bound by their different brushes with death and by Joshy's intense camera wielded by DOP Mahesh Madhavan who does not know a word of Bengali! Is it a self-reflexive film, a tribute to Gautam Sen or a tribute to death as perceived from the perspectives of two people who have experienced death at a close hand? Perhaps the film is all of these and more.

CONCLUSION

An ethnographical documentary can emerge from an anthropological content and, alternatively, can offer readings as an investigative documentary because, along the way, an ethnological issue unfolds the truths that become investigative journalistic documents on celluloid. Several ethnographic, investigative and other similar genres evolve into powerful political statements in their own right and face problems with the Censors. For purposes of simplified understanding, in this chapter, the author has merged the ethnographic with the investigative and kept out of the box perspectives that could also be labelled miscellaneous in a different segment in the last part of this chapter. This is perhaps the most problematic area in terms of classification because there is defiance to categorization in terms of genre either through conscious design or without conscious design.

'Out of the Box' refers specifically to explorations into little-known areas, subjects and issues and experimentations across genres. However, the classifications are extremely subjective, determined as they are, by the author's perceptions of the term 'out of the box', which may differ from different groups of readers, cineastes and film-makers. Some of the films in this group offer point-of-view perspectives by the subjects in a few cases and by the film-maker in others.

SUMMING UP

The outstanding quality of the independent documentary movement is that the film-makers, technicians and producers do not allow power relationship to grow between the film-maker and his subject. They take care not to interpret the subject as the inheritor of a specific mentality, which can place qualitative limitations on the subject. They do not perpetuate definite modes of objectification.

Today, when one teaches a course in documentary and non-fiction cinema, one has access to extensive material on DVDs. Propaganda films from the 1930s, such as Leni Riefenstahl's *Triumph of the Will* and *Olympia* (her masterpiece on the 1936 Berlin Olympics), can be screened, analyzed and discussed. The great British documentary tradition of John Grierson and others are available at the National Film Archives. The films of the Dutch master, Bert Haanstra, are in pristine condition on DVD. Students can have an intelligent perspective on the grand sweep of the documentary tradition around the world. And then they can place the Indian documentary in that global context.[1]

As channels of the mass media become a part of the corporate structure, television and image-making have increasingly withdrawn into an artificial world of make-believe and propaganda, and it has increasingly been left to documentary films to tell the other stories. In trying to evolve this 'alternative language' through an 'alternative cinema', crusaders of public causes are struggling to bring about a happy marriage between art and activism and between creativity and political action. This struggle is full of seemingly insurmountable hurdles because of the structural lack of basic needs of film-making. Post-production work has to be done with either personal funding or infrastructure or by making use of one's friends' network for free use of someone's editing studio. Few documentary film-makers can afford the hiring costs of camera, lights, sound recording equipment and skilled technicians. When the film is complete, financiers shy away from buying it because the country does not have exhibition channels.

It is crucial to reflect on the various sets of relationships that documentary film-making involves: (i) between the author and the narrative—the question of realism; (ii) between the author and the subjects filmed—the question of ethics and politics of representation; (iii) and between the narrative and the audience—the question of effects and audience reception. With new technologies such as digital image manipulation and inexpensive and portable camcorders that are redefining the realm of the real, the project of recording reality has never been more problematic.[2]

"It is not easy to be a crusader film-maker but one can always keep trying. No matter how much you criticize, there is always a bit of hope here, for at least there is a passion that is linked with the lives of people and the struggle for justice," says Amar Kanwar.[3]

FROM CONTROL TO INNOVATIONS, INVENTIONS AND MERGERS

In an insightful essay[4] Sandeep Vishwanath opens his article with, "Rejected by conventionally organized film festivals on account of exhibiting 'uncomfortable' content, independent documentary film-makers take on the task of showcasing their work by creating their own public viewing spaces with their own rules." His essay fleshes out the history of censorship imposed on the independent documentary by the Mumbai International Festival of Documentary and Short and Animation Films tracing the dictatorial control and curbs blocking the screening of certain films at the festival.

He goes on to describe how the call for entries for MIFF 2004 introduced a clause that made it mandatory for Indian film-makers to produce censor certificates for their films in order to be eligible for participation in the festival. The history of MIFF had never seen a clause like that since its inception in 1990. In fact, the Ministry of Information and Broadcasting relaxes the 'censor certificate' rule for films that are showing at film festivals and exhibitions. MIFF and other festivals like it were known to be an avenue for film-makers to express themselves freely and exhibit their work to an audience.

MIFF is the Mumbai counterpart to festivals at Kolkata, Bangalore and Trivandrum. Most of the documentary films are politically and socially relevant and tend to assume strong stances quite unlike the staid and politically inert mainstream cinema in India.

Widespread agitation and collective protest by documentary film-makers finally led to the withdrawal of the clause. Yet, Vishwanath elaborates that the selection process itself incorporated tacit censorship. Films eliminated by what was read as political pressure were those that were direct exposes and critiques of the establishment and its organizations—such as Rakesh Sharma's *Final Solution* and Sanjay Kak's *Words on Water*. They perhaps made the powers-that-be quite uncomfortable and, therefore, deemed unfit because of their content.

These restrictions to their right of expression led film-makers to join together and embark on an interesting and courageous campaign against censorship. With this regard, Patwardhan writes, "Over 275 film-makers exchanged ideas, drew up action plans, organized a CAC and threatened to boycott MIFF if the censor certificate requirement was not withdrawn. As a result of a united and popular campaign, the rules of MIFF were amended again and the censorship clause withdrawn." And it didn't just stop at that; the united members who worked for this campaign went on to create a festival and hold screenings parallel to the screenings of MIFF. Since they were denied space to express themselves openly at avenues like MIFF, they created a space for themselves where there would be no such restrictions. The festival/movement was christened Vikalp—films for freedom.[5]

So after pooling in INR 1,000 each, the film-makers embarked on a search for a venue to screen their films and found an appropriate place close to the venue of the MIFF. An erstwhile printing press of the CPI that was converted to a screening hall, with curtains on windows and a screen on one of the walls, served as their initial space for resistance. Surabhi Sharma, an independent film-maker reiterates the view that Vikalp was born from a protest. "Vikalp has its roots in a very different moment as opposed to other film societies. Vikalp was born out of a protest of independent film-makers to the censorship at MIFF in 2004. A counter film festival was organized parallel to MIFF that year. It was a brief moment that brought us all together."[6]

It would be in the fitness of the subject to draw inspiration from what Fischer wrote in his seminal essay.[7] He was exploring the independent political documentary in India whereas this work is concentric on different kinds of documentaries within the independent movement because this writer believes that every documentary is, at its root, a political documentary because it does take sides and must take a definite standpoint never mind how objective the film-maker might be in his/her approach towards his subject. For example, when a film-maker chooses to make a biographical documentary, his/her choice of the subject reveals his bias for the given subject over others. If the film-maker chooses to make a documentary on Buddhadeb Dasgupta, it means that he prioritizes Dasgupta as a 'subject' over other contemporary Indian film-makers.

One welcome transition has been the involvement of FD that has been lending its support to the independent documentary since 2012. Under its new director general, FD has organized regular screening facilities in its auditorium in Mumbai under the label of FD Zone. This 'Zone' presents weekly screenings that offer a fine blend of FD archive films and contemporary independent films. It also organizes mini documentary film festivals, sometimes presented and conceptualized by the film-makers themselves. But for these weekly screenings, films, such as Surabhi Sharma's *Bidesia in Mumbai* (2013), would have died a silent death. Produced by Sharma with dialogue in Bhojpuri and Hindi, the film explores the lives and struggles of migrants into Mumbai who speak in Bhojpuri; *bidesia* means 'the one who leaves home'.

Says Sharma about her film, "Like most migrants in this 'global city', the 'bidesia' inhabits its remotest and sometimes most precarious edges. These are places that he tries to make his own and attempts to establish fragments of his own culture. This film follows a set of musicians who negotiate their way through the landscape of this city that was once alien to them, practicing their—a music that is frequently sexually charged, often religious, sometimes lyrical and occasionally political." She goes on to add, "The migrant is both the subject of and the audience for this music. In the present day, mobile phones bridge a tenuous connection between home and the city, often interestingly becoming a motif in the music itself. This feature-length film attempts to make the migrant visible by celebrating the musical sphere that he inhabits, in a city that renders him illegal and unwanted."

Sharma is an FTII graduate following her degree in anthropology and has been making documentaries since 2000. Her key concern is documenting cities in transition through the lens of labour, music, migration and reproductive labour. Her films have been screened at museums, universities and at international film festivals where these received awards too.

TECHNOLOGY AND CHANGE

One development that has truly liberated the documentary from the shackles of its propaganda past is technology. It was with the arrival of the digital, handheld camera. No longer does a film-maker have to shoot on grainy 16mm film that would then be transferred to magnetic tape and lose a few generations of visual quality on the way to telecast. No longer does a documentary film-maker have to acquire raw stock, deal with an expensive laboratory and submit his/her film to paperwork, including the Censor Board. He or she can shoot, edit and send the finished film for selection to film festivals abroad. It is relatively inexpensive, a far greater number of people had access to it, and it could be updated and reedited at any point in time. It was as if a writer had suddenly discovered that he did not need a publisher to be in print. The documentary film movement in India received a major thrust with the digital revolution.[8]

The advent of modern technological mutations, especially in the technological shift from film to digital, has brought about corresponding changes in film-making, both documentary and other kinds of films. Documentary has been specially impacted due to what is seen as a shorter and cheaper way to make documentaries on the one hand and make distribution and exhibition more mobile and flexible on the other.

Across the world, the documentary is growing at a tremendous pace in terms of quantity, status and accomplishments. Digital, high-definition (HD) video equipment and desktop computer post-production have revolutionized screen production and displaced film from its elite and excluding position as the medium of choice.[9] The future has never looked more exciting for independent documentary film-makers across the world in general and in developing countries like India in particular.

Rabiger goes on to add: "Using even the simplest video equipment, extensive and fascinating study is immediately possible"[10] because video shooting gives the director the space and opportunity to watch his online monitor about how each shot is going, whether it is an okay shot or needs a retake. Given that the documentary mostly tries to resort to candid and cinema verite methods of filming, this retake is not always possible or acceptable or both. But the fact remains that constant monitoring becomes an advantage unless the director gets overwhelmed by this technique of depending too much and becoming insecure and less confident of his own ability and command over this medium and subject.

Shooting on video delivers results immediately and time is saved. Some experienced veterans still believe that film gives a superior image, but one must constantly worry about the amount of stock consumed. Video editing has become a universal practice today. Film equipment today is cumbersome, and raises problems of portability and mobility, is expensive and difficult to handle. If there are differences between the end product of a work captured on film and a work captured on video, the audience can hardly make out the difference, if any.

Choice of technique is another creative and technical option the director has. There have been instances of a film having been originally shot on analogue Betacam video and then transferred to 35 mm in finished form for theatrical release with very good results. Some film-makers have shot originally in a variety of video formats and then transferred to 35 mm with excellent results. Besides, Rabiger insists that HD video removes gaps, if any, between video and film. With the proliferation of camcorders and desktop non-linear editing, one can now learn film-making easily and rapidly and also at low cost. Most of the veteran documentary film-makers in India possess their own editorial console where the investment may be high initially but the returns are many—in terms of time, money, quality of the final product and independence in functioning minus interference of any kind.

Sahib Biwi Aur Gangster (2011) was the first Hindi film to be shot on Alexa. The biggest advantage in my mind is the ability of a digital camera to reproduce dark and very low-lit images without any grain or under exposed quality. The good digital cameras give you very good shadow detail, which gives me as a Cinematographer the ability to experiment with very dark moody images. Convenience is also an advantage. The fact that there is no more dependence on a photochemical process and you are assured of clean images that will be true to the exposure you set," said Aseem Mishra, cinematographer of Tigmangshu Dhulia's wonderful film *Paan Singh Tomar* (2012).[11]

Cinematography has pushed its borders. RED Digital Cinema enables high-resolution, file-based cinematography through cameras that capture images with more than four times the resolution of the best HD cameras. RED dispenses with the need for raw stock and the sophisticated movie camera can decode light by itself. Then there is Blu-ray (not Blue-ray) also known as Blu-ray Disc (BD), which is the name of a new optical disc format jointly developed by the Blu-ray Disc Association (BDA), a group of the world's leading consumer electronics, personal computer and media manufacturers. The format was developed to enable recording, rewriting and playback of HD video, as well as storing large amounts of data. The format offers more than five times the storage capacity of traditional DVDs and can hold up to 25 gigabyte (GB) on a single-layer disc and 50 GB on a dual-layer disc.[12]

In an interview with this writer in August 2006, Rakesh Sharma, one of the most aggressive and commanding members of the independent documentary movement, states: "DV (digital video) has created new opportunities for independent film-makers to explore subjects for which funding has become scarce in the last few years. Film-making is no longer a capital-intensive medium; especially for documentary film-makers, as the technology itself (cheap, easy-to-handle cameras, and edit-at-home solutions) and the raw material (digital tapes) have become more accessible. In the Indian context, it has virtually given a new lease of life to this genre, as there is very little financial support for documentary-there is neither a well-developed network of funds/foundations nor a single broadcaster interested in acquiring/commissioning documentary films."

"The new PCs with windows XP," adds Rakesh, "actually come with a firewire port. So you do not even need the $800 video card anymore! There is any number of cameras now available in the middle class universe. I borrowed one tiny handycam to make

Aftershocks, which later picked up 10 international awards! Anyone can borrow one of these handycams—if you want to buy one, the price range is between 50K and 100K."

And how does he solve the problem of exhibiting his films? "As opposed to a film print, an 80 minute film on video CD costs less than ₹15.00, if you make professional labels and jackets too! A DVD will cost less than ₹40 or 50. There are many groups showing these films around. As a film-maker, I draw the line at handing out DVDs or VCDs. I leave it to others to organize a college with a projector or even show it on a 29" TV. The good news is—there is a big audience. The bad news—neither these audiences nor film-makers are able to access each other readily. It is something I want to work on—but then I want to make films too!" says Rakesh.

THE SHOW MUST GO ON

The questions that come up after this exploration and analysis are:
1. Will the independent documentary film-makers be able to sustain their messages and aesthetics as the genres continue to evolve?
2. Will these film-makers be able to face the threat posed by official documentary bodies such as the FD in terms of viewership as the FD is believed to have a more ensured audience than the independent film-makers?
3. Will new sources of funding such as (a) crowd funding, (b) decreased production costs because of technical innovations, (c) switching from film to digital, allow independent film-makers to compete with FD films, films by corporate houses and so on? These must be considered as most corporate films are in reality promotional films disguised as films with a social agenda. One may note that corporate houses' films have specific market-dictated agendas.
4. Will the possibility of securing funding from NGOs and other non-profit-making bodies place pressure on independent documentary film-makers in terms of distorting their original messages?
5. How will these film-makers come to a mutual agreement with NGO funders if the specific agendas of the film-maker and the NGOs concerned are different?

6. How will the film-makers resist falling into the trap of globalization on equipment prices or adopting aesthetic and technical flourishes of Western documentary film-makers to gain prestige and awards at international film festivals which might possibly run counter to the original 'Indian' voice so distinctly visible in Indian documentaries?

In other words, with one obstacle seen through and resolved with some degree of success, others appear across the horizon. Ultimately, the future of the independent documentary movement in India remains uncertain. In the meantime, these film-makers continue to struggle to have their messages heard by the Indian people.

According to Sanjay Joshi, National Convenor, Jan Sanskriti Manch, a strong activist of the independent documentary movement and one of the founders of Cinema of Resistance, "India is experiencing monopolistic aggression of capital on an unprecedented scale. And this aggression is not confined to mining and land-grab alone. The cultural sphere is not being spared. Over 90 percent of our cultural space is dominated by big players like UTV, Reliance, or Ekta Kapoor's Balaji Telefilms. All our news and electronic media are owned by a handful of select companies. They are carrying out corporate propaganda like never before. Bollywood is churning out films by certain formulae, like the 'gangster formula', the 'terrorist formula' or the 'mafia formula'. And the entire distribution network is again controlled by the big sharks themselves. How must we confront this scenario other than building a strong alternative model? We must use technology in a radical manner. This brings me to the closing anecdote of this piece. In 1969, the Argentinian film-maker Fernando Solanas gave a radio interview to Jean-Luc Godard, after the release of the iconic *The Hour of the Furnaces*. After a while when Solanas asked Godard about his views, Godard said he wanted to use the camera in the same way as the Vietnamese fighters had used the bicycle against the US aggression. We must have a radical mindset to similarly use all the technology currently at our disposal."[13]

Dziga Vertov, in his *Kinok manifestos*, said: "I am kino-eye, I am a mechanical eye. I, a machine, show you the world as only I can see it. Now and forever, I free myself from human immobility, I am in constant motion, I draw near, then away from objects, I crawl under, I climb onto them. I move apace with the muzzle of a galloping horse. I plunge full speed into a crowd, I outstrip running soldiers, I fall on my back, I ascend with an airplane, I plunge and soar together with plunging and soaring bodies. Now, I, a camera, fling myself along their resultant, maneuvering in the chaos of movement composed of the most complex combinations. Freed from the rule of sixteen-seventeen frames per second, free of the limits of time and space, I put together any given points in the universe, no matter where I've recorded them. My path leads to the creation of a fresh perception of the world. I decipher in a new way a world unknown to you."[14]

NOTES

1. Ibid.
2. K.P. Jayashankar and Anjali Monteiro, "Counter Images–Reflections on the Independent Documentary," Festival Brochure—Films for Freedom, Bangalore, 2004, 20. Organized by Campaign against Censorship.
3. Amar Kanwar, "The Search," Festival Brochure—Films for Freedom, Bangalore, 2004, 25. The quotes in this chapter, wherever not accompanied by a footnote or reference, are based on the author's interviews with the film-makers—personal, telephonic and/or through e-mail.
4. Sandeep Vishwanath, "Documentary Filmmakers—A Room of One's Own," *Footnotes*, March 2014.
5. Ibid.
6. Ibid.
7. John Fishcher, 2009, "Oppression: The Indian Independent Political Documentaries and the Ongoing Struggle for Viewership," *The Columbia Undergraduate Journal of South Asian Studies*, 1 (1): 41–53.
8. Ajit Duara, *The Indian Documentary Has Arrived*, http://www.openspaceindia.org/essays_48.htm
9. Mike Rabiger, *Directing the Documentary*, 5th ed. (Elsevier: Amsterdam, 2009), xii.
10. Ibid.
11. Bikash Misra, "Future is Digital but I Miss the Joy of Seeing the Rushes," Interview of Aseem Mishra on *Dear Cinema.com*
12. Shoma A. Chatterji, *Of Jump-Cuts and Fade-Outs —100 Years of Indian Cinema—Tracking Change* (Delhi: Rupa Publications, 2014).
13. Sanjay Joshi, *Gorakhpur to Kolkata: Eight Years on the Road of Resistance* (Unpublished paper, 2014).
14. Dziga Vertov, "Kinoks: A Revolution," in *Kino Eye: The Writings of Dziga Vertov*, ed. Annette Michelson, trans. Kevin O'Brien (Berkeley: University of California Press, 1923[1984]). Also available online at http://monoskop.org/images/2/2f/Vertov_Dziga_Kino-Eye_The_Writings_of_Dziga_Vertov.pdf

BIBLIOGRAPHY

BOOKS AND JOURNALS

Abraham, Thomas. 1996. *Who's Afraid of the Commercial Wolf?* Interview with Satish Bahadur published in Spectrum India, 29th January to 5th February.

Althusser, Louis. "Ideology and Ideological State Apparatuses." In *The Norton Anthology of Theory and Criticism*, edited by Vincent B. Leitch, trans. Ben Brewster. New York and London: W.W. Norton & Co.

Bandi, Swati. 2008. "Films From the Margins: Women, Desire and the Documentary Film in India." MFA diss., State University of New York at Buffalo.

Barnouw, Erik, and S. Krishnaswamy. 1963. *Indian Film.* New York: Columbia UP.

Baskaran, Theodore. 2007. "Non-fiction Cinematic Work." *The Hindu*, September 25.

Butalia, Pankaj. 1988. *The Indian Documentary in the '80s.* Paper on tendencies of development in the three continents.

Chakrabarty, Atanu. 2010. *Cinema, sangeet O Satyajit*, (Bengali). Nandan Publication: Kolkata.

Chatterjee, Niladri R. 2009. "'Now I'm Chapal Rani': Chapal Bhaduri's Hyperformative Female Impersonation." *Intersections: Gender and Sexuality in Asia and the Pacific* (22).

Chatterjee, Saibal. 2009. *Gutsy Reels, Real Voices.* The Tribune, Chandigarh, Sunday Cover Story, July 5.

Chatterji, Shoma A. 1996. *The Ethnographical Documentary.* Spectrum India, 4th Mumbai International Film Festival for Documentary, Short and Animation Films, 29th January to 5th February, 11–13.

———. 2014. *Of Jump-Cuts and Fade-Outs—100 Years of Indian Cinema—Tracking Change.* Delhi: Rupa & Co.

Dasgupta, Chidananda. 1980. *The Cinema of Satyajit Ray.* Gaziabad: Vikas Publishing House.

Dutta, Madhusree. 2007. *In Defence of Political Documentary.* Infochange Film Forum, online magazine.

Fischer, John. 2009. "Oppression: The Indian Independent Political Documentaries and the Ongoing Struggle for Viewership." *The Columbia Undergraduate Journal of South Asian Studies*, 1(1): 41–53.

Flaherty, Robert. 1950. "Tanking." In *Cinema 1950*, edited by Roger Malin Manvell. London: Pelican.

Garga, B. D. 2007. *Raj To Swaraj—The Non-fiction Film in India.* Penguin-Viking: India.

———. 1988. Essay. The Indian Documentary.In *Cinema in India* 2, no. 2.

Hasan, Bilquis Zafirul. 2002. *Mohasiron Ka Shahar*. Translated from Urdu by Diba Zafir, as quoted in Seagulls 5, April-May-June.
Jayashankar, K. P., and Anjali Monteiro. 2008. *Counter Images–Reflections on the Independent Documentary*. Bangalore: Festival Brochure – Films for Freedom.
———. 2001. "Images of the "Other" in India." *Media Development* 3.
Joshi, Sonam. 2010. *Turning Around the Camera*. Caravan, April 1.
Kanwar, Amar. 2004. "The Search." Festival Brochure – Films for Freedom, Bangalore.
Malhotra, Priya Deepti. 2009. The Politics of Popular Culture. *Infochange News and Features*, April.
Minha, Trinh T. 1992. "Rethinking the Subject of Ethno-documentary." In *Visual Anthropology and India*, edited by K.S. Singh.
Miquet Francis. 1996. "*From The Polemical Heart*" taken in December 1995 published in *Spectrum India*. 29th January to 5th February.
Myerhoff, Babara. (1935–1985) anthropologist, filmmaker, and founder of the Center for Visual Anthropology at theUniversity of Southern California.
Narwekar, Sanjit. 1992. *Films Division and the Indian Documentary*. Ministry of Information and Broadcasting, Government of India, Publications Division.
Pendakur, Manjunath. 1995. Cinema of Resistance: Recent Trends in Indian Documentary Film. *Documentary Box* 7.
Pestonji, Meher. 1985. *Getting Rid of Slumdwellers is not the Solution. Express Magazine*, July 21.
Priyadarshini, S. 2012. "Celluloid Biographies." *The Hindu*, February 22.
Rabiger, Mike. 2009. *Directing the Documentary* (5th ed.). Focal Press: UK, p. xii.
Raman, S. V. 2004. "Cutting Edge: Senseless Censors." Paper presented at the Centre for Civil Society Liberty, Art and Culture Seminar, Kolkata, India, November 6 2004.
Ramnarayan, Gowri. 2000. "Limited Appeal." *The Hindu*, March 12, Entertainment Section.
Ramnath Nandini. 2010. "Reel Change, Revolution flows from the lens of a Camera." *Time Out*, Mumbai, online magazine. Also available online at https://mlfblog.wordpress.com/2010/01/
———. 2011. "Kashmir Calling." *Time Out*, December 9.
Raqs Media Collective, ed. 2000. *Double Take: Looking at the Documentary*. New Delhi: Foundation for Universal Responsibility of His Holiness the Dalai Lama in association with the Public Service Broadcasting Trust.
Roberge, Gaston. *Problems and Prospects of Short Filmmaking in Third World Countries*. Deep Focus.
Ruby, Jay. 1991. "Speaking For, Speaking About, Speaking With, or Speaking Alongside-An Anthropological and Documentary Dilemma." *Visual Anthropology Review* Fall 7(2): 50–67.
Rutherford, Anne. 2006. '*Buddhas Made of Ice and Butter*': *Mimetic Visuality, Transience and the Documentary Image*, Third Text, 20(1), Routledge.
Sanjana. 2004. "Batte Cinema" Festival Brochure – Films for Freedom, Bangalore, 30–31.
Sarris, Andrew. 1993. "Towards a Theory of Film History." In *Movies and Methods*, edited by Bill Nichols—vol. I, pg. 237. Seagull Books: Kolkata.
Sen, Gargi. 2013. "More than 'Earnest' and 'Real'." *Himal Magazine*, October 1.
Sengupta, Shuddhabrata. 2013. "A Long March—Sanjay Kak's Cinema of Rebellion." *Caravan*, July 1.

Seton, Marie. Portrait of a Director: Satyajit Ray.
Sukhdev, S. Filmmakers Purpose- Personal Cinema or Social Relevance—Paper, 1971.
Vertov, Dziga. (1984). "Kinoks: A Revolution." Translated by Kevin O'Brien. In *Kino Eye: The Writings of Dziga Vertov*, edited by Annette Michelson. Berkeley: University of California Press.
Vishwa Priya. *Patwardhan's Bombay, Our City:A Blueprint for Irrational Development*. Deep Focus.
Vishwanath, Sandeep. 2014. *Documentary Filmmakers—A Room of One's Own*. Footnotes, March.
Waugh, Thomas. 1998. "Independent Documentary in India: A Preliminary Report." *Visual Anthropology Review* 4(2): 164–175.

WEBSITE REFERENCES

http://www.patwardhan.com
Duara, Ajit. "The Indian Documentary Has Arrived." http://www.openspaceindia.org/essays_48.htm
http://www.csds.in/sites/default/files/Banner/FD%20Zone%20Details.pdf
http://www.upperstall.com/films/2002/tell-them-the-tree-they-had-planted-has-now-grown
http://www.upperstall.com/films/2004/wapsi
http://windsfromtheeast.blogspot.in/2009/01/is-anyone-watching-indian-documentary.html

INDEX OF FILMS

CHAPTER 1
In the Land of Head Hunters, 1
Siddheshwari, 2, 13, 14
Khayal Gatha, 2, 25,
Dharmayuddha, 4
Nasoor, 4
Bombay:Our City, 153
The Clap Trap, 9, 66
Dhrupad, 13
The Inner Eye, 13, 137, 141
Another Way of Learning, 10
Freedom Marches On, 12
Our National Anthem, 12
New Era, 12
Face to Face, 12
This Bit of That India, 12
Explorer, 12
Flashback, 12
Lamp in the Dark, 14
Nargis, 14
Eyes of Stone, 14
Prisoners of Conscience, 13, 153
War Game, 2

CHAPTER 2
Arzoo, 24, 225–27
The Salt Stories, 24, 59–60
Bhavantarana, 25
Pandit Bhimsen Joshi, 14, 25, 26
Colours of Absence, 26
A Dream Takes Wings, 26
B.N. Sircar, 26
Creative Artist: Satyajit Ray, 27
Hrishikesh Mukherjee, 27, 41
G. Aravindan, 27
Anil Biswas, 28
Pankaj Mullick, 28

Salil Chowdhury, 28
Naushad Ali—The Melody Continues, 29
Immortal Martyr Jatin Das, 29
Natak Jaari Hai, 30–31
Vision Unveiled, 32
Mrinal Sen, 14, 33, 34
Ekti Nadir Naam, 34, 35
Eka Ebong Kayekjon, 35–36
Collage, 36
Pakhira, 36
Third Theatre in Bangla, 36
Ebam Badal Sircar, 36
The Last Lady, 37, 250
Melody in Mass, 38
Portrait of a Pioneer, 38
Padatik, 39
Remembering Bimal Roy, 40
Soumendu Roy, 41–43
Subrata Mitra, 41, 42
Bansi Chandragupta, 45–47
Celluloid Man, 47–49
An American in Madras, 49–52
In the Land of Chhinnopatro, 53–54
Images Unbound—The Life and Times of Rabindranath Tagore, 54–57
Jeebon Smriti, 57
The Loom, 58–59
The Salt Stories, 59–60
The Saroj Khan Story, 60–63
Pancham Unmixed: Mujhe Chalte Jaana Hai, 63–64
Ragpickers, 63
I'm The Very Beautiful, 65
Way Back Home, 65, 175
The Other Song, 65
Hyderabad: A Place in the Heart, 67
Manjuben Truck Driver, 67
Pala, 67
The Bioscopewallah, 68
Performing the Goddess—Chapal Bhaduri's Story, 69–71
Making The Face, 71–73

CHAPTER 3
The Martial Dances of Malabar, 76
The Oraons of Bihar, 76
The Flute and the Arrow, 76
The Vanishing Tribe, 76
Tree of Wealth, 76
The Nomad Puppeteers, 77
Chitrakathi, 77

Main-Taris of Assam, 77
Gothrasmriti, 77
Mithak Bhan, 78
Songs of Abitani: The Missings, 78
Sabzi Mandi Ke Heere, 78
The Vehicle with the Soul of a Man, 78
Lyrics of Life, 79
Buddha Weeps in Jadugoda, 79
Colours Black, 79
Jari Mari: Of Cloth and Other Stories, 79
In The Land of Hidden Treasure, 80, 81
If It Rains, 80
Khepar Mon Brindabon, 82–86
Bottle Masala in Moile, 86–90
Dancing for Themselves, 90–93
Where are You, 93–96
Divine Drums, 95–98
The Shillong Chamber Choir and the Little Home School, 98–100
Little Magaziner Katha, 100–03
Bilal, 104, 113–14
Ab Aur Waqt Nahin (WAQT), 104–05
Known Strangers, 124–27
The Conflict—Who's Loss, Who's Gain, 109–11
Apna Aloo Bazaar Becha, 111–12
Loha Garam Hai, 114–19
Crosswinds over Icchamati, 119–20
This Land is Mine, 120–24
Whose Land is This Anyway, 120–24
Sons and Daughters, 232
Yamuna Gently Weeps, 132–34

CHAPTER 4
Child Artistes and Satyajit Ray, 150
A Perfect Day, 136
Quest for Health, 136
Our Children Will Know Each Other Better, 136
Rabindranath Tagore, 54–57
Sukumar Ray, 139
Sikkim, 80–82
Bala, 142
Ray, 136
Satyajit Ray, 27, 141
The Music of Satyajit Ray, 147–49
Ghare-Baire, 146, 148
Pather Panchali, 39, 45, 147, 151
Aparajta, 210
Apur Sansar, 149
Agantuk, 151

CHAPTER 5

A Time to Rise, 153
In Memory of My Friends, 154
Ram Ke Naam, 154
Father, Son and Holy War, 154
Jang Aur Aman, 154
Jai Bhim Comrade, 155
A Season Outside, 156
A Night of Prophecy, 156, 157, 158
The Lightning Testimonies, 157, 158
Aftershocks: The Rough Guide to Democracy, 159
Final Solution, 158, 159, 162
Khedu Mora Re, 160
Chet'ta Rejo, 161
Words on Water, 163, 165
In the Forest Hangs a Bridge, 163
One Weapon, 163, 164
A House and a Home, 163
Until My Freedom Has Come—The New Intifada in Kashmir, 163
Jashn-e-Azadi, 162, 164, 172, 173
One Weapon, 162, 164
Red Ant Dream, 166
Tell Them, The Tree They Had Planted Has Now Grown, 167, 168
Wapsi, 167, 169, 170
Apour Ti Yapour, 169, 170
Voices from Baliapal, 171
Forever Young, 171, 173
In Camera – Diaries of a Documentary Cinematographer, 171
Follow the Rainbow, 172
Bhiwandi, 173
Abak Jaye Here, 173
Wait Until Death, 173
The Dream of Hanif, 174
The Nest, 174, 175
Way Back Home, 65, 97,175
Hope Dies Last in War, 176
Wagah, 177
Sarang—Symphony in Cacophony, 177
And the Bamboo Blooms, 178
Making the Face, 71–73
Journeying with Mahasweta Devi, 178, 179, 180
One Day from a Hangman's Life , 179
Mukti Chai, 183
A Poet, A City and A Footballer, 269
Hungry Autumn, 183
An Indian Story, 183, 190
Tiger—the death chronicles, 180
The Forgotten Tigers, 182, 183

The Godfathers of Dhanbad, 181
The Revolution and After, 181
My Camera and I, 182

CHAPTER 6
Brides of Hyderabad, 187
Women in Conflict, 187
Parenting Alone, 187
Seismograph, 187
Can't Take It Anymore, 187
On My Own, 187
Missing Young Women, 188
The Women of Kisani Sabha, 188
Cotton for my Shroud, 188
Candles in the Wind, 188
Gandhari, 189
Half-Way Home, 189
Uttaradhikar, 189
Najaayaz, 189
The School That Karmi Soren Built, 189
Understanding Trafficking, 189
An Indian Story, 183, 190
Beyond Genocide, 183, 190, 191
Citthi, 190
The National Art Gallery of India, 190
And Miles to Go, 190
The Advocate, 192
Nari Adalat, 192, 196
Itta Hejje Mundakka Thegiya Bediri Hindakka, 192
The Legacy of Malthus, 192, 196
Something like a War, 192, 196
Sudesha, 192
Invoking Justice, 195, 196
I Live in Behrampada, 197
Memories of Fear, 197, 198
Scribbles On Akka, 197, 200
Sundari—An Actor Prepares, 126, 197
7 Islands and a Metro, 201
Annapoorna: Goddess of Food, 201, 203
Cosmopolis: Two Tales of a City, 201, 203
Defeat of a Minor Goddess, 201, 202
Q2P, 202, 203, 204
Where's Sandra, 202, 203, 204
Unlimited Girls, 202, 203, 204
A Short Film About Time, 202, 204
Morality TV Aur Loving Jehad: A Thrilling Tale, 203, 204
Kamalabai, 205, 206
Skin Deep, 205, 206

On an Express Highway, 206
City of Photos, 207, 208
Gulabi Gang, 207, 209
Family Album, 207
At My Doorstep, 207
6 yards to Democracy, 207, 208
Call it Slut, 207
Aparajita, 210
Kaveri, 210
BOL, 210
Autumn's Final Country, 210
Mann ke Manjeere, 211
Amra Padatik, 211
Soldiers in Sarong, 211
Paradise on a River of Hell, 212

CHAPTER 7
Changing Currents, 214
Plumbing the Rights—Part 1, 214
Tell-Tale Signs, 214
Jal Bharo Jal Dharo, 214, 215
Ek Ropa Dhan, 216, 218
Niyamgiri—You Are Still Alive, 219-22
Johar—Welcome to Our World, 222-25
Arzoo, 24, 225-27
Earth Witness: Reflections on the Times and the Timeless, 227-28
There was a Queen, 229-33
Have You Seen the Arana, 233-37

CHAPTER 8
Exploring Madness, 240
Nirastra Padatik, 240
Nakusha—The Unwanted, 240, 251-54
Angels of a Troubled Paradise, 240-54
Ocean of Tears, 255-57
Char—The No Man's Island, 260-62
Different Strokes, 241
Three Women and the City, 241, 267
Once Upon a Madman, 242
King of India, 173, 242-46
Between the Devil and the Deep River, 246-49
Lyrics of No Life, 250
The Last Lady, 37, 250
Kalo Shekh, 249-51
110002, 257-59
Supermen of Malegaon, 260
Char—The No Man's Island, 260-62

INDEX OF FILMS

Flickering Angels, 262–65
Our Family, 265–69

SUMMING UP
Triumph of the Will, 274
Olympia, 274
Final Solution, 158, 159
Words on Water, 163, 165, 276
Bidesia in Mumbai, 277

INDEX

9th National Film Awards, 139
10th Jeevika Asia Livelihood Documentary Festival, 2013, 90
32nd National Film Awards, 149

Academy of Fine Arts, 38
Act Now for Harmony and Democracy (ANHAD), 129
Agnihotri, Anita, 17
AIR. *See* All India Radio (AIR)
Aljazeera Golden Award, 114
Aljazeera International Documentary Festival, 114
All India Radio (AIR), 28, 97
American Indians, 1
ANHAD. *See* Act Now for Harmony and Democracy (ANHAD)
Anthropological Society of India, 80
APDP. *See* Association of the Parents of Disappeared Persons (APDP)
Arambam, Lokendra, 211
Artscan (television series), 112
Ash, Timothy, 75
Association of the Parents of Disappeared Persons (APDP), 231, 257
autonomous documentary film-makers, 5
Award for Best Documentary at Festival de Cine de Pobre Humberto Solas in Cuba, 114

Banerjee, Jagadish, 28
Banerjee, Nishith, 27
BD. *See* Blu-ray Disc (BD)
BDA. *See* Blu-ray Disc Association (BDA)
Best Documentary Award, 139
Best Environmental Film Award, 115
Best Short Documentary Award, 90

Bhowmik, Someswar, 3
Bhushan, Brij, 28
biographical documentary, 10, 24, 27, 73
bioscope, 68
black and white (B&W), 27
Blu-ray Disc (BD), 280
Blu-ray Disc Association (BDA), 280
Board of Film Censorship in India, 3
Bose, Krishnendu, 180–3
Bose, Tapan, 12, 183
Bosu Cultural Academy, 38
British India Government, 76
Bronze Remi Award, 90
Brothwick, Jessica, 1

campaign against censorship (CAC), 16
CBFC. *See* Central Board of Film Certification (CBFC)
censorship paradigm, 3
Central Board of Film Certification (CBFC), 3
Central Bureau of Investigation (CBI), 256
Centre for Science and Environment (CSE), 112, 214
Centre of Indian Trade Unions (CITU), 31
Chakraborty, Utpalendu, 12, 183
Chatterjee, Ananya Chakraborty, 188–90
Chatterjee, Saibal, 5
Child Rights and You (CRY), 211
chronologically-sequenced story, 7
Cinema and Censorship: The Politics of Control in India (Bhowmik, Someswar), 3
CITU. *See* Centre of Indian Trade Unions (CITU)
Community Claims Provision of the Forest Rights Act, 221

Coomaraswamy, Anand, 25
CSE. *See* Centre for Science and Environment (CSE)

Datta, Madhusree, 196–201
DD National, 34
Devi, Siddheshwari, 14
Dewan, Saba, 4
Dhanraj, Deepa, 191–96
Dhar, Aniruddha, 34
digital camera, 279
director of photography (DOP), 42
Directorate of Film Festivals, 9
divine drums, 95–98
docu-fiction, 2
documentary format, artificial classifications of, 25
documentary, definitions, 1, 2
Doordarshan, 66
Dungan, Ellis Roderick, 49
Dutt, Priya, 14
DV (digital video), 280

Eastman Colour, 43
economic bankruptcy, 15
Edinburgh Festival, 77
ethno-documentary, 76
ethnographical film, 75, 80–82, 103–09

Falcon, Francisca, 88
FD. *See* Films Division (FD)
fiction films, 14
Film and Television Institute of India (FTII), 22
film critic, 11
films
    counter-movement, 11–14
    criteria for choice of, 7–8
Films Division (FD), 11–12, 24
films for freedom, 16
foreign voluntary agencies, 15
Forest Advisory Committee (FAC), 222
Forest Protection Committee in Kundrijhoor, 108
Francis Miquet at the Montreal Film Festival, 8
Frontline, 16
FTII. *See* Film and Television Institute of India (FTII)

Gandhi, Mahatma, 60
Ghose, Goutam, 12, 136, 183
Ghosh, Suman, 11
globalization, 6
Golden Jubilee of Queen Victoria, 88
Gorakhpur to 'Kolkata: Eight Years on the Road of Resistance (Joshi, Sanjay), 20
government-produced/sponsored documentaries, 215
Grierson, John, 2
Gujarat Mineral Development Corporation (GMDC), 159

high-definition (HD) video, 278–81
hindi film, 44
Hindustani classical music, 25
Hoso-Bunka Foundation TV Documentary Competition in 2001, 244
Houston International Film Festival, 2013, 90

IAWRT. *See* International Association of Women on Radio and Television (IAWRT)
IDRC. *See* International Development Research Centre (IDRC)
IFAD. *See* International Fund for Agricultural Development (IFAD)
IFI. *See* Information Films of India (IFI)
independent films, 3–5
    classifying and categorizing, 8–11
independent movement, 7
India Foundation for the Arts, Bangalore, 93
Indian Catholic community, 88
Indian Documentary Producers Association (IDPA), 115
Indian film-makers, 5
Indian People's Theatre Association (IPTA), 30
Information Films of India (IFI), 76
International Association of Women on Radio and Television (IAWRT), 186
International Development Research Centre (IDRC), 112
International Documentary and Short Film Festival of Kerala's Competition Section, 2013, 90

International Documentary Film Festival, 16, 93
International Film Festival of India (IFFI), Goa, 61
International Fund for Agricultural Development (IFAD), 112
International Public Television (INPUT), 19
investigative film, 103–9
IPTA. *See* Indian People's Theatre Association (IPTA)

Jain, Nishtha, 207–10
Jan Commissions' investigation, 256
Jan Sanskriti Manch (JSM), 20
Jatin Das Centre of Art, 16
Joseph, Joshy, 177–80
Joshi, Pandit Bhimsen, 25
Joshi, Vasudha, 171
JSM. *See* Jan Sanskriti Manch (JSM)

Kak, Sanjay, 13
Kak, Sanjay, 162–67
Kanwar, Amar, 14, 156–58
Kapoor, Meena, 28
Kapoor, Wasim, 32
Kapuscinski, Ryszard, 3
Karnad, Girish, 14
Kaul, Mani, 2, 13, 14, 77
Kendro, Roopkala, 17
Khan, Raja Shabir, 254
Khayal School of Music, 25

Locarno International Film Festival, 138
Ladakh International Film Festival's Competition Section, 2013, 90
Las Vegas International Film Festival, 114
London Smog Disaster of 1952, 117

M.K. Thyagaraja Bhagawathar (MKT), 53
magazines, 100
Magic Lantern Foundation, 13
mainstream cinema, 5
Marudhur Gopalan Ramachandran (MGR), 51
Marxists, 8
Meitei society, 72
Mexican Film Festival, 114

MIFF. *See* Mumbai International Film Festival (MIFF)
milestone, 152
Ministry of External Affairs (MEA), 141
Ministry of Information and Broadcasting, 9
Misquitta, Jill, 8, 9
MKT. *See* M.K. Thyagaraja Bhagawathar (MKT)
MNCs. *See* multinational companies (MNCs)
Mohan, Reena, 205–07
Mukherjee, Chhandita, 10
Mulay, Suhasini, 12, 183, 190–91
multinational companies (MNCs), 110
Mumbai International Film Festival (MIFF), 16
Murzello, Walter, 89
mythological characters, 92

Namjosh, Madhav, 252
National Award, 116, 137, 138, 146, 153, 183
National Center for Performing Arts, Bombay, 142
National Convenor, 20
National Film Archive of India (NFAI), 47
National Film Awards, 9–10
National Film Development Corporation (NFDC), 35, 149
Naxalite movement, 12
New York Review of Books (Plumb, J.H.), 15
NFAI. *See* National Film Archive of India (NFAI)
NFDC. *See* National Film Development Corporation (NFDC)
NGOs. *See* non-governmental organizations (NGOs)
Nippon Hoso Kyokai (NHK), 81
non-governmental organizations (NGOs), 13
non-resident Indian (NRI), 10, 252
NRI. *See* non-resident Indian (NRI)

out of the box, 239–42

P.K. Nair, 53
P.V. Thampy Endowment Award, 234

INDEX

Pali, Ranjan, 171–4
Pan India Paryatan Pvt. Ltd (PIPL), 89
Panchayat Extension in Scheduled Area (PESA) Act, 118
Pandey, Mike, 10
Patwardhan, Anand, 8, 9, 12, 13, 153–55
Pedestrian Pictures, 109
People's Union for Civil Liberties (PUCL), 111
Phalke, D.G., 26
political control, ambience of, 3
political documentaries, 10
political prisoners, 13
political statement, 103–9
positive stories, 213
prisoner of war (POW), 76
promotional and advertising films, 5
propaganda films, 5, 10
PSB system, 33
PSBT. See Public Service Broadcasting Trust (PSBT)
Public Diplomacy Division, 99
Public Service Broadcasting Trust (PSBT), 18
PUCL. See People's Union for Civil Liberties (PUCL)

question of realism, 275

R.D. Burman's (RDB), 63, 64
Rabiger, Michael, 2
Raina, ajay, 167–71
Raindance Film Pitch Competition at Edinburgh, 62
Ramchandra, C., 29
Ray, Satyajit, 13
Ray's documentary films, 136–44
RDB. See R.D. Burman's (RDB)
RED Digital Cinema, 280
Riefenstahl, Leni, 274
right to information (RTI), 16
RTI. See right to information (RTI)

Sarangi, Saurabh, 113
Satyajit Ray Film and Television Institute (SRFTI), 42
Sen, Amartya, 11
Sen, Aparna, 46
Sen, Gargi, 5, 13

Sen, Supriyo, 174–7
Shahani, Kumar, 2, 25
Sharma, Rakesh, 158–62
Shell Film Unit of London, 76
Silver Ace Award, 114
Silver Palm, 114
Sircar, Shoojit, 211
Social Communications Film Conference, 17
South Zone Culture Centre, 93
special economic zone (SEZ), 89
Special Investigation Team's (SIT's) investigation, 256
Spivak, Gayatri Chakravorty, 239
SRFTI. See Satyajit Ray Film and Television Institute (SRFTI)
SRI method, 212, 218
Subbulakshmi, M.S., 51
Suman, Sudhir, 20
sustainable development, 213

Tagore, Rabindranath, 28
tamil films, 44
Tata Institute of Social Sciences (TISS), 58
technology and change, documentary, 278–81
TERI. See The Energy and Resources Institute (TERI)
Thaiyya community, 77
The Art and Culture Trust of Sikkim, 141
The Damodar Valley Project, 107
The Energy and Resources Institute (TERI), 112
third theatre, 36–7
TISS. See Tata Institute of Social Sciences (TISS)
transgender people, 72

UAIL. See Utkal Alumina International Limited (UAIL)
UCIL. See Uranium Corporation of India Limited (UCIL)
United Nations Organization (UNO), 159
University of Southern California's (USC), 51
Uranium Corporation of India Limited (UCIL), 79
Utkal Alumina International Limited (UAIL), 110

Vachani, Nilita, 14
Vishwa Hindu Parishad (VHP)! 162
Vohra, Paromita, 201–5

Watkins, Peter, 2

Youthquake (television series), 112

ABOUT THE AUTHOR

Shoma A. Chatterji is a freelance journalist, film scholar and author based in Kolkata. She contributes to around a dozen print media and net publications. She has won two National Awards for Best Writing on Cinema: Best Film Critic in 1991 and Best Book in 2002 for *Parama and Other Outsiders: The Cinema of Aparna Sen*.

Chatterji won the Bengal Film Journalists Association's Best Critic Award in 1998 and the Bharat Nirman Award for excellence in journalism in 2004. She is the recipient of a research fellowship from the National Film Archive of India (2005–06) and the Senior Research Fellowship from the PSBT, New Delhi, for research in the politics of portrayal of gender on Indian television in 2006–07. She has authored 22 books on cinema and gender, which includes three short story collections and one work of translation, besides one on the history of the city of Kolkata. She has been a jury member at several film festivals in India and abroad. After her PhD in History (Indian Cinema), Chatterji won a Senior Research Post-doctoral Fellowship from the Indian Council of Social Science Research, New Delhi. In 2009–10, she won a Special Award for consistent writing on women's issues at the United Nations Population Fund's UNFPA-Laadli Media Awards (Eastern region). In 2010, the Kalyan Kumar Mitra Award for excellence in film scholarship and contribution as film critic was bestowed upon her. She also received the Lifetime Achievement *SAMMAN* (honour) by the Rotary Club of Calcutta-Metro City under the auspices of Rotary International in July 2012.

Among books authored by Dr Chatterji are: *Subject-Cinema, Object-Woman: A Study of the Portrayal of Women in Indian Cinema*; *Parama and Other Outsiders: The Cinema of Aparna Sen*, which bagged the National Award for Best Book on Cinema (2002), and the soon-to-be-published *Charu and Her Lorgnette: The Material Universe of Ray's Works Based on Tagore's Writing* and *Reading Rituparno*.